Digital Poetics

Digital Poetics

The Making of E-Poetries

Loss Pequeño Glazier

The University of Alabama Press
Tuscaloosa and London

Copyright © 2002
The University of Alabama Press
Tuscaloosa, Alabama 35487-0380
All rights reserved
Manufactured in the United States of America

1 2 3 4 5 6 7 8 9 . 10 09 08 07 06 05 04 03 02

Designer: Paul Moxon
Typefaces: Janson, Frutiger, Interstate

The paper on which this book is printed meets the
minimum requirements of American National Standard
for Information Science–Permanence of Paper for
Printed Library Materials, ANSI Z39.48-1984.

Library of Congress Cataloging-in-Publication Data

Glazier, Loss Pequeño.
  Digital poetics : the making of E-poetries / Loss
  Pequeno Glazier.
      p. cm. — (Modern and contemporary poetics)
  Includes bibliographical references and index.
  ISBN 0-8173-1074-6 (cloth : alk. paper) —
  ISBN 0-8173-1075-4 (pbk.: alk. paper)
  1. Poetry—Marketing. 2. Poetry—Data processing.
3. Poetry—Computer network resources. 4. HTML
(Document markup language) I. Title. II. Series.
  PN1059.M3 G58 2002
  808.1'0285—dc21
                          2001001826

British Library Cataloguing-in-Publication Data
available

For My Parents

Each art has a duende different in form and style, but their roots meet in the place where the black sounds of Manuel Torre come from—the essential, uncontrollable, quivering, common base of wood, sound, canvas, and word.

Behind those black sounds, tenderly and intimately, live zephyrs, ants, volcanoes, and the huge night straining its waist against the Milky Way.
—Federico García Lorca, *In Search of Duende*

The intention is not a fixed ideal form, but a process of synthetic utilization and transformative integration. . . . It's got to take you and keep you with/in the process of becoming what it is itself. Nowhere to get, of course, nothing ever finally resolves. Things take form and then disintegrate to reconstruct, reassemble, rearrange in another temporary configuration. The point is to work with that continual rearrangement, the redefinition.
—Johanna Drucker, "Process Note"

The poet's eye, in fine frenzy rolling . . .
The forms of things unknown, the poet's pen
Turns them to shapes and gives to airy nothing
A local habitation and a name.
—Shakespeare, *A Midsummer Night's Dream*

Contents

Acknowledgments

Thanks to my dissertation committee members, Charles Bernstein, Robert Creeley, and Susan Howe, who were influential in the formative stages of some of these ideas. Critical to the development of this work were members of the early 1990s innovative poetry community, Poetics Program, State University of New York at Buffalo. In this regard, Charles Bernstein and Robert Creeley have been unwavering supporters of the Electronic Poetry Center, a significant site for the development of these ideas; vital support has likewise come from Dennis Tedlock, Raymond Federman, Gerard Bucher, the English Department, and the Dean of the College of Arts & Sciences, State University of New York, Buffalo. Special thanks to Hank Lazer for his encouragement of and patience with this project. Finally, thanks to all who have contributed to the building of the Electronic Poetry Center; it has been the beneficiary of contributions from an entire community of generous and talented poets and writers.

Portions of this book have appeared elsewhere in substantially different versions or were presented at conferences as follows:

Parts of "Language as Transmission" were presented at the "Present(ations) of the Future" Conference, sponsored by *The Little Magazine*, Albany, New York, Jan. 1995; at the Twentieth Century Literature Conference, University of Louisville, Feb. 1996; at the Poetry and the Public Sphere Conference, Rutgers University, New Jersey, April 1997; at the Governor's Conference on Arts & Technology, New York State Council on the Arts, Palisades, New York, March 1998; and at Digital Arts & Culture 2001, Providence, Rhode Island, April 26, 2001; and at "The Brave New World," Guggeheim Museum, New York, June 3–4, 2001.

"Jumping to Occlusions" was presented in earlier states at the Assembling Alternatives Conference, University of New Hampshire, Durham, New Hampshire, Aug. 1996; the Association for Computers and the Humanities Panel I, Modern Language Association Annual Conference, Washington, D.C., Dec. 1996; and Hypertext 97: The Eighth ACM Conference on Hypertext, University of Southampton, England, April 1997. A hypertextual version of the essay was published in *Postmodern Culture* 7 (1997) and an earlier pamphlet version as *Electronic Projection Poetries* (Buffalo, N.Y.: RIF/T, 1995).

"Our Words Were the Form We Entered" was presented at the program "The Convergence of Science and the Humanities: Internet Technologies and Scholarly Resources," State University of New York, Buffalo, 1995. Versions of this essay appeared in *Witz* 4 (1996) and in *Hypertext 97: The Eighth ACM Conference on Hypertext* (New York: Association for Computing Machinery, 1997).

"Home, Haunt, Page" was written for *Chloroform: An Aesthetics of Critical Writing* (1997).
"The Intermedial: Investigating the Medium" was written for *Chain* 3 (1996).
Parts of "Coding Writing, Reading Code" and "Hypertext/Hyperpoeisis/Hyperpoetics" were presented as a lecture for the Wednesdays @ 4+ Series (Poetics Program), State University of New York, Buffalo, Feb. 1998.
"The ABC's of Coding" appeared in *Doc(k)s*, Série 3, no. 21/22/23/24 (1999).
"Grep: A Grammar" appeared in *Witz* 7 (1999).
"A Grep of 'Methods for Reading and Performing Asymmetries'" was published in part in *Crayon* 1 (1997).
"Ego non baptiso te in nomine: A grep on Y" was published in *Salt* 10 (1997).
"On Mouseover" includes panels from "Mouseover: Essay in JavaScript," which appeared in *The Electronic Book Review* 7 (1998).
Differently focused sections of "E-Poetries: A Lab Book of Practice, 1970–2001" appeared in *The Poetry Project Newsletter* 174 (1999) and are forthcoming in the *Talisman* issue titled *The World in Time and Space: Towards a History of Innovative American Poetry, 1970–2000*.
Previous versions of "Future Tenses / Present Tensions: A Prospectus" and "Tin Man Weeps Straw Break" were delivered at Digital Arts & Culture 98, SKIKT Program (Norwegian Research Council) and the Cyber/Media/Culture Project (University of Bergen, Norway) Nov. 1998.
A previous version of "Between the Academy and a Hard Drive" was delivered at Digital Arts & Culture 99, Atlanta, Georgia, October 1999, and appeared in *Open Letter* 10th series #9 (Fall 2000), "Cyperpoetics" issue. For Real Media video versions of the conference presentation (as well as a reading of the digital poem, "Bromeliads"), see the conference Web site at http://www.lcc.gatech.edu/events/dac99/webcast.html.
"[Mayapán]: A Poetics of the Link," appearing in John Kinsella's *Salt* 10 (1997), presented a landmark early assemblage of selected themes related to this book, as did the visual compilation "Writing, Chmodding, Linking," which appeared in *Basta* 3 (1999).

The author expresses his gratitude to the following people for permission to reprint material used in this book:
From Caroline Bergvall, "Writing Out of Space: The Performance of Writing as Sited Practice," paper presented at Assembling Alternatives, U of New Hampshire, Durham, 29 Aug.–2 Sept. 1996. Used by permission.
From John Cayley, "Re: Norway" (5 Oct 1998), e-mail to the author. Used by permission.

From Jackson Mac Low, "Re: My Article" (25 Oct. 1998), "Re: Aleatoric" (31 Oct. 1998), "Re: A Footnote" (7 Mar. 1999), e-mails to the author. Copyright © 2000. Used by permission.

Introduction
Language as Transmission: Poetry's Electronic Presence

> Do rivers not render an increase in letters by going where they're
> going and not stammering.
> —Jackson Mac Low, "See"

> Poets understand texts better than most information
> technologists.
> —Jerome McGann, *Textual Condition*

> To make a prairie it takes a clover and one bee,
> One clover, and a bee,
> And revery.
> The revery alone will do,
> If bees are few.
> —Emily Dickinson, *Complete Poems*

The Electronic Medium

Digital Poetics is an introduction to the making of the new digital poetries. From code to code, whether a Web page in Moscow, a speaking clock in Kentish Town, a computer-generated Buffalo, or a bot inhabiting an archive in Melbourne, the making of poetry has established itself on a matrix of new shores. From hypertext to visual/kinetic text to writing in networked and programmable media, there is a tangible feel of arrival in the spelled air. New possibilities stand out as intriguing, while technologies that once seemed futuristic now have all the timeliness of World War II bunkers overlooking an unperturbed Pacific. But arrival where? I argue that we have not arrived at a place but at an awareness of the *conditions* of texts. Such an arrival includes recognizing that the conditions that have characterized the making of innovative poetry in the twentieth century have a powerful relevance to such works in twenty-first-century media. That is, poets are making poetry with the same focus on method, visual dynamics, and materiality;[1] what has expanded are the materials with which one can work. Such materials not only make multiple possible forms of writing but also, in the digital medium, contribute to a re-definition of writing itself. By recognizing the conditions of such making of innovative poetry, and by appreciating the material qualities of new computer media, we can begin to identify the new poetries of the twenty-first century.

Putting together such a vision is more than a simple concatenation of strings of practice; it involves recognizing the interwoven matrices through

which e-writing makes its way. In this model, writing is not a single monu-
mental totality that can be measured. Rather, what can be charted is writing
as an overlapping, hybrid, and extendible terrain of *parts* of writing, parts
that fit together at times awkwardly and out of joint, to compose a textual
continuum through which writing practices weave. Moreover, charting the
production and circulation of poetry is germane to any study of this art,
because poetry's circulation has always been related to its making. The same
was true of poetry in the twentieth century, when its means of production
and distribution was a crucial consideration of writing.

Indeed, the rise of the little magazine and small presses, from hand presses
of the fifties through the mimeo, Xerox, and offset production of the fol-
lowing decades, exemplifies not only poetry's engagement with making, its
mode of production, but also its means of dissemination. What has existed
is a union between poetry and its technologies of dissemination. Poetry's
path through these technologies has been one of appropriating "discarded"
technologies or subverting primary economic intentions of technologies
(publishing *C* or *The World* with tossed mimeo machines, running off a po-
etry magazine on the photocopier at the law firm, or pirating a NATO-created
military network to distribute writings on nomadology). As such the pro-
duction and consequent distribution of poetry texts lagged behind publishing
and distribution channels more current with production technologies. For
example, letter presses, mimeo machines, early photocopy machines, and
daisy-wheel printers passed from businesses to small presses as they were
superseded by newer technologies. Paper-based dissemination has its limi-
tations. Paper is expensive to purchase and to transport. Distribution, because
of postage costs, import restrictions, and currency exchange, is limited by
national boundaries, effectively restricting international dialog. (Why does
it cost more, for example, to mail a postcard from Buffalo to Toronto than it
does to mail one to Anchorage?) The nineties presented even greater chal-
lenges with the collapse of poetry distribution channels (Segue, Inland, and
others) and the nearly totalizing rise of bookstore chains. The decade finished
with an even more debilitating blow delivered by online book merchandis-
ing companies, companies bound neither to serve any community nor even
to make a profit. In this light it is surprising that some poets choose to list an
online book merchandiser as a source for their books, when they could as
easily list a small press bookstore. (Often these also offer ordering through
e-mail, phone, and the Web.) Because online book merchandisers have not
committed to ongoing support of small-circulation books, it might be naive
for poets to support them without questioning the impact of this practice.
Poetry's distribution problem was further compounded by the practically
nonexistent means of distribution for poetry in other media such as sound,
performance, and the visual.

The possibilities for poetry's writing in electronic space are to be reck-
oned with. Electronic technology offers unprecedented opportunities for

the production, archiving, distribution, and promotion of poetry texts, but the most important aspect of electronic space is that it is a space of poeisis.

Several computer-poetry[2] production efforts were made from 1980 to 1990;[3] yet during that decade, poetry's victories in the electronic realm remained scattered, and the texts themselves often proved elusive. (Divergent programs were required for operation. Moreover, some of the publishers involved were arguing the proprietary status of their texts and fighting distribution battles tougher than those of the small press.) The nineties also compounded the difficulty of access to specific electronic texts with the rise of the Internet and the Web. Though this might seem a contradiction, the sudden proliferation of electronic texts of all varieties has made access to specific types of writing even more challenging. What have become crucial in the climate of this textual dystopia are (1) gathering places or subject villages for texts with related engagements, and (2) a recognition of the materiality of digital poetry texts.

Sites

Central to the success of electronic poetry is the notion of a "subject village," a site for the access, collection, and dissemination of poetry and related writing. Such a site provides a gathering ground, floodplain, mortar for the pestle of poesis. It should be understood that such a subject village neither attempts to collect everything, nor does it exert "control" in a traditional sense. Rather, it does the following:

• It collects materials according to an editorial policy. Its contribution to the Web lies in its provision of a focused collection of texts.
• It facilitates the dissemination of print publications (resulting ultimately in royalties for authors) through the maintenance of bibliographic and promotional vehicles. It also makes possible other types of publications that may have been unprofitable in the print medium.
• It serves as a gateway to relevant, externally available electronic resources.
• The circulation of texts becomes its primary mission.
• It exists in the context of the Web. That is, it not only delivers texts but also offers slow connect times, error messages, misgivings, and is interwoven with the megabytes of misinformation that typify a largely undisciplined textual space.
• Most important, the creation of a poetry archive of this order rests on the realization that the Web is itself an instance of writing.

Such sites can do much to locate the overlapping fields of practice that, taken together, begin to suggest the contours of digital poetry. Notable among such sites are the Electronic Poetry Center (EPC), Ubuweb, and Burning Press.[4] The EPC, founded and directed by the author of this book, operates under the aegis of the Poetics Program, Department of English, and

the College of Arts & Sciences at the State University of New York at Buf-
falo. The EPC served as a laboratory for the development of some of the
ideas presented in *Digital Poetics*. These three sites are described in fuller
detail in chapter 7 of this book.

Materials

Much as with earlier technologies, the electronic medium not only pro-
vides a means of publishing and distribution but also, as a technology, enters
the materials of writing. What writing *is* becomes altered by how it is physi-
cally written through its production technology, its files, codes, and URLs
(sometimes called "earls"). We are living in a material world, and these are
material URLs; that is, the URL itself contributes to your experience of
reading. What are you thinking as you key in those symbols, fragments of
names, tildes, and guttural utterances that invoke Web screens? For example,
how is your experience different approaching a writing at a URL containing
the path /authors/glazier/theories/hypertext.html versus /authors/glazier/
tomfoolery/hypertext.html? Such text strings are not transparent paths to
destination; rather they form part of the material of the page.

The same material influences occurred in the media of clay tablets, papy-
rus, and the codex, and the situation is no different now. Is there a parallel
for such an engagement with the material in the twentieth century? Think,
for example, of film—not when it attempts to reproduce reality but when it
functions as a medium consciously constituted of pans, camera angles, lens
effects, and montage. There are certain limits and specific effects concomi-
tant with the materials of a given medium. Further, the medium affects the
materiality of the work. An example of this is the way distortion, once a by-
product of electric instrumentation in rock music, has now become an
aesthetic element in the music. (The rock group Orgy's use of distortion in
their 1998 hit song "Blue Monday" is a prime example of this.) As a writing
medium, online electronic space depends on the fact that the Web is itself
an instance of writing. Not only do Web pages contain writing, but these
pages are presented through the medium of the home page and are them-
selves written in HTML (Hypertext Mark-up Language).[5]

In *Digital Poetics*, I look at such writing. Picture yourself with two win-
dows open on your computer screen: in one you are editing pure ASCII text
using the glistening, black Model T Ford of EMACS and sputtering through
the black-and-white fields of VT100.[6] In the other window you have Netscape
open,[7] that graphical but heinously sloppy browser that seems out to get
you with its delays, bull-headed error messages, and proclamations that it
just found you 750,000 items that exactly match your search for the term
"phanopoiea." You are editing not on some back-up system, then upload-
ing, but on the server itself; and every time you save your work in
progress—improvements, tests, errors—it is immediately available to the

world. The process has all the risks of live television; but there is an added excitement, because it is the act of writing that is the performance. In this investigation we will write, read, and breathe within the UNIX C-shell environment—a C-shell so efficient you swear you can hear the ocean if you put your ear to the monitor. This is a dynamic, expansive writing space, a pixelated "meadow" on a revolving disk inside a UNIX box. It is a field for which permission is an actual fact of the UNIX environment, in Robert Duncan's words (with the meadow representing creative space for Duncan):

Often I am permitted to return to a meadow
as if it were a given property of the mind
that certain bounds hold against chaos . . .

(Duncan, *Opening* 7)

The Web is a representational discourse cast from natural language cradled in the matted barbs of mark-up. If a field has it prose and versus, these are its verses, nested within a frame of webbed electronic poesis. Our task is to explore the texture of the clods the plow leaves behind; to celebrate its nitrogen, iron, and mulch, to furrow the "everlasting omen of what is" (Duncan, *Opening* 7).

Digital Poetics attempts to take on a task different than other books. First, this is a book about Web-based electronic writing viewed through the lens of *poetic* practice. It is not another book about "la vie en prose." Second, rather than idealize, hyperbolize, speak in the abstract, propose egolessness, waltz around conjectured possibilities, deny intention, postulate, berate, or generally irritate, the goal here is to argue electronic space *as a space of poesis;* to employ the tropes, hypertextualities, linkages, and static of the medium; to speak from the perspective of one up-to-the-elbows in the ink of this writing machine. (Though in this metaphor, the ink in question would be less like that of the printing press and more like the obfuscating fluid of the squid.)

It is also important to acknowledge that electronic writing has crossed the threshold into our common conversation. Indeed, our collective vocabulary is steadily growing: by some estimates, 25 percent of the new words entering the English language each year are now related to computing. Accordingly, *Digital Poetics* has only a brief glossary; the terms used here will be glossed whenever necessary, but I look toward the day when they become part of our collective vocabulary. I hope to suggest that one may go beyond looking at technology as something that should be on a shelf, labeled, and out of reach; there is much to be gained by simply investigating it *as writing.*

The digital field is a real form of practice and immediately relevant to any informed sense of what we will call "poetry" in coming years. But one must learn to see through a new lens, one with expanded focal points. Trying to understand the digital work solely through codex practice is like trying to understand film, for the person who has never seen one, by looking at a still. It is this general lack of understanding of the electronic text file as a physical, visual, and verbal writing *material* (akin to a Pollack-painted, barn-sized wall of dizzying links, splotches of error, and black holes of hang time) that is addressed here.

This study presents not a theory of electronic textual artifice, not emotion as represented by the emoticon (;>), but an investigation into the materiality of electronic writing. It addresses, to varying depths, the three principal forms of electronic textuality: hypertext, visual/kinetic text, and works in programmable media. (Though by the end of this study the goal is to emerge with a clear sense of the relative importance of these three forms.) It does not try to determine what might occur under ideal conditions. Rather, it looks at electronic textuality as writing per se and investigates how the materiality of electronic writing has changed the idea of writing itself, how this writing functions in the real world of the Web, and what writing becomes when activated in the electronic medium. A sense of "active" is being argued here, similar to what William Carlos Williams argued for the print poem. As Robert Creeley mentioned at a reading in Buffalo (5 Nov. 1999), Williams's insistence was not on the poem as afterthought (the classic concept of "recollections collected in tranquility") but on the poem as itself an instrument of thought. He has written: "I've never forgotten Williams' contention that 'the poet thinks with his poem, in that lies his thought, and that in itself is the profundity. . . . ' Poems have always had this nature of revelation for me, becoming apparently objective manifestations of feelings and thoughts otherwise inaccessible" (*Essays* 572). The poem is not some idealized result of thinking: the poet thinks *through* the poem. Similarly, investigated here is not the idea of the digital work as an extension of the printed poem, but the idea of the digital poem as the process of thinking through this new medium, thinking through *making*. As the poet works, the work discovers.

Documentary Materials

> threatening construction on its very
> printed page, corrector fluid
> swashbuckling first words
> formatted like a river ending
> in a window . . .
> —John Kinsella, *The Undertow*

Curiously, though material about the Web and its various practices and manifestations, both in print and online, is more voluminous than one might easily enumerate, well-written literature on electronic poetries is sparse. Indeed, many areas overlap, and it can be easy to make mistakes about what material might be relevant to the study of digital poetics. What is helpful here, before looking at the small number of sources on digital poetries, is to

delineate areas tangential to this topic. The areas that follow are not neces-
sarily germane to digital poetry per se but are mentioned here in order to
map the parameters that form the point of departure for this study.

The Digital Context

The present field of digital media studies developed from a diverse mix of
lines of inquiry, a mix that interweaves sociology, computer science, literary
theory, and science fiction, among other fields. The earliest of these works
include Marshall McLuhan's *The Gutenberg Galaxy: The Making of Typographic
Man* (Toronto: U of Toronto P, 1962) and *Understanding Media: The Exten-
sions of Man* (Cambridge: MIT P, 1994, originally 1964). Emergent theories
of the text as pioneered by Roland Barthes in *S/Z* (New York: Farrar, Straus,
& Giroux, 1974) and Jean Baudrillard in books such as *Symbolic Exchange
and Death* (London: Sage, 1993) and *Simulacra and Simulation* (Ann Arbor:
U of Michigan P, 1994) provided key terms and concepts for conceptualiz-
ing the field. Theodor Holm Nelson's *Literary Machines 93.1* (Sausalito, CA:
Mindful, 1992, originally 1980) was an insightful early theorization of net-
worked textuality, whereas William Gibson's *Neuromancer* (New York: Ace,
1984) was singularly influential as the first conceptualization of cyberspace.
Books such as *Cyberspace: First Steps*, edited by Michael Benedikt (Cambridge,
MA: MIT P, 1991) and Ed Krol's *The Whole Internet User's Guide & Catalog*
(Sebastopol, CA: O'Reilly, 1992) served as landmarks in early efforts to,
respectively, theorize and provide subject access to the medium.

Since the original issuance of such works, varying digital investigations
have progressed, allowing numerous distinct fields of practice to emerge as
key fields of inquiry. These include cyberpunk and science fiction, informatics
and information theory, scholarly textual editing and humanities comput-
ing, hypertext and hypertheory, hypertext fiction, digital culture, digital art,
and media studies. Obviously, different fields of inquiry are never entirely
independent, and I will touch upon some of these areas in the course of this
book, most notably hypertext and hypertheory, hypertext fiction, and, to a
much lesser extent, scholarly textual editing and humanities computing.
Though, for the most part, these fields lie outside of the focus of this book,
it is important to note some of the more important points of difference and
convergence, admitting that some generalizations are necessary in order to
provide a quick sketch of the context of this book.

An area not directly related to *Digital Poetics* is the field of scholarly tex-
tual editing and humanities computing. One of this field's most prominent
spokespersons for the application of technology to literary studies, Jerome
McGann, has written convincingly of the importance of digital media to
scholarly editions. Jerome McGann's essays, "The Rationale of Hypertext"
and "Radiant Textuality," extend ideas introduced in his books *The Textual
Condition* (Princeton, NJ: Princeton UP, 1991) and *Black Riders: The Visible
Language of Modernism* (Princeton, NJ: Princeton UP, 1993). These essays

reflect the importance of the electronic medium to the future of scholarly textual editing. McGann suggests that "scholarly editions comprise the most fundamental tools in literary studies" ("Rationale"). Considering that such editions have been limited by the codex format, he notes that this situation can now change: "We stand at the beginning of a great scholarly revolution. Even now we operate under the extraordinary promise this revolution holds out: to integrate the resources of all libraries, museums, and archives and to make those resources available to all persons no matter where they reside physically" ("Radiant"). His project involves not only the expansion of the role of the library to include digital texts but also the investigation of new methods of criticism and interpretation for the scholar, as he illustrates through numerous examples.

Clearly, McGann's work provides an eloquent and extensive argument for the importance of digital media to scholarly editing and should not be overlooked. Also of note in this field is the Institute for Advanced Technology in the Humanities at the University of Virginia, Charlottesville,[8] an organization that furthers the use of digital media for scholarly purposes. The Center for Electronic Texts in the Humanities[9] is a central source of information about the tools, standards, and practices that constitute scholarly textual editing, text encoding, the building of repositories of electronic texts and corpora, and related electronic text projects. Linguists, historians, textual theorists, literary historians, and other scholars employ such tools and corpora in their research. For those interested in this field, the "Selective Bibliography for Humanities Computing" provides an excellent source of information.[10]

Similar to the concerns of humanities computing is the field of hypertheory. Practitioners in this field—David Jay Bolter, George Landow, Michael Joyce, Jakob Nielsen, and others—focus less on standards and methods of literary investigation; instead, their attention is on the relation between hypertext and literary practice. Some of these practitioners are also keenly interested in the consonance between some post-Structuralist theory and hypertextual practice, though these connections are sometimes evoked rather than systematically argued. Most of these are writers are primarily concerned with the academic possibilities of hypertext and the relation of hypertext to teaching literature, providing alternate forms of criticism and enabling varieties of annotation to literary works. Some of the most influential texts in this field include *Hypertext and Hypermedia* by Jakob Nielsen (San Diego: Academic, 1990); *Writing Space: The Computer, Hypertext, and the History of Writing* by Jay David Bolter (Hillsdale, NJ: Lawrence Erlbaum Associates, 1991); *Hypertext: The Convergence of Contemporary Critical Theory and Technology* by George P. Landow (Baltimore: Johns Hopkins, 1992); and *Of Two Minds: Hypertext, Pedagogy, and Poetics* by Michael Joyce (Ann Arbor: U of Michigan P, 1995).

Related to and overlapping with the interests of hypertheorists is the practice of hypertext fiction, which is often confused with digital poetics. Michael Joyce and Stuart Moulthrop are two major names in hypertext fiction, a field that has been heavily influenced by Eastgate Systems (developers of Storyspace hypertext authoring software) and Robert Coover's hypertext fiction workshops at Brown University. "Hypertext at Brown" (http://landow.stg.brown.edu/HTatBrown/BrownHT.html [15 Jan. 2000]) provides useful information about events at Brown, and the Eastgate Web page (http://www.eastgate.com [15 Jan. 2000]) offers information about Storyspace, information on writers connected with Eastgate, and a hypertext bibliography (http://www.eastgate.com/Bibliography.html [15 Jan. 2000]). For a thorough look at a variety of forms of hypertext, however, the RMIT HyperText Project at RMIT University, Melbourne, Australia (http://hypertext.rmit.edu.au [15 Jan. 2000]), is probably the best resource available. This project, written by Adrian Miles, offers a collection of texts about hypertext that have been meticulously culled by a search robot; it is a valuable site that is updated frequently.

Readers interested in the topography of digital studies are encouraged to consult Matthew Kirschenbaum's "A White Paper on Information" (http://www.iath.virginia.edu/~mgk3k/white [15 Jan. 2000]). Kirschenbaum's essay provides a thorough and exacting outline of these disciplines and detailed analyses of visual aesthetics and information theory and of the history of theories of cyberspace. He also encourages us to hone our critical tools and to interrogate our assumptions about information more thoroughly. Indeed, Kirschenbaum's studies of information and aesthetics are crucial, and readers are also encouraged to consult his essay, "Machine Visions: Towards a Poetics of Artificial Intelligence" (http://www.altx.com/ebr/ebr6/6kirschenbaum/6kirsch.htm [15 Jan. 2000]), as well as his dissertation, "Lines for a Virtual T[y/o]pography: Electronic Essays on Artifice and Information" (http://www.iath.virginia.edu/~mgk3k/dissertation/title.html [15 Jan. 2000]), of which "A White Paper" is a chapter.

Of the scholars and writers mentioned thus far, the most influential to *Digital Poetics* is Jerome McGann. Though McGann's emphasis on the preparation of electronic scholarly editions is outside the scope of the interests of this book, his concept of "the textual condition" is central to the type of materiality discussed here. Speaking of the network of exchanges that constitute human communication, he writes, "Even in their most complex and advanced forms—when the negotiations are carried out as textual events—the intercourse that is being human is materially executed: as spoken texts or scripted forms." The "textual condition" defined by McGann is foundational to the concept of the conditional text put forward here, writing that exists within the material dynamics of electronic space. This is a conditionality that Matthew Kirschenbaum also explores at length, especially in relation to the visual aesthetics of information.

In terms of literary theory about alternative textuality, Charles Bernstein's

A Poetics (Cambridge: Harvard UP, 1992), Marjorie Perloff's *Radical Artifice* (Chicago: Chicago UP, 1991), Adalaide Morris's *Sound States* (Chapel Hill, NC: U of North Carolina P, 1998), and *Experimental—Visual—Concrete* edited by K. David Jackson, Eric Vos, and Johanna Drucker (Amsterdam: Rodopi, 1996), though not direct analyses of the poetics of electronic space, are works that exemplify productive ways of thinking about alternative textualities. A key work of theory in this regard has been Espen Aarseth's influential book, *Cybertext: Perspectives on Ergodic Literature* (Baltimore: Johns Hopkins UP, 1997). In this book, Aarseth delineates numerous new forms of technology, and it is a crucial work to any consideration of the plural forms of "writing" present in the digital medium. An important update to some of the issues raised in Aarseth's book can be found in Marie-Laure Ryan's *Cyberspace Textuality: Computer Technology and Literary Theory* (Bloomington: Indiana UP, 1999), a useful collection of articles illuminating various issues in digital textuality.

Writings in electronic format have also provided significant discussions about digital textuality. *Postmodern Culture*'s 1997 hypertext issue,[11] edited by Stuart Moulthrop, is an important resource. It contains hypertexts by Michael Joyce, Diana Reed Slattery, John Cayley, and by "The Tribe of the Chalk," hypertextual articles by Matthew G. Kirschenbaum and me, and an article by Craig Saper. Of crucial interest are three issues of the *Electronic Book Review*,[12] including the "Image+Narrative" series edited by Steve Tomasula and Anne Burdick, *EBR 6*, Part One (Winter 1997/98) and *EBR 7*, Part Two (Summer 1998), as well as EBR 5 "(electro)poetics" (Spring 1997) edited by Joel Felix. These issues cover much territory, with contributions by Charles Bernstein, John Cayley, Eduardo Kac, Steve Tomasula, Kirschenbaum, Marta Werner, and J. Hillis Miller, among many others.

Finally, it must be noted that innovative poetry in the print medium has contributed a crucial context for the types of textuality investigated in this book. As will be discussed later, the procedures and practices of poets as diverse as John Ashbery, Bruce Andrews, Joan Retallack, Susan Howe, Robert Creeley, Charles Bernstein, Jackson Mac Low, Rachel Blau DuPlessis, Larry Eigner, Fluxus and Oulipo writers, and many poets featured in *Poems for the Millennium* (Berkeley: U of California P, vol. 1, 1995, and vol. 2, 1998), as well as writers of prose or mixed genres, such as Jorge Luis Borges, Gertrude Stein, James Joyce, and William Carlos Williams, have opened paths of understanding key to this study. It is important to recognize the lines of continuity between innovative practice in print and digital media and to be aware that many of the concepts pioneered by innovative poetry practice offer us the chance to understand digital practice much more clearly, a point central to this investigation.

Poetry in Electronic Media

News of computers and poetry have appeared in the mainstream media: one occasionally hears references to Robert Pinsky arguing in the *New York Times* for the "fundamental affinity between poetry and personal computers" (Mirapaul). Pinsky has had an ongoing interest in computers, a fact that may have added to his desirability as U.S. Poet Laureate. He is the author of an interactive text adventure game, "Mindwheel," which he created in 1983. Of the affinity between poetry and computers, Pinsky argues that they both offer "the discovery of large manifold channels through a small, ordinary-looking or all but invisible aperture," because both can evoke worlds from small amounts of text. "This passage to vast complexities," Pinsky notes, "is at the essence of what writing through the machine might become," emphasizing the compression made possible by digital media. Besides such statements in the *New York Times*, one also hears the argument for hypertext in popular media for writers. For example, Robert Kendall's 1995 article in *Poets & Writers Magazine*, "Writing for the New Millennium: The Birth of Electronic Literature," in which Kendall asserts the ability of electronic literature to break "the bonds and stasis imposed by paper." He details some of the advantages of digital poetry—its ability to enjoy increased circulation, employ multimedia, and be interactive. Though he embraces various qualities of the digital medium, and he does this enthusiastically and encouragingly, his vision of the digital text seems to be related to narrative rather than materiality. Of his own work, "A Life Set for Two," for example, he notes in the same article that "the reader roams through ruminations and memories of failed love, as if following different trains of thought" (Kendall), suggesting a story-based approach to his text. Nonetheless, Kendall's article identifies some useful points in the transition to writing beyond paper, and the appearance of such articles demonstrates increased general consciousness of poetry in electronic space. These articles by Pinsky and Kendall, however, contribute little to the exploration of the material nature of electronic writing.

Of the small number of print publications presenting digital poetry or the results of e-poetry procedures, a few stand out as particularly important. These are *Sentences* (Los Angeles: Sun & Moon, 1995) by Charles O. Hartman and Hugh Kenner; *Virtual Muse: Experiments in Computer Poetry* (Hanover, NH: UP of New England, 1996) by Charles O. Hartman; and Jackson MacLow's *Barnesbook* (Los Angeles: Sun & Moon, 1996). *Sentences* uses computer-executed deterministic methods to generate the text of the published book. That is, first the computer executes specified procedures; then the authors make revisions according to their vision for the text. *Sentences* contains a useful afterword by Kenner, who has had a long-standing interest in technology's relation to literature. (He is the author of *The Mechanic Muse* [New York: Oxford UP, 1987], a look at the impact of technology on selected modernist writers, and also has co-written, with Joseph O'Rourke, the computer program *Travesty* published in 1984 in *Byte* magazine.) *Virtual Muse* is a collection of thoughtful essays on the topic of using computers to generate poetry and on the relationship between computers and poetry. Hartman is a key contributor to all of the books mentioned here. Not only is he the author or co-author of the first two, but he is a less-than-obvious contributor to the third, since he wrote the programs that made it possible for Mac Low to generate *Barnesbook*. Hartman is also the author of significant books of literary theory and brings an important perspective to a discussion of computers and poetry. "When poetry is treated as the hallowed repository of sacred Culture, it's dead," Hartman writes, arguing that poetry involves *doing*. Hartman's argument is crucial, framing an approach that makes computer generation of text a natural interest of innovative poetry; a field, as we will see, with few tools.

The most important book published in this area is *Barnesbook*, which, like *Sentences*, is the result of computer-assisted deterministic processes. Mac Low is the winner of the 1999 Tanning Prize from the Academy of American Poets, a prize that recognizes outstanding and proven mastery in the art of poetry. This mastery extends to a number of books he has written using deterministic procedures, of which *Barnesbook* is but one example. *Barnesbook* also contains a very useful afterword, detailing his work with computers and procedures over the years. One additional source should be added to the category that includes these three books: It is *Poems for the Millennium*. This important anthology of innovative poetries in the twentieth century includes a section on e-poetries, "Towards a Cyberpoetics: The Poem in the Machine," a small but important acknowledgment of the place of e-poetries within the avant-garde tradition.

Documentary material on e-poetries has been sparse; however, two major collections of articles have been issued. First, the important resource, the "New Media Poetry: Poetic Innovation and New Technologies" issue of *Visible Language*, offers one of the best collections of essays on the genre. Included are essays by Eduardo Kac (holography), Philippe Bootz (location poems), E. M. de Melo e Castro (videopoetry), André Vallias (diagrammatic poetry), and Ladislao Pablo Györi (virtual poetry), as well as John Cayley (programmable media), Jim Rosenberg (hypertext), and theoretical writing by Eric Vos. Cayley's "Beyond Codexspace: Potentialities of Literary Cybertext" describes some of Cayley's e-poetic compositions and also argues for a poetics of electronic space that moves us from simple hypertext into the "scoring of the spelt air" that might be the standard for electronic textuality in the future (Cayley, "Beyond" 169). An expanded collection of these essays is also scheduled for publication in book form by the University of Chicago Press. Second, the special combined issue of the magazines, *DOC(K)S* and *ALIRE*, *DOC(K)S ALIRE* 3, 13–16 (1997) provides a superb selection of articles in various languages about digital poetry, including numerous theoretical works (Augusto De Campos, Jean-Pierre Balpe, Philippe

Bootz, Philippe Castellin, Clemente Padin, and others) along with a CD containing digital works (Balpe, Bootz, Cayley, De Campos, Kac, Rosenberg, and others).

Sidebar: On Techne

On the Web, writings converge, a flickering cellulose nitrate film stream of texts, malformations, kinetic plays flickering in close proximity to the blaze of the projector arc lamp. Webbed information speeding in an onslaught of virtual fire, scripts, and rapid links. Jack Spicer as an antenna receiving transmissions or Rimbaud thought through. In this case, however, it's not "On me pense" but "Oh me pense on fire."
—Loss Pequeño Glazier, *Tango*

At this point it is useful to focus specifically on some aspects of techne and look at the context within which one can "make"—a crucial concern for the poetics of any medium, documented at least since the time of Aristotle. Techne, with its resonance with "technical," may be even more important in the digital environment, a medium where materials are not always apparent.

On UNIX

It should indeed be admitted that there is a UNIX bias to computing as described in this book. Despite the incendiary rise of the NT server paradigm, a product that may very well seize the entire market, there is UNIX.[13] The open and collaborative basis of UNIX—and the fact that it has developed into a shared programming space with access to source code for the user—may be much more fruitful as a metaphor for the more interesting possibilities for digital writing. UNIX has developed so that a number of users can simultaneously use a computer and also so that software can be ported among disparate computer systems; in this sense it may have been the first networked system to exist on an extended scale.

From early on, UNIX embodied a visionary sense of system, or "distributed intelligence," that recognizes the need for computers to be interlinked. Such a vision of interconnectivity, as John Cage suggested in "Aspects of a New Consciousness," extends the idea of the individual nervous system to a worldwide scale, with the possibilities that such a sense of scale presents. Certainly, the continuing enthusiasm for Linux (UNIX's PC avatar, a system conceived precisely in the spirit of shared, noncorporate computing) suggests that there is an interest in this approach to technology. *UNIX was designed as a networked, collaborative, and shared programming environment;* NT is a proprietary imitator of those concepts, though we must be fair and admit its prevalence—and cost effectiveness—for many small providers. NT's ties to a model of corporate control can further be seen by the fact that some organizations have implemented NT instead of Windows 98 in order to restrict the ability of individual computer users to install their own software. In such cases, though a user may be classed a "superuser," the "administrator" category is usually reserved for the computing department. Among several reasons for withholding such an ability, is to allow administrators the ability to verify that each piece of software is licensed. Thus we have a proprietary system designed to make its *own* interests a higher priority, in some cases, than those of the user.

Someone who is familiar with NT only, may not have experiences outside of that system: for those readers, it is urged that you let your imagination run free. Imagine worlds within worlds where metaphors of the shell, permissions, the command line, and symbolic links suggest productive ways of viewing a computing environment. Imagine an arcane, foreign language, that at first seems like a tar baby of befuddling syntax, embarrassing slips of the tongue, and the ever-present faux pas. But in this quagmire you experience the exhilaration that knowledge of other languages brings: the new forms of expression and turns of phrase that make fluid what was once awkward, the opportunity to re-view your own ideas in a different discourse, to find new tools for abstract thought. Such a language, once learned, allows you to be precise and efficient in your interactions, not dependent upon programs written for the lowest common denominator user or obtusely unresponsive in their prêt-à-porter generic design.

UNIX has certain possibilities that do not carry over to its commercial competitor. The command system, error messages, and conventions in UNIX may at first seem difficult, but UNIX professionals see it as simple, modular, flexible, and extensible. It can also be seen as highly poetic, employing sparse, condensed syntax for powerful effects. The UNIX system, as it developed, has made possible collaboration, free access to code, and end-user customization of the computing environment. It offers possibilities for conceptualizing space that are compelling. For example, the fact that, in UNIX, "a directory is simply present and rarely gives any clues as to its physical location or nature" (Heath, *Newnes* 8) makes for a very poetic nesting of writing within the flexibility that virtual space offers. (This concept is one that also forecasted the Web, years before it actually appeared.) The symbolic link, as a second example, allows one to place a pseudo-link in one directory to simulate a different directory's being within it. Yet it does so in a way that the information is not merely simulated but, for the reader, is functionally in both places at once. The long directory listings format ("ls -lag") provides a powerfully concise numeric "mapping" of access levels. These and many similar features suggest that UNIX is a system with intensely compelling poetic features. For that reason, metaphors of UNIX are referred to here and are used to invoke such qualities.

On HTML

HTML is usually thought of as being much more complicated than it is. Referred to as mark-up or code,[14] HTML is simply a system for marking documents that has, as its fundamental premise, the placement of tags. Tags describe how text will look or where text will appear when viewed through a browser program such as Netscape or Internet Explorer. For the most part, HTML mark-up consists of simple on and off tags. For example, <i> will begin a section of italics and </i> will end it. Thus <i>italics</i> will display as *italics* and bold will display **bold**.

In addition to their state of being on or off, some tags have attributes, elements that qualify what the tag does. For example, if <H1>Welcome</H1> describes text to be represented as a heading (larger and bolder than the text's base font), the attribute ALIGN=CENTER, in the form <H1 ALIGN =CENTER>Welcome</H1> will not only represent the word "Welcome" as heading text but also center it on its line within the browser window. Tags may also have multiple attributes, making the mark-up at times even more difficult to read. Additionally, there are always exceptions. For example, some tags do not require both on and off elements to be present.

Facilities introduced in HTML 4.0 extend HTML's layout capabilities somewhat, but HTML can never sustain a "fixed" text. Indeed, HTML's most appealing quality is its lack of fixity. Because all browsers and all configurations of all browsers cannot be anticipated, HTML mark-up, in poignant contradistinction to typesetting for printing, proposes a provisional or conditional text. (Innovative poetry, it will be argued, has a historic interest in such a vision of the text.) HTML markup details a general layout, a skeleton or arrangement of the *parts* of the document, over which the displayed version of the writing is draped like cloth or a very loose skin. The fact that HTML operates within such a conditional space for the text brings a significant fluidity to textual practice in the Web environment. The shift from the paradigm of print, where all details can be specified down to the millimeter (or ems and ens), changes the writer's relation to the text. Writing in this environment consists of proposing a text that will withstand changing conditions, a text that will deliver its message despite widely varying conditions (e.g., the reader may not receive any images, hear sound, or may not see items in the position where they were placed). Because much or all of your text may not be received, you must, to be successful, create a text that is somehow suspended between various possibilities of reading; such an e-text is provisional, conditional, and characterized by its multiple renderings. Writing thus becomes less a matter of a canonical "laying down the law" and more of a dance between possibilities of representation.[15] It requires a writer who can create a work that aims for a proposed rendering—a work with a program not a floor plan—a rendering that is adaptable, flexible, and able to communicate by placing writing in a suspension between possibilities, not by fixing it with any given finality.

Although a wide array of WYSIWYG software exists for the creation of HTML pages, most purists would probably argue for HTML written by hand. There can be immense benefits to writing in "raw code." Among these benefits are certain kinds of control, structure, and style not available through all HTML generating programs. For example, some of these programs only insert HTML in all uppercase letters. Can you imagine a word processor that only allows the creation of uppercase text? Other programs automatically insert code to credit themselves for creating the document. There are many benefits to writing HTML directly. Key is the ability to position comments or subtextual writing with precision and to be able to insert special types of comments for access by programs. Not all readers will choose to write code directly. Nevertheless, being able to at least **read** the code, as will be argued in this book, can be immensely valuable, if not essential. (The "view markup" option of most browsers allows almost universal access to code, benefitting both beginners and advanced readers of HTML.) "Read" is used here in the sense of not only reading the narrative of the coded page but also reading the ideological implications and textual strategies that certain choices in mark-up suggest.

State of the Art

Charisma of morning oxygen,
totally numb with vista.

An unparalleled and
very nervous breakdown of underground
Mirror Doors.
—Kevin Davies, "Thunk"

Now one realized the book and the labyrinth were one and the same.
—Jorge Luis Borges, *Ficciones*

As if from a Pandora's box of cross-purposes, the Web's growth has been rapid and mostly unplanned. The Web began in 1969, when the very first nodes of the ARPAnet were wired for military and research purposes; it was the same year that human beings landed on the moon and the last year of the cultural revolution of the sixties, marked by Woodstock. The year 1983 saw the introduction of the Internet protocol. In 1987, the Department of Defense removed itself from the management of the network, launching the Internet into an unbridled, free-ranging, and chaotic era of development. The popularization of the Internet followed directly thereafter. Espen Aarseth notes: "The idea (and ideology) of the Internet seems to have crystallized around 1988–89, when the number of users reached the critical mass sufficient to catch the interest of the mass media, helped by such major events as the 'Internet worm' incident" (98), the first mass-media virus scare. The fact that such a scare attracted the attention of the mainstream media meant that the Internet had come of age.

From this point, coinciding with the availability of increasingly affordable personal computers, the Internet grew at an astronomical rate,[16] and the problem of how to manage and navigate this flood of information emerged as a pressing issue. At first, FTP and telnet were dominant modes of retrieving files and accessing remote sites. These were efficient protocols, quirky and enigmatic, almost poetically abstract. For most users such forms of access were cumbersome, necessitating a bevy of vexatious commands. Moreover, such commands differed from platform to platform, making mastery of these tools even more elusive. What became necessary was a protocol that could combine different functions into one interface.

At this point the specter of the Web's previous iteration must be raised. How many Web surfers would be able to name the Web's precursor? Would the name "gopher" draw blanks? And yet, gopher was an important step in the gathering of the protocols that has become the Web. Gopher was named for a rodent that burrows, since the metaphor for the Net at the time was a series of "underground" tunnels, a metaphor that carried with it the suggestion of a sixties-like counterculture or an alternative information culture. As yet the Web was thought of as an "underground" operation. Compare this with the present connotations of "the Web" as a virtual mall!

Gopher, a text-only interface, solved many problems and initiated the Internet revolution. Indeed, the whole context of that network was different, because the user had to commit to multiple metaphors of access in order to succeed. Such metaphors were embodied in the separate processes for file handling, indexing, and searching that had to be mastered—telnet, FTP, Archie, Veronica, and WAIS, among them. The user had to achieve mastery of the idiom and be fluent in the fundamentals of the Internet. This is unlike the present incarnation of the Web, which requires little knowledge of what is going on, an indication that passive consumption is a key to the paradigm of the Internet as it has been reinscribed in the form we know as the Web.

Gopher's major drawback, in today's terms, was that gopher did not display images. Instead, it was predominantly text. The system did allow the retrieval of images, but first you had to download them, then open them with a separate image-displaying program on your computer for viewing. That is, you could get images, but you could not see them before you saved them, and downloads could take substantial amounts of time. You had to be committed to get the picture! An interesting characteristic of gopher was that it amounted to a flood of text. There was text everywhere, and you could get it all—even on a 1200-baud modem. It was a day when minimal technology resulted in maximum (textual) results. Somehow, one might say that it was a wholly lexical era that preceded the advent of the Web as we know it.

In certain ways, the textual nature of gopher defined its providers and users in a way that was unique to the period. In fact, if we think of all the exchange of text that took place, gopher and the system of text-based hypertext it employed, may have marked a kind of age of innocence for digital poetry, a last great days of print.

Next came the World Wide Web. Released for use by CERN, the European Particle Physics Institute in Geneva, Switzerland, in May 1991, the Web offered an interface that allowed images and text to coexist in the reading area. Suddenly, a whole new group of users, most notably commercial ones, became interested in the medium, partly because of the possibility for these images to be advertisements. Some problems still existed in the Web's first phase, such as the lack of common formats for some files, especially audio and video, and the problems associated with having to download some large multimedia files before they could be used. This period was followed by the birth of the Web as we know it: as technologies were introduced that let files stream, or be used as they were being received, the Web became alternately multimedia and full-color advertisement. Now we are almost flooded by media, including images, audio, video, animations, and more. Now the resources of the Web include a plurality of forms. It is a totally new terrain, but certain facts remain unchanged.

The basic concept of hypertext, the linchpin of the gopher world, almost goes unnoticed amidst the Flash animations, video, and sound of the new world. Of course, hypertext is the basic grammar of Web navigation and must be investigated extensively. Further, the gamut of decisions that have resulted in the consensual experience that constitutes a network must be evaluated. When you consider the basic functions of such a system, you must think about the decisions that have been made. (Why, as one example, is the Web user not allowed to turn off a designer's "spawn window" capability, that function that allows each click to result in more and more browser windows? How could such an invasion of one's desktop—and mental space—be permissible?) What should be questioned? What should be accepted? What terms, structures, nomenclature, should be accepted or rejected? One should not consent to protocols, default settings, interface design without question. Such parameters of online reading and writing, like the format of "the book," do not serve as a transparent conveyance for meaning. Rather, they define the possibilities for meaning in a given medium. We need a critical view of the Web, not one that is New Critical, presenting its content with an uncontested authority. Nothing should be accepted blindly! Our metaphors, our preconceptions, and the sales pitch that is everywhere—even preloaded on the desktop of your out-of-the-box computer—should all be questioned without surrender.

The E-Writing Condition

> the words are meaningless
> until they emerge in the action
> —Robin Blaser, *The Holy Forest*

> Pensé en el fuego, pero temí que la combustión de un libro
> infinito fuera parejamente infinita y sofocara de humo al
> planeta.[17]
> —Jorge Luis Borges, *El Libro*

> Writing is for me the most viable and open condition of
> possibility in the world.
> —Robert Creeley, *Collected Essays*

In "The Book of Sand," a story by the Argentinean poet, writer, and librarian, Jorge Luis Borges, a traveling Bible salesman sells the story's narrator a book that is different every time you open it. (The fact that the salesman sells Bibles suggests an ironic play on the idea of a book as being "the word."[18] This irony is reinforced later, when the salesman is referred to as a "Bible peddler," a disparaging term.) Of the book, the peddler instructs, "Look at it well. You will never see it again" (*Collected* 481). The book is called "The Book of Sand," because, like sand, it is described as being without beginning or end. How does the book work? "The number of pages in this book is literally infinite. No page is the first page; no page is the last" (482). The narrator purchases the book and eventually becomes a prisoner of his desire to master it. His obsession with the book propels him to believe that "It was a nightmare thing, an obscene thing, and that it defiled and corrupted reality" (483).

Borges's story provides, like many of his stories, a premonition of the dilemma of the book of the future. Though published in 1975, eight years before the introduction of the Internet protocol, it seems to describe well the crisis in textuality that is presently being explored by poets, writers, and literary scholars. The narrator in the story experiences a rift between the old textual order and the new. Because he is a bibliophile (one with a vested interest in the book and also one whose aesthetic is intricately tied to codex technology), the resistance to this "conditional" text is especially strong willed. The narrator goes to extraordinary lengths to defuse the book's potential. Finally, after being unable to document a pattern to its shifting pages, the narrator finally decides get rid of the book in some definitive way. Ironically he hides the book in the national library. He swears that he will never again even walk down the street the library is on. (A library is the last place anyone would ever look for a book of the future!) It is important to note that

Borges can be considered the father of Latin American fiction, an experimental form that features extra-rational texts able to embody both the contradictions of post-colonial Latin American history and the complex religious beliefs of Latin American peoples. Thus, he could be considered to have a special interest in alternatives to dominant paradigms of power. This story is even more extraordinary if one looks on "The Book of Sand" in light of the Web, the "book" of the third millennium A.D. context. This "book" is one that similarly is never the same, whose pages can never be trusted to be there when one returns, one that seems to threaten the traditional dominance of the static, printed text.

Most important, "The Book of Sand" illustrates quite tangibly the idea of a conditional space for writing, a concept that *Digital Poetics* seeks to illuminate. Specifically, the argument is as follows: Writing in electronic media, whether simple Web pages, text generated by an algorithm, or pages that display kinetically, is writing that exists within specific *conditions* of textuality. Such writing has different properties than the writing to which we are accustomed. These properties include the fact that the text is not physical but is displayed (similar to film, holograms, and other "projected" media). Further, the characteristics of such a text points to the idea of an "intelligent" work: it can move according to a predetermined sequence, it can be produced on the fly, or it can respond to the input of the user. Under certain conditions, it can be cognizant of who the reader is, where the reader has been, what kind of machine he or she is using to access the text. Conceivably, it could enter the reader's machine and replicate and/or store itself without the reader's permission. These qualities evoke, at times, nightmarish visions (like Borges's story); but conversely, what interesting material this is for writing! Digital media offers a pliant, reusable, programmable, responsive material from which to construct a text.

"The Book of Sand" stands in opposition to the arguments of a number of leading hypertext practitioners who interpret the textual frontier as centering around the issue of narrative. This constant reliance on the idea of prose as central to digital writing demonstrates a singular pursuit and limited perspective. In the case of this story, for example, it is reductive to look at it as being solely about the crisis of conventional narrative. The narrator here is not trying to piece together a narrative; he is trying to fathom a post-Relativity pattern of textuality. Describing how such a book is possible, the Bible peddler comments, "If space is infinite, we are anywhere, at any point in space. If time is infinite, we are at any point in time" (482). The narrator is tormented because he is faced with the lack of a possibility of narrative. This is especially unsettling for a man whose most prized volume is the paragon of traditional narrative, a copy of Wyclif's black-letter Bible. When the narrator tries to penetrate the mystery of "The Book of Sand," he does not try to piece together a narrative; rather, a "prisoner of the Book," he tries to find a pattern to the text; that is, he tries to decipher the text's "algorithm": "I found that the small illustrations were spaced at two-thousand-page intervals. I began noting them down in an alphabetized notebook, which was very soon filled. They never repeated themselves" (483).

By this account, it is not a conventional hypertext that is being described.[19] Rather, it is a textual experience that is more dynamic, random in nature, more like a programmed text—one that is less about telling a story and more like a plunge into pure textual possibility. Accordingly, in terms of the digital possibilities for writing, it seems shortsighted to think that such possibilities should be explored solely within prose or solely by using narrative as a term of inquiry. In fact, the contrary could be argued; that is, twentieth-century art has managed to carve new possibilities for numerous disciplines, painting, sculpture, and music among them, through a refusal of the ideological baggage of narrative. Writing may be the last theater of this confrontation. Within the practice of writing, poetry has certainly been active in inventing the future of the word. Indeed, the processes of innovative poetry may be uniquely qualified to equip us to enter and investigate the expanded textuality of digital writing.

How could poetry be best suited to help us understand writing in the digital realm? Jerome McGann notes: "The object of poetry is to display the textual condition. Poetry is language that calls attention to itself, that takes its own textual activities as its ground subject. . . . Poetical texts operate to display their own practices, to put them forward as the subject of attention" (*Textual* 10-11). Therefore, one very interesting mission of poetry is to put forward investigations of textuality. This can occur in diverse ways, ranging from examining the conditions of the sonnet and its codes in Shakespeare, for example, to investigating code-like surfaces of text, as in David Melnick's *PCOET*.

PCOET is an intriguing work and is worth examining momentarily. Beginning with the typo in its title, it seems to be a book of typos and strikethroughs. From the first page it presents line after line of unintelligible, jumbled letters that seem to eschew any possibility of conventional meaning:

    t'inalie thodo
    to ~~tala~~
    ienstable
    ate sophoabl
    (16)

What is amazing, however, is that it is not just a few isolated lines that appear this way, nor is it solely one poem in the book—it is the entire book. These poems seem to conjure a tangled barrage of nonsense. *PCOET*, however, resembles good code, and after one examines it for a while, a certain field of action becomes clear. Clearly, the unit of "the poem" is claimed. Each of these units asserts a format of the poem: each is generally left-justified, numbered, and generally fits on one page. Once this general format is established, certain poems can stand in opposition. These include number 45, a dispersal of text fragments defying standard horizontal orientation on an expanded field of the page, reminiscent of some work by Susan Howe. Also departing from the general format of the poem is the series of mostly one-word poems in sections 62 to 83, the concluding section of the volume. Curiously, after a time, we can "read" these variations, because we begin to notice how the patterns of text change. Such perceptions give a sense of how the text progresses. One cannot argue that such perceptions constitute a literal reading of it, for very few words of the text are understandable. Yet *PCOET* does show how a text can be conditional, because "meaning" emerges once its conditions have been identified. Further *PCOET* shows one way that poetry, as a genre that investigates textuality, is uniquely qualified to offer a perspective important for the understanding of the conditional nature of digital media.

Indeed, poetry does offer a unique perspective, providing a vocabulary—such terms as metonymy, ambiguity, metaphor, conceit, concrete poetry, abstract poetry, measure, and meter[20]—terms congruous with the conceptual space of the digital medium. Within the field of poetry, and more directly applicable, are *innovative* poetry practices. Such practices have at their core the investigation of key issues relevant to e-poetries.

First, innovative poetry offers the perspective of the multiple "I." Because non-innovative writing centers on the exposition of a world as perceived from a self-constituted, monolinear, and sometimes solipsistic "I," it is not adequate to see the potentials of e-writing. (The old, "I write because I have my story to tell," offers neither an engagement with the materiality of new media nor with a society that needs to increasingly accept plural and non-egocentric viewpoints.) As McGann has noted, "to be human is to be involved with another, and ultimately with many others" (McGann, *Textual* 3). McGann suggests that the relation between persons needs to be emphasized over the viewpoint of the solitary ego. Of the position of the "I," Robert Creeley writes: "There is nothing I am, / nothing not. A place / between, I am. I am // more than thought, less / than thought" (*Poems* 317). Thus Creeley suggests that the "I" can be more broadly defined and more subtly dispersed than the identity present in an individual human ego. Accordingly, innovative poetry's historic concern with the multiple in discourse, perspective, and textual constitution, positions it uniquely to approach the multiple "I"s that are collapsed to form the polysemous, constantly changing multiple-author text known as the Web.

Second is the recognition of the importance of the materials of writing to writing itself. From Blake's investigation of image and text (as printer, poet, and artist), to Ezra Pound's typographic imagination, to the efforts of Charles Olson and Robert Duncan to argue the relation between the typewriter's machinations and the work itself, materiality is key to understanding innovative practice. In this regard, for example, a poem like Bernstein's poem beginning "I and the" (*Sophist* 59-80) shows the natural interchange between words in their poetic context and linguistic corpora studies, as if there were a natural affinity between computer analysis of text and innovative poetry. This range of interests from Blake to Duncan, to the writers associated with L=A=N=G=U=A=G=E and further to Susan Howe and Joan Retallack, helps to establish the field of concern with materiality from which a digital poetics can emerge.

The materials of the work are what count. William Blake, for example, combined word and image in his self-produced books. Blake's use of word and image was singular. As William Vaughn notes, "[Blake's] own position as being equally gifted in both [media] enabled him to explore the interchange in a unique manner. For with him painting was not simply the illustration of poetry, or even its rival. It was a counterpart, a genuine other half. Indeed, one might see the relationship as that of two voices singing a duet" (27-28). This inter-relation between media is crucial to digital space because the multimedia work is not a collection of different media that are juxtaposed but an arrangement of media that are interwoven in their interests. Further, in areas such as hypertext fiction, as text-based hypertext gives way to text-and-image hypertext, such concepts of hybrid activity are critical.

Materiality is important because writing is not an event isolated from its medium but is, to varying degrees, an engagement with its medium. This concern with the material has been a constant element in modern and contemporary innovative literature and is highly relevant to e-poetry. It is a trend that has continued through generations of innovative practice. Of Ezra Pound and the material, McGann writes:

> One of Pound's greatest contributions to poetry lies concealed in his attentiveness to the smallest details of his texts' bibliographical codes. Along with Mallarmé, Apollinaire, and many other modernist innovators, Pound felt that the renewal of the resources of poetry in an age of advanced mechanical reproduction required the artist to bring all aspects of textual production under the aegis of imagination. Nothing was to be taken for granted: the poetry would be brought forth not simply at the linguistic level, but in every feature of the media available to the scriptural imagination. (*Textual* 137)

McGann's insistence on "every feature of the media available to the scriptural imagination," is one that can illuminate immensely the field of e-poetic practice. It allows that e-writing infiltrate and investigate every corner of the digital palette—JavaScript, strands of poem in code, animated poetry text—a palette bursting with digital materiality. The machine itself, like Jackson Pollack's paint can, is a component of the process, a fact that Charles Olson emphasized, discussing his concept of projective verse, in respect to a previous writing technology, the typewriter:

> The irony is, from the machine has come one gain not yet sufficiently

observed or used, but which leads directly on toward projective verse and its consequences. It is the advantage of the typewriter that, due to its rigidity and its space precisions, it can, for a poet, indicate exactly the breath, the pauses, the suspensions even of syllables, the juxtapositions even of parts of phrases, which he intends. For the first time the poet has the stave and the bar a musician has had. For the first time he can, without the convention of rime and meter, record the listening he has done to his own speech and by that one act indicate how he would want any reader, silently or otherwise, to voice his work. (Olson, *Selected* 22)

Olson's reflections on the typewriter sound a call for the scriptoral imagination to engage the materiality under one's fingers. Thus, Olson suggests, literary form can be revitalized. Such a freeing of the word comes through recognition of how closely the machine's operation and writing are connected. This relation is so important that it becomes key to the reading or execution of the poem itself. As Robert Duncan explains about the relation between typography and his text, *Ground Work: Before the War:* "The caesura space becomes not just an articulation of phrasings but a phrase itself of silence. Space between stanzas become a stanza-verse of silence: in which the beat continues" (Duncan, *Ground* ix).

Such relations extend past the machine to include multiple elements of the text-producing activity. One must really expand one's concept of the production of writing to be able to see the plethora of variables present. As Jerome McGann has noted: "Most important . . . is to demonstrate the operation of [textual] variables at the most material . . . levels of the text: in the case of scripted texts, the physical form of books and manuscripts (paper, ink, typefaces, layouts) or their prices, advertising mechanisms, and distribution venues" (McGann, *Conditional* 12).

In the digital medium, these material levels include elements of electronic materiality: the magnetic medium, its compactness and rewritability, its transmissibility. For example, anyone who has painted or sculpted in both traditional and digital media can testify about the comparative pliancy of magnetic media. How easy it is to wipe it clean, to put something there and remove it, to copy specific motifs and then replicate them in the same or other files. Such properties allow one to stretch, to push, and to experiment in ways that other media do not allow. (There is still resistance in the medium, but it is of a completely different order.) Likewise, the properties of e-media (the ability to reproduce work in color, to instantaneously be able to give a copy to a collaborator in a distant land, to have a virtual gathering with other colleagues in other countries) introduce previously unheard of social and production factors. Finally, the ability to give a composition kinetic qualities, to have it move while displayed, or to be able to program permutations or variations into a work, makes it possible for the work to leave the world of rigidity and enter a textuality that is more multiple, variable, and vibrant.

Such e-poetic features were anticipated by a technology used from the 1950s to the 1970s for the circulation of poetry in what has come to be called "the Mimeo Revolution."[21] In this case the mode of production, the raw, on-the-fly appearance, uneven inking, often low-quality paper, and 8½-by-11-inch or 8½-by-14-inch format, seemed to directly or indirectly relate to the works being transmitted. First, these publications were characterized by inventiveness that seemed to declare them as "new poetry." Steven Clay notes: "The books and magazines of the Mimeo Revolution appear imbued with a vivid purity of intention which it is nearly impossible to conceive of creating in today's publications" (Clay 14). Secondly, the work itself seemed to share qualities of rawness or improvisational production. Though this is difficult to argue in any empirical way, there does seem to be a consonance between handmade or natural production quality and the straightforward language and subjects of Berrigan, the rough-edged drawings by Brainard, and the mix of genres in magazines like *C* or *Adventures in Poetry*. (I would suggest that the relation between hand-coded HTML and the e-text has a similar resonance.) Indeed, it is these production qualities that made it possible for material in French to be included in *C* in a nonpretentious, straightforward manner, because no claim is made, through production, for any aspiration to high culture. Moreover, it was especially important that poets had taken over the means of poetry production, a fact that Robert Duncan declared instrumental to the work of the poet: "This very matter of the typewriter and the author's work and the emergence of the idea of our taking over the means of the production of our copy into our own hands is where we must start out" (Duncan, "Preface" 6).

Like Blake's experiments with image and text (his efforts were successful because he self-produced his works), mimeo-produced works exhibit a clear intimacy. Even when a publisher was involved, there was a much closer relationship between publisher and author. Important to the Mimeo Revolution was one aspect that McGann would consider part of its materiality, the circumstances of a text's circulation and distribution. As if following Duncan's dictum that "the poet's own time is . . . not to be at the command of a publishing opportunity or inopportunity" (Duncan, "Preface" 13), poets became free to circulate texts according to their artistic imagination: "Direct access to mimeography machines, letterpress, and inexpensive offset made these publishing ventures possible, putting the means of production in the hands of the poet" (Clay 14).

The results of this self-empowerment in production include an abundance of texts and speed in circulation. This speed, as Ron Loewinsohn has commented, gave poets a sense of instant response, suggesting that a work published one week could be responded to the following week. Speed of production, abundance of texts, and immediacy of circulation engendered a new sense of poetry's possibilities. Such factors are part of the materiality of Mimeo Revolution writing, and the resonance with digital poetry is obvious: e-poetry allows rapid dissemination by placing production back in the hands of the artist.

Such materials, the pliancy and programmable qualities of the digital text, along with its distribution mechanisms of immediate speed and unlimited geographic and social reach, are elements that determine the conditions of the digital text. What, then, is the conditional text?[22] To take an example from jazz, it is said that Charlie Parker would astonish his fellow musicians by simultaneously working within multiple contexts, including those that seemed outside traditional ideas of the materiality of the music being performed. For example, if he were playing a solo, and a woman dressed in red walked by the stage, he was known for being able to seamlessly weave elements of "Lady in Red" into the solo he was performing. This reflected Parker's confidence in his improvisational abilities. More important, he recognized music as existing in relation to the location in which it was being performed.

Another example lies in the seamless manner in which Parker could separate a song's melody from its chord changes, creating a space where the textuality of the music became conditioned by the art of improvisation. In one case, Parker did not want to pay royalties for his arrangement for strings of Fat Waller's "Honeysuckle Rose," so he borrowed Waller's chord changes and wrote a new melody; the result became another classic, "Scrapple from the Apple." By contrast, in his solo for the Gershwin ballad, "Embraceable You," Parker invented his own melody and sustained it for the entire thirty-two bars of his solo without playing one note of George Gershwin's melody. In this case, he would not have had to pay royalties except that he elected to use Gershwin's title, something he did to emphasize the degree to which a melody could be removed. It is this kind of fluidity between performance and structure of the text that illuminates the conditional nature of the digital work.

Innovative poetic practice has investigated both materiality and the conditional dynamics of writing. Indeed, it is important to note that digital poetries are not print poetry merely repositioned in the new medium. Instead, e-poetries extend the investigations of innovative practice as it occurred in print media, making possible the continuation of lines of inquiry that could not be fulfilled in that medium.

If one considers the visual work of any number of innovative writers, the connection between materiality and the conditional dynamics of writing begins to become tangible. Guillaume Apollinaire's *Calligrammes*, composed early in the twentieth century, offers clear indications of this type of continuity.[23] Apollinaire's "Coeur Couronne et Miroir," as one example, presents the items described in the title, a heart, a crown, and a mirror, in a very visual manner. That is, the relation between word and image is highlighted because the letters of this poem are arranged to form the objects they evoke. This is, in a sense, ASCII art at its finest.[24] Further, the letters that are arranged to form these objects interrogate the connotations of each object. "Coeur" states: "My heart like an inverted flame" (99). Such an interrelation between image and text, an interest that has been present in writing since the days of ancient Crete, is quite germane to the digital medium. Such pattern poetry confronts us with the double textuality with which we must contend: in Western languages, the image of the word is separate from the image it invokes. (By placing his name within the mirror, Apollinaire also quite wittily plays on the meaning of the "I" in the work of art, a topic that also extends to digital media.) Finally, the arrangement and size of the letters suggest motion. The letters in "coeur" invoking a heart that is moving, as if the little letters that make it are coursing around and around. Similarly, the words and letters in "mirror" can be seen as varying in position to suggest not just a framing but a sense of motion.

A similar sense of motion occurs in Apollinaire's "Il Pleut" (where lines of letters rain down across the page), "Le Petit Auto" (where wheels formed of letters seem to want to gyrate on the page), and works such as the extraordinary "La Colombe Poignardée et le Jet d'Eau" (where the whole page turns into a gushing fountain of typography). The letters that constitute these works are like "so many explosives just about to be ALIVE!" (Apollinaire 289); they vividly convey energy and motion. Of course, text in motion would not have been possible at the time these typographic works were created. Yet one can easily see them as precursors to animated text.

What is important to recognize is the continuity of innovative practice that leads directly into the digital medium. The work of Apollinaire's *Caligrammes* can be seen as taken up by the Concrete poetry movement of the fifties and sixties, Charles Olson, and Susan Howe, among others. For one illustration of these connections, the lineage that extends from Apollinaire's "Visée" (150–51) through Olson's "I have been an ability—a machine—up to now" (*Maximus* 498–99) through parts of Howe's "A Bibliography of the King's Book or, Eikon Basilike" (see *Nonconformist's Memorial* 78–79) to Jim Andrews's "Seattle Drift"[25] is striking indeed. Innovative print works find a very natural extension into the digital medium where the kinetic and nonlinear qualities of text can be made literal.

Natural extensions can be seen in works by a number of poets currently working in new media. In Darren Wershler-Henry's "Grain: A prairie poem," for example, the same type of rain evoked in "Il Pleut" is realized in tiny g's that rain and make the grain grow. A similar work is my "(Go) Fish," where a pattern poetry method is used to create streaming fish shapes from blocks of text; these works are discussed later. As another example of such extensions of tradition, in Miekal And's "After Emmett,"[26] concrete poetry is put into literal action as a tribute to the poet Emmett Williams.

A continuity of practice can also see in the procedural tradition that extends from the very interesting Fluxus projects known as "Flux-boxes" or "Flux-kits," boxes that contained instructions for the generation of a work.

Such instructions would be performed in a different order each time; thus a different work would be produced each time the Flux-box was used. Because the Flux-box contained a procedure for generating a work, the Flux-box could be considered a kind of early programming, one that is inherently multigenre. Thus, the present practice of writing in networked and programmable media can be seen not only as an offshoot of standard programming practices but also as an extension of the projects of Fluxus and, of course, Oulipo, as will be discussed later in this book. There are many such continuities between innovative practice and e-poetry; these continuities provide compelling testimony of innovative poetry's relevance to digital media practice.

The digital medium is a real and present form of writing, one that has changed the idea of writing itself. Indeed, it is becoming common knowledge that this change has occurred. Even in *Designing with JavaScript*, a basic how-to manual about writing for the Web, the shift to e-writing is clearly expressed. The author, David Siegel, notes that "documents are becoming applications" (vii), a statement that unintentionally sums up the nature of e-writing. "Since the day someone put the first 'submit' button on the first Web page, the nature of [the] Web was not 'electronic paper,' but something much more" (vii). Thomas Powell in *HTML: The Complete Reference*, notes that "a transition is already underway from a page-oriented view of the Web to a more program-oriented view of Web sites" and that these days, "Web sites sound more like software. The truth is, many sites *are* like software" (655). What is this "much more" that now constitutes writing? E-writing is not fixed; it is not just an arrangement of static symbols on a fixed page; it *does* something. It can interact with the reader. It can change in real time or as programmed. As Marie-Laure Ryan notes, "The digital revolution of the last decade has let words on the loose, not just by liberating their semantic potential, as most avant-garde movements of the past hundred years have done, but in a physical, quite literal sense as well" (1).

Further, the digital text signals not just a change in writing practices but part of a change in consciousness of the entire culture. Writing about identity in the age of the Internet, Sherry Turkle suggests that Internet experiences should be understood as "part of a larger cultural context." That context, Turkle argues, "is the story of the eroding boundaries between the real and the virtual, the animate and the inanimate, the unitary and the multiple self, which is occurring both in advanced scientific fields of research and in the patterns of everyday life" (Turkle 10). If indeed the patterns of everyday life are being transformed, writing is one of the key areas where this transformation is occurring. The e-business writer J. Neil Weintraut considers this reinvigorated use of writing to be one of the major benefits of the Internet age. Contrasting how broadcast media have inculcated society into being "passive observers" and how telephone communication ushered in the sunset of the "art of writing," he suggests that things have now changed. "The

Internet will . . . recover great things lost; notably writing as an art form, a communications medium, and a lubricant within our society—lost for the past 40 years—is rapidly resurging on Internet E-mails and chat forums" (xv). (The importance of e-mail to literary conversation is evident in the recently published *Poetics@*, edited by Joel Kuszai [New York: Roof Books, 1999], according to its cover note, "the first book of poetics to emerge from an electronic community.") Though Weintraut may idealize the effect of the Internet, writing certainly has a new communality: communicating through writing, whether by e-mail, Internet Messenger, or chat rooms, is now a practice common even to teenagers. Indeed, "letter" writing is no longer viewed as an antiquated form of communication, the relic of an epistolary past or academic practice but, when undertaken through programs like Internet Messenger, as daring form of social intercourse.

What's more, e-writing has an increased appeal since it can be nearly instantaneously transmitted to any other connected computer on the planet. Such an idea has returned a palpable sense of power to the written word. That old phrase "would you put that in writing" now suggests not just that writing adds legitimacy to an utterance but that, in the electronic realm, it can also be delivered. Similarly, it was the potential for dissemination that fueled numerous historical writing movements, including the Soviet Samisdat, various fine and little press movements, mail art movements, the Mimeo Revolution, the photocopy press of the 1970s, "the PageMaker Press"[27] of the 1980s, and the Zine movement of the 1990s. These are all traditions where the writer took control of the production and circulation of literature.

Now, even more tools have become available. Weintraut notes the nature of the new materials now at hand: "The Internet provides essentially anyone with electronic canvas—be it audio, graphical, textual, animated, or video content—and a means to make available creative work to the masses" (xli). This has a direct impact not only on writing, but on what writing *is*. The digital medium has reinvigorated the idea of writer as maker because this medium allows the author to be typesetter, graphic artist, and director of the work. The change? Agoraphobics who have cowered in locked rooms can now adopt a "handle" and roam dungeons in search of prey. Artists and authors in countries on opposite sides of the earth can hang works side-by-side in virtual galleries, real-time collaborations can occur regardless of time zones. Further, conferences such as "Digital Arts & Culture," "Beyond Art: Digital Culture in the 21st Century," and "In the Event of the Text: Ephemeralities of Writing" are occurring with increasing frequency and attest to the magnitude of this change,[28] a change that is both social and textual—and permanent. But this change is not just about writing but about how writing is *made*. Word processors, image manipulation programs, animation tools, HTML generators, and other tools witness the implications of this change in writing: it has shifted from latent to hyperactive that quality of writing we can call "making"—or poeisis.

Though it might seem that the questions raised here are strictly tied to digital technology, the issues that dominate this flood of activity are in many senses the same ones that Aristotle and the librarians at Babylon dealt with. The questions of how to organize information, what ideology is implied by that organization (interface[29] and order of links), and what relation the mechanics of given functions have to meaning, must be addressed. For the writer, artist, and programmer, more specific questions arise. One of these is, "What can you do here—in this medium—that you could not do before?" The second, "How does one characterize this medium as 'writing' or 'text' or 'making,' and what are the specific materialities of this activity?" These are the questions central to *Digital Poetics*, published as writing has entered its fifth millennium. As we engage the present, entering choreographies of JavaScript, database-generated Web pages, Flash, virtual reality, frames, dynamic fonts, style sheets, DHTML, VRML, and XML, these questions endure. Indeed, given the possibilities of programming, the emergence of the poet/programmer, and the horizon of artificial intelligence, quite extraordinary developments are a certainty. It behooves us now to begin to map this terrain and locate our position within it.

To do so, it is crucial to delimit this field critically. There are a number of points that need to be clarified. What constitutes innovative practice in digital media? Is the dominance of hypertext practice to be questioned in this field? What are the defining features of the e-text, what is the relation of code to textuality, and what new parameters do we need to *read* in this medium? What criteria do we use to identify works that advance the possibilities of this field? How do we identify emergent works of lasting interest? Finally, we must see the intricate interrelation between innovative poetic practice and digital media. As no understanding of digital media can be complete without considering innovative poetic practice, no assessment of contemporary poetry can be complete without a consideration of works in digital media. This is an interesting relationship and one that is fruitful to examine. What must be done? It is time to map a poetics that brings the experiments of the twentieth century into the medium of the twenty-first. This is a poetics that will increasingly address questions of the material nature of electronic writing, one that will establish the parameters by which we can start to identify issues central to this crucially important field of practice.

1
Jumping to Occlusions
A Manifesto for Digital Poetics

> fret which is whirled / out of some sort of information
> —Charles Bernstein, *The Sophist*

> Precipitation: violent passages: from which we each emerge:
> rending: stuffed: awkwardly shaped by the heat of such and such
> a system
> —Caroline Bergvall, "Fourth Tableau"

Poetry has entered the electronic landscape. Even if such a landscape suggests images of electronic video games or machine-readable iambs swooning under a science fiction lexicon, the fact is that the electronic world is a world substantially of writing. Though this writing often seems eclipsed by its mode of transmission (e-mail, chat rooms, the World Wide Web, and Flash as primary instances), it is not unlike all previous writing, which has also been eclipsed by modes of transmission (the book, the stone tablet, the scroll).[1] We write in words—but also in the grammar and politics of code (HTML, JavaScript, and more). Electronic writing, like previous instances of writing, equally engages the double "mission" of writing: that is, writing is about a subject—but it is also about the medium through which it is transmitted. "Transmission," then, suggests both the circulation of texts and the cross-purpose ("trans" = across or cross + "mission" = purpose or intention) of inscription.

How does transcription have a cross-purpose? The language you are breathing becomes the language you think. Take for example in UNIX (and UNIX is the wellspring from which the World Wide Web was drawn) to "grep" or "chmod," things done daily, possibly hundreds of times a day.[2] When you grep ("global/regular expression/print") a given target, you search across files for instances of a string of characters, a word. To chmod ("change mode") is to use a numeric code to grant, in an augenblick, permission to read, write, and/or execute a given file to yourself, your community, and your world. These are not mere metaphors but new procedures for writing. How could it be simpler? Why don't we all think in UNIX? If we do, these

---

This essay was released in two different earlier versions. In the Web version of this essay, images and sound form components of the writing, sound icons being used at various points in the text to indicate the availability of a sound component. Web versions may be found at the Postmodern Culture Web site (http://muse.jhu.edu/journals/pmc/v007/7.3glazier.html), or for those who are not Muse subscribers, a courtesy copy is available (http://epc.buffalo.edu/authors/glazier/essays). The version of the essay included in this book contains substantial additional text not available in previous Web or print versions of this work.

ideas are a file: I am chmoding this file for all of you to have read, write, and execute permission—and please grep what you need from this! What I am saying is that innovative poetry itself is best suited to grep how technology factors language and how this technology, writing, and production, are as inseparable as Larry, Moe, and Curly Java.

Why poets? Numerous poets working within innovative practice have explored language as a procedure to reveal the *working* of writing. Poets endeavor, as Emily Dickinson has written, to "Tell all the Truth but tell it slant" because "Success in Circuit lies" (506). That is, rather than focusing on the information of the text, poetic practice has explored the conditions that determine that information, the procedures, processes, and crossed paths of meaning-making, meaning-making as constituting the "meaning." Unlike information itself, which can vary limitlessly, such mechanisms often reveal something about writing that might not otherwise be apparent. Innovative writing in electronic media has for its charge the *processes* of meaning-making, hoping to extend Dickinson's success from "in Circuit" to the circuit board, exploring the procedures, loops, and processes of digital writing. Such a focus on making's relation to the machine has been a preoccupation of poetry throughout the past century, present in numerous engagements.

How can materiality influence the meaning transmitted by a text? If one looks at works from the Mimeo Revolution, for example, one can see the intrinsic relation between text and its means of transmission. There were several features that seemed to typify mimeo: rough textured, elementary-school-thick pages, pages printed on one side, and uneven and faded courier or gothic type. These are not merely incidental facts about this publishing means, but are facts related to the content that is transmitted by such texts. Specific works from this movement illustrate this point. If one looks at *Adventures in Poetry* 3, one gets a sense, from the black-and-white graphic on the cover, the 8¹/₂-by-11-inch size, and the signature three staples at the left margin, that a particular spirit defines the magazine. This spirit is reinforced by some of the snappy, direct works, such as Berrigan's "Black Shoe Face" presented in its pages. Many of the magazine's details, such as its unnumbered pages, its inclusion of poetry, line drawings, and short, colloquial prose, bespeak a sense of mission for this mimeo production. (Similar details can be seen in magazines such as *Tom Veitch Magazine*, which also includes the use of multicolored pages, the use of underlining instead of italics, blocky iconographic images, and contents such as "The Hippy Termites.") Such a mission seems to be characterized by a literary spirit that calls for a directness, an urgency, and a nonacademic posture toward literature. What I argue for is an approach that looks at the *writing* on the screen. Just as the mimeo brought its "style" of writing, and the perfect-bound offset book brought its typical page size and length of text—factors which influenced the *writing* of texts *for* these technologies—the World Wide Web factors its texts.

On the Web, the actual language (HTML) and scripts that enable the circulation of texts *are* writing, and the way texts are displayed is an *activity* of writing. Further, the Web we read is the Web we write on. Writing enters the Web not only as technique but as "transmission."[3] This fusion is unavoidable. Charles Bernstein has commented that "language is the material of both thinking and writing. We think and write in language, which sets up an intrinsic connection between the two" (*Content's* 62). This same kinship applies to writing and the computer.

Recent poetic theory is particularly relevant to electronic space. Robert Duncan, writing about Charles Olson, suggests that one of Olson's messages was adjusting the scale of the poem's activity to new contexts. This has particular relevance to an electronic poetics, where assumptions about specific formal qualities must be converted from assumptions about the print medium. The breakthrough? As with any development in technology, writing does not stay the same, but the writing technology becomes an expanded way to *perceive* under the aegis of the writing activity. This scale, Olson suggested, extended "from Folsom cave to now—the waves of pre-glacial and post-glacial migrations out of Asia, the adventuring voyages out from the Phoenician world, the Norse world, and then the Renaissance, as coming 'home,' 'back' to their origins. 'SPACE': I spell it large because it comes large here. . . . Large, and without mercy" (Duncan, "Introduction" 80).

Olson's historicizing of poetic space suggests movement into larger scenes of activity. This movement can also be seen as extending into electronic space. The sense of "home" here resonant with a home page that can be fragile, fleeting, "historic," obnoxious, pretentious, or revelatory but that stands as a point of application juxtaposed against the merciless immensity of online space.[4] With Olson's work, Duncan writes, "the opening up of great spaces in consciousness had begun, and in the very beginning, it its origins, he moves in, as he knows he must, to redirect the ideas of language and of the body, of Man, of commune, and of history" ("Introduction" 80). This "consciousness" includes a consciousness of the space of the page, and writers of Olson's circle, Duncan and Robert Creeley among them, addressed the physical space of the page.

The question then becomes how, on the Net, writing intersects with its materials. What specifically is the difference between a paper poetry and an electronic one? The paper press certainly offers parallels. The avatar of small circulation, fine press, has clearly been concerned with its materials. Those who work in fine printing can speak of sensuous relations between text and materials. (The "press" in fine press insists on "impression"; the act of physical impression carries through to tactile qualities in the printed object.) Thus fine press also engages transmission; what is transmitted is the tactile record of the act of impression. The term "small press," in contradistinction, more clearly insists on transmission.[5] "Press" here refers to the machinery of reproduction and the social institution of disseminating information. It is small, non-corporate, a pequeñismo, privileging content over profit. Its machinery becomes a part of the materiality of the text, grepping writing through such called for material facts as $8^{1}/_{2}$-by-11-inch paper, black-and-white reproduction, and (before the microcomputer revolution) a fairly standardized set of fonts.

Electronic texts also have material properties—the size of the electronic "page," the structural tropes (frames, tables, layout), the quality of HTML mark-up, the factors of plug-ins and file formats, the action of programming[6]—and the materials of this technology have a direct effect on the actual path of writing. In the electronic environment, the materials shift into a different grid of properties, propensities, and resistances. In addition, as fonts rage wistful or out of control and the writing "canvas" becomes unlimited, texts become constituted as physical *pieces* of a never complete and constantly reconstituting whole (the network).

Ron Silliman introduced his influential anthology of new writing, *In the American Tree*, citing a statement by Robert Grenier that "'PROJECTIVE VERSE' IS *PIECES* ON" ("Language" xv). Silliman was suggesting that his anthology extended Olson's theory of Projective Verse as realized in Creeley's breakthrough collection of poems *Pieces* (New York: Scribner's, 1969). (*Pieces* also insisted on poetry's possibilities, as pieces of text, outside externally mandated form.) This statement has resonance in new terrain and might be re-stated: *electronic verse is pieces online*. Thinking of Creeley's "form is never more than an extension of content" (*Charles* 79),[7] what avenues of content have been opened by such vastly different possibilities for "form"? The medium gives the poem added potential for "making"; hence electronic poetries are positioned to enter and extend a number of investigations of language into a new poetic terrain where words are mutable and embody transmission. These are words that do not merely name; they approach an added potential for "activity." As Charles Bernstein has written, speaking of visual poetry: "For words are no more labels of things than the sky is a styrofoam wrap of some Divine carryout shop. And letters are no more tied to words or words to sentences than a mule is tied to its burden. Letters in liberty. Words freed from the tyranny of horizontality, or sequence" ("Response" 3).

These words have equal significance in the electronic realm. Bernstein's allusion to Marinetti's great Futurist declaration, gestures toward the advancement of writing's physicality. Electronic texts provide the subsequent step, projecting writing into charged space, where words themselves extend beyond sequentiality. From context to "dystext," pieces or fragments of text. This is a Texas-sized shift in potentiality, a dance outside the linear, outside the line, an interesting and real place for writing; as they say in Texas, "real cowboys don't line dance." Analogously, the real poem extends beyond the line.

Thus we look at online hypertext. (Here we investigate link-node hypertext that is generic and Net disseminated, as opposed to proprietary "closed" hypertext or other hypertext systems.)[8] Importantly, electronic poetics are not tied to the linearity of the page; this is not an end of linearity but an emergence of multiple linearities. The connection between these multiples is the link, a signal word or conjunction of letters, Bernstein's mule unharnessed, free to jump into a lateral or completely irreverent context or medium (graphical, sound, video).

Links bring to the text the riddle of discovery experienced by the anthropologist stepping onto the soil of a previously undiscovered culture: once the imprint of such a footstep is on the sand, the culture is no longer "native." Once a link has been taken, it is no longer a link but a constituted part of the already traveled narrative; the link loses its potentiality, but in doing so, it opens up the possibility of other links. And what if some of these links fail? What we have is not a failure of the internal system but a triumph of internal workings over any possibility of external order. As Gregory Ulmer puts it: "There is no 'central processor' in hyperrhetoric, no set of rules, but a distributed memory, a memory triggered by a cue that spreads through the encyclopedia, the library, the data base (connectionism suggests that the hardware itself should be designed to support the spread of memory through an associational network)" (346).

Hypertext allows sequences beyond sequence; however, a serious point of difference must be taken with some Web utopianists: despite tendencies in this direction, the point is not that *everything* is linked through these sequences. The constitution of any such whole could only be a misrepresentation of stability—another pursuit of the mirage known as the encyclopedia. The arrangements of the internal orders of texts do not add stability to the text, rather they add a perplexing layer of instability; it is the "failure" of the links, whether they connect or not, that gives them their activity. It is through this activity that electronic writing departs irreversibly from the world of print.

This post-typographic and nonlinear disunion is no news to poetics. The argument that "Pound's significance lies in his having anticipated the end of 'the Gutenberg era,' the age of print" (Davie 5), rings true in works of many experimental movements and authors who problematized the medium in which their work appeared or the act of writing itself. These include such movements and authors as the following: Futurism, Gertrude Stein, and Dada; the textual webs of Jorge Luis Borges; Gabriel García Márquez and Julio Cortázar; following World War II, the exploration of system in Charles Olson, Robert Duncan, and Robin Blaser's serial works; Larry Eigner's articulation; Robert Creeley's numeric determinations; Jack Spicer and Ed Roberson's split pages; Charles Bernstein, Steve McCaffery, Ron Silliman, Robert Grenier, Alan Fisher, Robert Sheppard, Emmanuel Hocquard, and Claude Royet-Journoud; the radical typographies of Susan Howe and

Johanna Drucker, David Antin's improvisations, Jerome Rothenberg's ethnopoetics; redeployments of language by Maggie O'Sullivan, Caroline Bergvall, Karen MacCormack, Nicole Brossard, Michele Leggott, Lyn Hejinian, Joan Retallack, and Hannah Weiner; and the procedures of Jackson Mac Low and John Cage, all which point in different ways to various forms of nonlinearity.

It is the play of *pieces* that forms the tropes of an electronic web. Speaking of Charles Bernstein's work, Marjorie Perloff writes that it "playfully exploits such rhetorical figures as pun, anaphora, epiphora, metathesis, epigram, anagram, and neologism to create a seamless web of reconstituted words" (*Dance* 231). Bernstein has called this weaving "dysraphism." "'Raph'. . . means 'seam,'" Bernstein explains, "so for me dysraphism is mis-seaming— a prosodic device!" (*Sophist* 44). (John Cage's mesostics, with their key words running through the middle of a poem, seem to dramatize this because they have an almost literal central "stitch" threading text along a vertical axis.) Bernstein's "sensitivity to etymologies and latent meanings is reflected in the poem itself," Perloff writes, "which is an elaborate 'dysfunctional fusion of embryonic parts' [and] a 'disturbance of stress, pitch, and rhythm of speech' in the interest of a new kind of urban 'rhapsody'" (*Dance* 230).

The weaving of disparate elements into such a larger "whole" is a prosody. As Ron Silliman writes, "When words are, meaning soon follows. Where words join, writing is" ("For L=A=N=G=U=A=G=E" 16). Gertrude Stein expressed a similar idea in her performative observation from *How to Write:* "A sentence is made by coupling meanwhile ride around to be a couple there makes grateful dubiety named atlas coin in a loan" (118). Such coupling can occur through many methods: various forms of automatic writing, Jack Kerouac's spontaneous improvisations, the cut-up techniques of William Burroughs, Antin's collage and talk texts, Cage's mesostics, Mac Low's deterministic procedures, the sound-text experiments of Henri Chopin or Kurt Schwitters, the procedures of text generation programs, among many others. One could even add to this list earlier "conventional" poetic techniques—Chaucer's use of the tale, Blake's images, and the white space of William Carlos Williams.

Additionally relevant is the work of an international group of Concrete and visual poets active in the 1950s and 1960s. Poets such as Eugen Gomringer, Augusto and Haroldo de Campos, Emmett Williams, Dick Higgins, Bob Cobbing, and Ian Hamilton Finlay, among many others, carried out essential investigations of non-semantic arrangements of text in visual fields; these poets broke valuable ground for the visual possibilities of e-poetries. These are all methods used by poets to investigate the poetics of juxtaposition, the weaving of texts. It is through this weaving that writing approaches its potential on the Web, a writing based on juxtaposition.

What are links but faults in the monolinear imagination?[9] In his "Parapraxes" essays, Freud has written about parapraxis, faults in reading, writing, and speaking, "slips of the tongue," as more possible when the mind shifts into an associative disposition.[10] (For example, at a recent videodisk viewing of cave paintings of Lascaux, I was struck by an enlarged detail as identical to a common image of open-heart surgery.) Though Freud would, as is his penchant, like to suggest that conclusions may be drawn from parapraxis, what is important is that he has documented it as a logic of association. Thus we can say that the ability to read linked writings calls on skills of association and depends not on conclusion but *occlusion*, or an aberration of the eye, literally and homophonously. (If the machine is meant to calculate, writing begins when its error is engaged.) This is a space where the minor matters: with monolinearity blocked, peripheral vision may again resume activity.

An electronic poetics alters the "eye" ("I") and also extends the physicality of reading. With the keyboard, literal manipulation is engaged with fingers determining different referentialities of the text—a sight more active than repetitious page turning. Again a fusion of parts extends into a plethora of directions, reminding us of Robert Duncan's reference to the traditional work of a poet as juggling a number of objects and Gertrude Stein's "a spectacle and nothing strange a single hurt color and an arrangement in a system to pointing" (*Tender* 9).

Writing's acute (hence "hyper") activity of movement and transmission—the thousands of Poetics list subscribers or the millions of transactions a year at the Electronic Poetry Center (EPC) (http://epc.buffalo.edu)—witness the merging of writing and transmission. When oral, the voice projects across the room, beyond rooms, and as a "system to pointing," its poetic is one of deflection. Texts move not only within themselves but into socially charged externalities: a webbed interference of junk mail, frets of information, systemic failures, ephemera, disunion—there is no resting place, only the incessantly reconstituted lexia dissolving each time a pathway is chosen.

As to the "resting place" in question, I am frequently asked what factor was so motivating that it caused a poet to enter the world of greps, chmods, kernels, and shells—not to mention to suffer the ignominy of being referred to as "one of the UNIX guys" and create the Electronic Poetry Center. The reason? Not only could we not get our early online texts correctly archived, we could not even convince the archival site to classify the texts as poetry. The administrators there insisted that the work we created did not look like poetry to them, and so our work was listed under "Zines." What more reason could there be needed for founding an online site? Further, beyond classification is language itself. With dimly veiled rancor, I have been asked, what is it about computer-related writing that interested me? Did I take up e-literature because I could not get a job as a programmer or as a sonneteer? I explain some of my reasons: For one thing, having grown up with two languages in San Antonio, I was always fascinated by how languages have a permeable seam between them. Indeed, poetic language is a seam through which seep multiple parts of language, multiple languages. Like all language, computer language is not limited to use within its primary field.

Indeed, its metaphors, its hype, and its vision is seeping into language at all levels, most opportunistically in advertising. Its relevance to poetry, especially when ironic, is quite natural. As might be evidenced in the poem that concludes this chapter, "Mendum," or in a poem such as my "Windows 95" (*Leaving Loss Glazier* 1),[11] poetry is the line where the impact of technology is explored. Thus, to those questioners who ask how I got "here," I explain that indeed I came from a background of poetics. When I discovered that, like my language-within-a-language experiences in the Southwest, I discovered the language-within-a-language structure of computer-based writing. It was a natural interest—and an affirmation that within the twisted barbs of any language, lie the strands, roots, and metaphors of language matter that make the field of poetry such a fertile one to plow.

An electronic poetics is a poetics. Like any other poetics that recognizes system—be it breath, a controversy of texts, or a nexus of interests—system is a determining factor. A poetics also involves a particular engagement or set of engagements, with its issuing "authority" and technology. The public life of a poetics has, perhaps, been nowhere more visible, with its incessant transmission, than in the electronic poetries. An electronic poetry is a public word, projected across a public world, across systems, itself as system.

MENDUM

italicized—"faulty text"
see *ambient transmission . . .*

Implacable pressure individual word
nor factor of its essay's plangent
technological writing finds its
shortened by speed's excess
prescribes the next case sensitive
frame interval back to LIT so that's
science vita as temporal release

Presumed oneself lost as at
anagram of lexis should not
moebius strip chain of linked
emend hot links simmer on grill
have turned set spills Norwegian
routing so trajectory across

the Atlantic call it bullish poets
television effect figurations desert
have gotten lost (a whirling disk)
both netted and offline turn on its
immunely dancing platforms
last year Southampton asymptotic

in olive phone calls ring your Fonseca
Marrakech relation to decadence
in anthology. Never thought to find
in effect "you get what you ASCII for"
to Royaumont gardens an illustration
another nine Dutch poets revisiting

Bergen in its custom prescribes that
swoop across the road as continents
transmit say a gathering to honor
Pacific write against this point
cross-current, visible vs. physical
extended serial sequences, beyond text

and voilà! hence antho-, ana-, autho-
got faults "mendum" gears affix
for public consumption into Veracruz
La Malinche's words ring of books then
radio drift, deep inflected tones fit
forget to send even-rendered domain.

2
Our Words

> The West is seized with panic at the thought of not being able
> to save what the symbolic order had been able to conserve for
> forty centuries, but out of sight and far from the light of day.
> Ramses does not signify anything for us, only the mummy is of
> inestimable worth, because it is what guarantees that
> accumulation has meaning. Our entire linear and accumulative
> culture collapses if we cannot stockpile the past in plain view.
> —Jean Baudrillard, *Simulacra and Simulation*

> I kept asking myself how a book could be infinite. I could not
> imagine any other than a cyclic volume, circular. A volume
> whose last page would be the same as the first and so have the
> possibility of continuing indefinitely.
> —Jorge Luis Borges, *Ficciones*

> Vast orange libraries of dreams stir inside "The Poems."
> —Ted Berrigan, *The Sonnets*

The Internet eludes definition. It is, of course, possible to point to the
physical composition of the Net: the Internet, through the connectivity made
possible by TCP/IP protocol suite,[1] is the sum of the information resources
made available through thousands of networks, allowing the interchange of
information between millions of computer nodes. But this definition does
not get us very far. Indeed, it is comparable to the kind of response you
might have gotten in 1450 asking the question: What is printing? To this
question an enterprising literalist might have responded: Through the con-
nectivity made possible by the replica-casting protocol, printing is the product
of single letters engraved in relief and then punched into slabs of brass to
produce matrices from which replicas can be cast in molten metal. Using an
ink that will adhere to metal type, a flat printing surface, and an adaptation
of the screw-and-lever winepress, printing allows the unprecedented pro-
duction and circulation of the Bible.

Before pursuing the immense cultural implications of such a parallel, it
might be worthwhile to consider how labor intensive both these technolo-
gies are, at least in their infant states. Anyone who has labored "engraving"
ideas and then punching them into the "brass slabs" of HTML is well aware

that the trek from the idea to the "screw-and-lever winepress" of a Web server is one of painstaking labor. The "matrices from which replicas can be cast" are not easily made and are equally vulnerable to the instabilities, uncertainties, and changeability of the "mechanism." Though there was no alt.replica-casting to record the anguish of early frustrations with print technology, we can be sure that it was laborious effort that made such early productions possible. Equally, that such an immense web of webs has presently been constituted is a tribute to the continued incessant labor of engaged human beings. The chaotic and unpredictable state of the Internet is equally a reflection of the human spirit. That such systems constantly escape their originally stated purpose may be more defining of both these technologies than their proponents would care to admit.

The Internet, like the interstate highway network, is a system designed originally for military purposes. (Thus the under-appreciated ironic ring to the term "Information Superhighway," because the interstate system was similarly designed for military deployment.) Indeed, the development of the computer was spurred forward not by any interest in information but by war needs. As Scott McCartney notes, the hallmark proposal for the first electronic computer, "The Use of High-Speed Vacuum Tube Devices for Calculation," was issued in August 1942, nine months after Pearl Harbor was attacked (49). Based on this proposal, Presper Eckert and John Mauchly built ENIAC, "the first digital, general-purpose, electronic computer. . . . ENIAC was a bus-size mousetrap of forty, nine-foot-tall cabinets filled with nearly 18,000 vacuum tubes and miles of wiring. It was developed as a weapon of war, a machine that could calculate trajectories for World War II artillery. Though unwieldy, ENIAC was wired with enough innovation and genius to provide the spark for computer development" (5). Indeed, the innovation that defines the later development of the Internet, its distributed structure, can be placed within the context of nuclear war. J. Neil Weintraut writes: "The design goal of nuclear resilience inspired a network architecture and technology unlike any other. . . . Where the telephone network architecture requires connection through a central switch (which by virtue of its centralization makes thousands of connections vulnerable to a single nuclear strike), the ARPAnet, and hence Internet, allows any computer to tap in anywhere" (xx).

Unlike telephone technology, which operates by sending a signal along a predetermined, singular path, Internet technology is "packet" based. The signal is sliced into small "packets" that then bounce along whatever path they can find until they reach their destination where they are reassembled. Weintraut suggests that "this packet technology . . . compliments nuclear resilience; if a nuclear attack compromises one path to a destination, each packet will just keep being rerouted between computers until it finds a path that still exists" (xx). This incredibly poignant design principle underlies the Internet. Its design is, in fact, a key reason that this system has been able to accommodate nearly unimaginable information flows.

Likewise, the Internet itself defies its original purpose. The predecessor of electronic data exchange (the Web) and electronic mail, ARPAnet, was pioneered to link NATO bases in 1969. The original technological objectives of ARPAnet are in the past, much as printing's original impetus to promulgate the Bible and other canonical works eventually passed. Similarly, NATO now exists as a defense superstructure in the face of no enemy. Both technologies originated as mechanisms to control the word; both began to attain their real potential when the opposite occurred, and the word was set free. What is most relevant, however, is how these technologies work *against* their original design. (For example, the Web must employ textual strategies rather than informational ones.[2]) The larger cultural implications of these technologies occur once they escape their original definition, subsequently engendering the proliferation of alternative content. At this point, the purpose of the technology no longer holds court; rather, the production of its rapidly diversifying subjects becomes its most remarkable outcome.

~

To this day I am so intimidated by the nature of libraries, the feel of them, the authority of their ordering of books on shelves, etc., that I rarely if ever go into them.

—Robert Creeley, *Essays*

In the late nineteenth century, library cataloging reached a crisis point. Until then, libraries were content to use a ledger system to record the acquisitions of books. Books added to the collection were sequentially entered in bound catalogs and inventoried according to a simple, sequential accession number. Someone seeking a title could always ask the librarian, who would examine the entries in the ledger. By the nineteenth century, however, book production had outstripped a single human mind's ability to monitor its products. What emerged were library classification systems: the Dewey Decimal System, the Universal Decimal Classification (a European adaptation of Dewey), and the Library of Congress classification scheme. Almost every library now uses one of these systems, including the Library of Congress, which presently owns about 100 million items.

What is the purpose of classification? Of the many possible theoretical positions from which to approach this question, one simple definition suggests that: "The library's catalog not only lists the library's contents but also analyzes them, so that all works by an individual author, all works on a given subject, and all works in a specific category (dictionaries, music, or maps, for example) can be easily located by readers. The modern catalog is a practical tool that is the result of the analysis of the subject, category, and contents of books, videocassettes, microfilms, compact discs, and a host of other informational vehicles" ("Catalog").

Classification, as a form of analysis, attempts to place products of one system into another system. To achieve the stated intention of this ordering, an analysis must be performed. Books must then be removed them from their "natural" order to accommodate the artificial positions of author, category, and subject.[3] In the Library of Congress system, creative works are arranged by author's nationality, and within that category, loosely by chronological period according to author's birth date. A particular author's work is further ordered according to whether each item is a collected work, an individual volume, or secondary work. There is little or no attention to the internal order of the book, the familiar divisions into preface, chapters, notes, and other bibliographical apparatus. Nor would there be any adjacency in ordering, for example, if two authors of different nationalities and of vastly different ages had a close working relationship. The science of ordering of books shows a remarkable similarity to what Baudrillard calls "the logical evolution of a science," which "is to distance itself increasingly from its object, until it dispenses with it entirely." Thus, he suggests, a science's "autonomy is only rendered even more fantastic—it attains its pure form" (8).

The phrase "pure form" suggests the creation of a second literary order. First, writing is placed in books, then books fall into their place in the order of books, and finally, in the catalog, they exist neither as writing nor as books. Consider the example of the Lascaux caves, where a replica of the caves stands five hundred meters from the original site. Visitors (who have in many cases traveled great distances to the caves) look at the original site through a peep-hole; then they are allowed to wander around the replica. In this way, "the duplication suffices to render both artificial" (Baudrillard 9), for neither one can be the real thing, only a variant. A library also produces a dual presentation of the printed object. The classification of books is an act of disinterment, similar to the exhumation of Ramses's mummy, where once the object is removed from its original order, strategies must be implemented to deter the natural decay of relation that is concomitant with dislocation.

The Fourth Media

> Speeding through space . . . speeding through heaven and the
> stars,
> Speeding amid the seven satellites and the broad ring and the
> diameter of eighty thousand miles,
> Speeding with tailed meteors . . . throwing fire-balls like the
> rest. . . .
> —Walt Whitman, *Leaves of Grass*

> Is the World Wide Web the "Fourth" Media, a technology
> positioned to take its place with the big three—print, radio,
> and television—as a mass-market means of communications?
> It's hard to create an argument against it. The Web has all of
> the social, technical and economic fundamentals which could
> help it achieve this prominence.
> —Paul Bonington, "Publishers Note"

Although it took four hundred years for the production of books to create the need for classification, the issue of order was immediate for the Internet. Its early history is an explosion of staggering proportions. In its first twelve years, 2.1 million files, or a fortieth of the holdings of the Library of Congress, became available. The number of host machines increased from four ARPAnet hosts in December 1969, to 3,864,000 Internet hosts in November 1994, with new domains being registered on an average of every two minutes during business hours.[4] This number, by January 1996, had risen to 9.5 million hosts.[5] As of January 2000, four years later, this number increased to 69.6 million hosts, according to NetSizer.[6] The dominant external Internet order is the World Wide Web; however, this was not always the case. Previously in Internet history there was another delivery system, gopher, as detailed earlier. Though passed over and now virtually forgotten, it is interesting that, as was the case with three-wheeled cars, there *were* other possibilities.[7] It is informative here to briefly compare the Web's architecture to that of gopher to help better understand how, once we limit ourselves to a single interface, that interface's limitations establish the limits of what we are able to do.

Both gopher and the World Wide Web collect protocols and standards used to access information on the Internet, but they do so in different ways. Gopher is a hierarchical system not unlike the alphanumeric hierarchies employed in library classification schemes (albeit without agreed-upon standards); the World Wide Web is a hypertextual network of links. (The Web must be accessed through an interface; early interfaces were Mosaic and Cello; now Netscape and Internet Explorer predominate. Again, there could be many possible ways to "browse" the Internet.) Internal orders include the ASCII text, a rather inert representation of the paper page on the screen, the HTML document, a text file bearing imbedded links to other Internet resources, and other more dynamic formats.

In terms of the relation of the textual unit, the file, to the controlling system, there are significant differences between gopher and the Web. For example, in the case of menus, gopher can only present an alphabetized list of files in a directory. This feature demonstrates a larger system imposing an "order" on an individual file. This is handled much differently with Web software when an index file is present. Because links form a structural part of HTML index files, Web software would have to intrude into an individual index file to exert the same kind of external order. Given the integrity of the individual file as a boundary that systems do not cross, clearly the order expressed *within* HTML documents guarantees the individual document a more faithful relation to the "world" of related documents. (Further, if files in a directory are *not* linked, Web software will, in contrast to gopher software, ignore them.) Looking at the library parallel, gopher assumes the librarian's sense of authority at classifying books according to a prevailing classification scheme. Web software shares what we can assume would be a librarian's resistance to entering a "file" (for example, altering the order of chapters in a published book) to extend the larger classification scheme into the internal order.

Printed texts have for many centuries made use of internal orders, employing mechanisms such as marginalia, in-text quotations, bibliographical apparatus, and various forms of textual notes, including footnotes, endnotes, and marginal notes (though, of course, some of these are fairly recent developments).[8] Earlier in the history of the book, layout could be incredibly important. The Biblia pauperum, for example, a block-book of the fourteenth and fifteenth centuries, employed elaborate arrangements of text, including different areas of the page to juxtapose images from the Old Testament and the New Testament, along with areas for commentary. Further, non-textual devices were variously important in different stages of the book's development. The illustrated book of the sixteenth century, was "intended to edify a huge public that could hardly read, to explain the text through the medium of pictures" (Febvre 96). In the seventeenth century, the engraving was "an essential medium of information" (102). Decoration was another non-textual element important to the book's meaning. Used both in early printing and in various printing revivals, decoration has had important implications: "By the disciplined uses of decorative borders and flowers, initials, head and tail pieces, charm and distinction may be given to the page without detracting from the main purpose of print—which is to be read" (Morison and Jackson 68). Such devices were an essential part of the text until economic pressures and standardization codified present conventions. What we presently know as the book could have gone in any number of directions. The present definitive format of the book is only one possible form; it just happens to be the form at which we have arrived.

The internal orders mentioned above suggest one way that the printed word can have hypertextual features; yet within writing itself are also found numerous other orders. Poets and writers have explored such possibilities extensively. William Burroughs (an icon of the cyberpunk movement) performed "cut-up" experiments using a compositional method that included slicing up a newspaper, throwing it into the air, and then reassembling it as it fell, a technique directly honored in the digital "Stir Frys" by Jim Andrews (http://www.vispo.com/StirFryTexts/index.html). David Antin composes from transcriptions of performative improvisations. Louis Zukofsky used musical notation script in his autobiography. Charles Bernstein has pioneered numerous inversions of expected literary form. Robert Creeley's early work investigated an authorial "I" as expressed in "pieces" of texts. Michael Joyce's disk-based hypertext novels make meticulous use of links. There are multimedia dimensions to many of Robin Blaser's works. His *Holy Forest* contains musical notation in section 11 of "Cups," red type in "Christ Among the Olives," and phonetic characters in "Image-Nation 10," among other forms of alternative textuality. William Carlos Williams, in *Kora in Hell*, and Jack Spicer, in *Homage to Creeley*, have written texts where footnote-like areas occupy nearly as much space as primary text. This format was more recently explored in "Eclogue" in Bob Perelman's *Virtual Reality*. Ron Silliman uses the idea of quadrants of a page to intriguing effect in his *Nox*, in which each page is divided into four areas by two intersecting blue lines. In addition, Silliman's procedural work also demands that we reconsider internal order. Silliman notes that "all poetry is procedure" and that writing involves solving the question of "how literally to proceed" ("Interview" 34). Internal orders are also foregrounded by serial practices, including Ron Silliman's alphabet series and the work of Robert Duncan, Robin Blaser, and Charles Olson. In the serial poem, sections of a longer "work" constitute discrete units in disparate volumes yet also form a bridge extending beyond individual volumes—a clear example of the published unit of the "book" perhaps not being synonymous with a "title." Charles Bernstein describes such texts thus:

> As to hypertext avant le PC, I am thinking, in the West, of the seriality already implicit in Buchner's *Woyzek*, or Blake's *Four Zoas*, Dickinson's fragments and fascicles, or in Reznikoff or Zukofsky or Oppen or Spicer or Stein; or in Grenier's great poem, *Sentences*, which is printed on 500 index cards in a Chinese foldup box; or Howe or Silliman or Hejinian; or the aleatoric compositions of Mac Low and Cage, Burroughs and Gysin; or prose works such as Wittgenstein's *Zettel* or *Philosophical Investigations* (and then the earlier history of philosophical fragment from Heraklitos on); or multitrack fictions by Federman or Beckett or Lydia Davis's *The End of the Story*; or let's not say only fragments and seriality but what

Viktor Schlovsky called the essence of prose in his *Theory of Prose*, writing at the beginning of this century: *digression*. . . . ("Mosaic") These textual alternatives provide many examples of internal systems redefining the notion of a bibliographical unit. Further, they allow for other internal pointing systems, imbedded links and programmatological components, in some instances even more significant than external orders. A final dimension of order arises when one considers that not every copy of a book necessarily needs to be identical. Such a dilemma of order characterizes the "Library of Babel" by Jorge Luis Borges. His library is one in which "each book is unique and irreplaceable." Yet for each book, "there are always several hundred thousand imperfect facsimiles—books that differ by no more than a single letter, or a comma" (*Collected* 116), an idea that seems to foretell both the Web and the inherent malleability of digital reproductions.

Sidebar: The "I" in "Internet"

> I celebrate myself,
> And what I assume you shall assume,
> For every atom belonging to me as good belongs to you.
> —Walt Whitman, *Leaves of Grass*

> Who
> am I—
> identity
> singing.
> —Robert Creeley, *Collected Poems*

> C'est faux de dire: Je pense. On devrait dire: On me pense. . . .
> Je est un autre.[9]
> —Arthur Rimbaud, *Collected Poems*

Non-innovative literature can be said to possess a number of distinguishing textual features. These can include narrative, plot, anecdotal re-telling of human experiences, logical descriptions, chronological sequences of events, a reliance on factual information, a view of language as a transparent (or at most, tinted) bearer of meaning, and an attachment to a Modernist aesthetic. Such texts often base their authority on the foundation of the certainty of semantic meaning. One can, of course, argue that the features I detail are too inclusive, exclusive, or that some features are too simplistically described. Such objections can be quite valid. (For example, it is not uncommon for non-chronological time to be used in non-innovative works.) Rather than addressing such possible objections here, however, I turn to a key feature that will even further distinguish such forms of textuality.

The position of the "I" is a crucial distinction between non-innovative and innovative literature. How the "I" is constituted in a text says much about that text's writing practice. Does the "I" assert forms of authority? Is it unquestionably a nonpermeable (or semipermeable) filter between the ego and the world? Is the relation between the "I" and the world characterized by conflict or even animosity?[10]

A poem such as Amanda Pecor's "Cinderella at Dusk, Before the Promenade," for example, is a poem about a troubled "I" who begins by reporting, "This yellow bothers me." Even grammatically, the verb sets off this "I" and the world as two distinct and antagonistic forces. We are drawn into the dilemma of this "I," who subsequently reports:

> I never see my boy
> as I loiter beneath the marquee.
> And well you may ask me why
> I go or at all bother.
> But where else shall I find
> sweeter chambers in this greenhorn town.
> (13)

Thus we begin to learn more about this "I" and its predicament.

Because of its colloquial tone and genial diction, this poem is clearly engaging; however, the perspective of the poem is one that does not attempt to investigate any other position than that of the self-constituted "I." This "I" is painfully separate from the world, separate from her child, starkly isolated beneath a marquee, so laden with loss that the ritual of observing separation offers the only respite this character knows. One can empathize with this character, and one can relate such a painful isolation expressed here to one's own experiences, yet I suggest that there are other positions for the "I" that might be more useful for a reading of the Web as writing.

How do poets deal with an identity not fixed beyond a given moment, an "I" that is not singular and isolated? There are many strategies for evading the misperceptions of the ego-oriented "I." William Carlos Williams argued for the individual to find "some approximate co-extension with the universe" (*Imaginations* 105). He also stated, "Whenever I say, 'I' I mean also, 'you'" (89), trying to break the bond between reader and writer, a usual separation of identities. The French poet Arthur Rimbaud was famous for saying, in a quote included at the beginning of this sidebar, that "'I' is an other." That is, of his role as author, Rimbaud argues that "'I' doesn't think," insisting rather that "one" thinks "through him"—meaning that the poet is a kind of transcriber for the poem that comes from "one," an intelligence that is larger than the individual. Jack Spicer took this idea further, likening himself to a radio that received a signal and then recorded it. Hannah Weiner considered that there were several "I's" in her work, her writing involving the transcribing of the voices she heard. One can see in Robert Creeley's work an expression of the distance between the New Critical "I" of the writer and the "I" on the page. His famous assertion that, "As soon as / I speak, I / speaks" (*Poems* 294), converts the "I" into a third person as soon as "I" is written, a compelling glimpse at the complexity of the written "I." Creeley also employs short sentences, compact phrases, words that are links, words from which associations can radiate in spoke-like patterns. Solid, outwardly gesturing words are also characteristic of the poems of the Spanish poet Pedro Salinas, who curiously does express a singular "I," but whose packing of meaning into individual word choices seems to make the *words* the subject, not the "I."

Deterministic processes for generating poetry similarly attempt to negotiate the interference of the "I." Jackson Mac Low has been forthcoming about describing what deterministic processes mean for him. As he explains, "Remember that the main motivation for using procedures of any kind is the Buddhist one of loosening and lessening the domination—in effect, the hegemony—of the artist's ego (in either the Freudian sense or the more inclusive Buddhist sense, which includes all of the Freudian institutions of the psyche, the Ego, the Id, and the Superego, in the ego)" ("Re: A Footnote"). Obviously, Mac Low notes, such an escape from the "I" is never literally possible, because "one realizes while working with methods meant to reduce the ego's domination that there is no such thing as nonegoic art" ("Re: A Footnote"). Even through procedures, anything you produce remains a product of your ego. Nonetheless, all of these strategies contribute to an awareness that there are other possibilities, to a lesser and greater extent, than the ego-centered "I." This can also result in crisper and more interesting writing.

Reading such poets, we begin to see alternatives to the head-on collision with which the personalized "I" confronts the world. Though such a self-constituted "I" may be necessary in certain survival scenarios, it is not the only way to view the world. When we think about it, there are indications that much can be gained by approaching the world in ways not limited to the singularized and solitary "I."

Indeed, the importance of the individual has been greatly exaggerated in our culture. When individuals act as parts of a collective body, the result is something much greater, in the words of the old adage, than the sum of the parts. This is evident in many such collectives: marriages, music groups, sports teams, communes, and communities. It explains the "mystical union" of marriage and the magic of dancing, the endurance of friendships and the allure of group-performed music. Such collectives are the webs that intrigue and inspire us. In fact, our life support itself is based on numerous overlaid webs—grids of wires and pipes from utilities, economic systems, food supply chains. And our identity does not reflect a solitary ego, like some granite boulder dominating a flat horizon, but is the result of numerous webs of relations—our genetics, how we were parented, the conditions under which we matured, and our associations: marital, family, and professional relations and friendships. Even on a molecular level the "I" is distributed more widely than a solitary ego, an assertion reinforced by animal genetics. British biologist W. D. Hamilton made a major contribution to science by answering a question directly related to this idea. The question facing Hamilton was why an animal would risk its own life to alert its kin to danger, when the rule of survival of the fittest would suggest that the animal should preserve itself first. Hamilton's answer was that, in these cases, the sacrificial act benefited the animal's relatives, that is, the animal's own genes as shared by its relatives—itself by extension. For human beings, equally, we are genetically parts of other people, and parts of us are other people.

The solitary "I" must be renegotiated as increasingly interrelated societies rely on cooperation, intertextuality, and senses of the multiple. Accordingly, many recent cultural developments have seen other forms of identity come to the front. The notion of our nation as multicultural, for one development, insists that a "nation" can be made of a plurality of identities rather than a sole stereotypical one. Such a perspective can be socially beneficial in a heterogeneous society as it obviates, for one thing, the need for one "I" to be more valid than others, a concept disruptive of social equality. The consequences can be horrible when we do not realize that everyone is "I" too, as witnessed by the holocausts, acts of genocide, and interpersonal violence that appear in the news more often than one would care to acknowledge. Many social and religious philosophies argue that recognition that "everyone is `I' too" is necessary for personal and social equanimity.

Such a sense of the multiple helps one understand the Buddhist goal of selflessness as necessary to a clear view of the world: "At the center of our desire for control is our sense of self. But with seeing, this sense loses its grip. What becomes extinguished is this false sense of self. We stop clinging to something that wasn't there to begin with" (Hagen 51). Such an assertion that "I" never existed at first seems not to make any sense. But it can be explained if one recognizes that, first, the "I" is subject to a web of relations. Such interconnectedness is something we tend to overlook. Secondly, we must note that, biologically, we are not technically the same person from moment to moment, for we are literally in a constant state of change: adding and losing cells, remembering and forgetting ideas, changing emotions, adding links to others, losing links. Thus "I" am no more than a kind of average of the "I" that varies from one second to the next. The "I" that argues its autonomy, that cuts another driver off to get the best parking space, that "I" is not as self-constituting as it thinks. Such an idea is even valid from the perspective of a computer scientist. As David Gelernter explains, even the simple act of observing a rose illustrates the fallacy of the autonomous "I": "That rose over there merely triggered, when you saw it, a barrage of neuron firings in your brain. But you have the sensation that some entity—namely, you . . . actually *saw* the rose" (21). Indeed, Gelernter suggests that the "I" is a marvelous fiction engineered for an organism to endure. "The brain is a lump of hardware artfully arranged so as to produce an I—to create the illusion that some entity inside you is observing the world that your senses conjure up" (21).

Although a role clearly exists for the "I," there are strong indications, I would suggest, to consider other possibilities. Thus we might be better able to inform our conceptions of identity and the text. If we choose to consider alternatives to the singular "I," we then turn to concepts of collective identity as evoked above. Such examples of the possibility of multiple or "distributed" identity lead us to consider the text as not singular and isolated but more like the "I" of the Internet. The Web can be seen as such a multiple text, being composed of endlessly varying pages or "I's." If the Web, in terms of computing, is based on distributed architecture, then, in terms of writing, it realizes distributed textuality. Such a distributed model introduces the concept that the text is not fixed. Rather, it is in the process of continual change. Control cannot be exerted over what everyone does, but neither is there a reason to want to exert such control. Textually, the Web is a dynamic organism that we read. Literally each instant, pages are added, removed, are read, are not read, go out of date, fail. Its pages are like the cells that fall off the "I" of the human body, similarly constituting a multiple sense of the "I" in writing. Its only unchangeable fact is that it will change, a tenet of Buddhism and Olsonian process-oriented poetry alike.

What we begin to discover is a larger sense of text in which individual writings are merely parts. Robert Creeley has described such experience as:

> a parts or pieces?—
>
> That tidy habit of sound
> relations—must be in the
> very works,* like.
>
> ───────────────
>
> *Words work
> the author of many pieces

(Poems 463)

After evoking "a parts or pieces," Creeley introduces a most compelling stanza. Here, one first notices the horizontal rule, a kind of fold that both divides and unifies. As I read it, the rule separates two concepts of authorship, the ego-centered author on top (author as practioner of "that tidy habit of sound / relations") and the egoless on bottom ("the author of many pieces"). Yet the connection between them is integral, as the asterisk indicates—linking and puncturing both texts at once. Writing, that "tidy habit of sound / relations," is not a process of the ego controlling words but is a recognition of those qualities of words that make them almost autonomous. The non-ego-centered "I" is characterized by the syntax of the argument that "words work." The subject of the sentence is the words themselves. The direct object of this sentence appears in the following line, as if words work the author (the inverse of the ego-centered approach to writing). The author is also described as *the author* of "many pieces," suggesting that texts are only pieces of writing, as the title of Creeley's landmark collection, *Pieces,* might also suggest.

The importance of pieces of writing is crucial to our discussion of digital writing. In this vein, I published a volume of poetry about the experience of the Internet as a writing space called *The Parts*. One reviewer responded to this collection as follows: "*The Parts* . . . is about parts—parts of writing. [Glazier] has gone so far into the Web world that creation and writing no longer are separate from web work/word. Parts on paper, in mind imagination and in that Web net cyber-space. Unified but parts. This is still the poem machine that William Carlos Williams defined but now the poem lives in a matrix of mediums" (Basinski). As the reviewer notes, *The Parts* argues that "there should be one book; writing weaves through that" (Basinski). The reviewer suggests a view of writing that allows for flux among its constituent elements. Such a view also recognizes distributed writing. This concept reflects the architecture of the Web itself, with countless pieces of writing coming from innumerable servers. It embodies and reflects the packet-based technology of the Internet, with parts of texts seeming to be able to take any path, to recombine in multiple manners, to be on the loose. As Roland Barthes remarks: "In this ideal text, the networks are many and interact, without any one of them being able to surpass the rest; this text is a galaxy of signifiers, not a structure of signifieds; it has no beginning; it is reversible; we gain access to it by several entrances, none of which can be authoritatively declared to be the main one" (*S/Z* 5–6).

Though Barthes refers to processes of meaning-making, his words seem to also evoke the notion of the parts from which Web and digital writings are fashioned. These parts come together, emerging and engaging multiple entrances and exits to form the digital text. The 1999 commercial that suggests that "in the time it takes for lightning to strike, the entire contents of the Library of Congress can be transported from coast to coast, flawlessly,"[11] shows that the advertiser has not grasped the paradigm shift that is upon us. Rather than looking at information in its new context (distributed in origin), the advertisement continues to view information as monolithic, authoritative, and singular. Such a misconception is common. The point here is not that this amount of information *can be* transmitted, nor how fast, nor that it can be done flawlessly. What is noteworthy is that information no longer exists in a single location; rather, in the new paradigm, a site of information simply offers a single window through which to view information residing in *multiple* locations, a number of locations so multiple that they can never actually be counted.

The Web, like numerous paradigm shifts in preceding decades (for example, the sixties), does not simply introduce new topics to our collective vocabulary. Instead, it has become a part of a transformed social fabric: writing will never be the same again, now that its linkages have been made manifest. The shift to interconnectedness presents a simple proposition: recognize the connectedness. The goal of interlinked writing is to put the weave back in "Web." Such a weave realizes a writing system that allows interdependence within an environment of constant flux. Indeed, meaning exists within the condition of what is present when the Web is entered, and this modulates according to the elements that change while you are there. That is, meaning is a *condition* of any number of transient, unbound parts of information.

Such a sense of the conditional is not new to innovative poetry. It is certainly not new to poets working in digital media, for whom hypertext, programmed, and kinetic poetry offer previously unavailable opportunities to work within changing conditions of meaning actualized through literal change on the screen. Writing in the digital medium, writing characterized by its connections to other writings, offers us the opportunity to re-imagine what writing is. We have the possibility of moving the "I" from a totalized entity in opposition to the totality of other entities to a sense of the "I" as one facet of a collective whole. This is an "I" that draws its meaning not from itself, but from its connections and disconnections with adjacent facets. This is similar to John Cayley's metaphor of "Indra's Net," a concept originating in Hinduism that, he explains, is "a network of jewels that not only reflect the images in every other jewel, but also the multiple images in the others" ("Indra's"). This is a strong metaphor for the kind of writing proposed here—a kind of writing that not only includes a sense of the seam (the edges of the facets) but also the interrelation of the messages, the endless interconnection between the "I's" that constitutes writing as a distributed network of parts.

The Classification

> Literature is an ongoing system of interconnecting documents.
> —Theodor Nelson, *Literary Machines*

> This "I" which approaches the text is already itself a plurality of other texts, of codes which are infinite or, more precisely, lost (whose origin is lost).
> —Roland Barthes, *S/Z*

> Il s'agit d'arriver à l'inconnu par le dérèglement de tous les sens. Les souffrances sont énormes, mais il faut être fort, être né poète, et je me suis reconnu poète.[12]
> —Arthur Rimbaud, *Collected Poems*

The purpose of classification is to arrange information systematically. One presumed reason for classification would be to allow people to find items of interest to them. How would you find something you wanted on the World Wide Web? Searching for material reveals much about the Web's resistance to classification. As Aaron Weiss argues, no "perfect" search tool exists for the Web: "Because of its nature, various search engines use different search techniques and yield different 'views' of the Web. Depending on what techniques they use, the automated search engines are sometimes referred to as 'robots,' 'worms,' or 'spiders.' One of the basic decisions a search engine makes is whether to follow a *depth-first* or *breadth-first* approach" (43). The difference between such approaches is large, ranging from having a universe of only the titles of series of books, versus one that contains not just all titles but all chapter titles. The problem with using such an in-depth query universe for the Web is not only that it is painstakingly slow but that the search engine "can also end up circling through loops of links that refer back upon previously covered tracks" (Weiss 43).

Another option is a weighted search. One search tool, LYCOS, does precisely this; however it bases its choices on: "a weighted random choice of which links to follow in a document." These are "biased towards documents with multiple links pointing at them (implying popularity) and links with shorter URLs, on the theory that shorter URLS tend to imply shallower Web links and, therefore, more breadth." Finally, LYCOS "not only catalogs a document's title and headings, but also the first 20 lines and the 100 most significant words, based on an algorithm" (Weiss 44). If one thinks about how arbitrary and frankly unsatisfactory such methods are for documenting each page of Web content, then multiply those inaccuracies by the millions of Web pages that have content, we find ourselves on truly questionable ground.[13] None of these approaches can effectively classify the Web, nor could they be said to rival even the most moderately competent human indexer, a situation that makes one think the Web is so inaccurately indexed that it is virtually uncharted.

~

The personal and social consequences of any medium—that is, of any extension of ourselves—result from the new scale that is introduced into our affairs by each extension of ourselves, or by any new technology.
—Marshall McLuhan, *Understanding Media*

Electronic space as literary space: one must begin by thinking of our attachment to texts as the embodiment of writing. What senses of writing are implied by this? First, the text is and has always been related to transmission. Transmission of what? A number of possible answers to this question arise: knowledge, experience, information, and thought, among them. Though these ideas are related to this question, what concerns us here is the transmission of literary material. Literary writing is writing that, whether or not it serves other ends, has an engagement with its own formal qualities. Whether this attention to formal qualities is conscious or not, reading texts as "literary" involves reading writing on formal terms.

Forms of verse, from traditional to experimental, are attentive to their formal qualities. Metrical verse differs from verbal communication in attention to the form of the text. Other poetic forms are defined by a number of "devices," from the foregrounding of their sounds to enjambment to interruptions as a metatextual procedure. In the modernist and postmodernist periods particularly, formal qualities have been foregrounded. Jerome McGann, among many scholars, has investigated typographic (and calligraphic) qualities as integral to the poetic project of specific authors. McGann's *The Textual Condition*, as discussed earlier, investigates the additional information that can be garnered from the typography of Ezra Pound's early publications. In *Black Riders*, McGann looks at the work of Emily Dickinson, Gertrude Stein, William Morris, and contemporary poets, such as Charles Bernstein and Susan Howe. Looking at the works of these writers, he demonstrates the importance of typographic practice to poetic writing. Following McGann's arguments, typographic and formal conditions not only inform, but *facilitate* the emergence of specific kinds of writing. McGann writes, "Stein's experimentalism was . . . licensed by the cultural scene in which she moved." That is, "Stein's *Stanzas in Meditation* . . . would be inconceivable without the late-Victorian Renaissance of Printing, just as Pound's *Cantos* and Yeats's 'The Circus Animals' Desertion' are inconceivable outside the same context" (*Black* 21).

If such a licensing occurs in typographic space, the possibilities for electronic space are truly copious. Indeed, the literary possibilities for writing in the technical and cultural context of online space are now an established part of contemporary literary activity. Such electronic journals as *RIF/T*, *DIU*, and *Passages: A Technopoetics Journal*[14] opened the gates in the mid-nineties, presenting works not only conscious of cultural space but exploring the technical possibilities of the medium. These efforts are now being fully demonstrated by such magazines as *Jacket*, *Riding the Meridian*, *How2*, *Deluxe Rubber Chicken*, and *Readme*.[15] The *Little Magazine* has delved into the rich and various the ramifications of electronic multimedia works through two CD-ROM and Web-based issues. The Electronic Poetry Center is also an example of a site that conceives of the presence of a text as nonspecific to its physical location. Many pages in the EPC re-position you in physical or conceptual space. Thus, echoing McGann, such experimentalism is licensed by the cultural scene of online poetic space. These are literary developments —developments in writing inseparable from the medium that transmits them.

George Landow has suggested that "since the invention of writing and printing, information technology has concentrated on the problem of creating and then disseminating static, unchanging records of language" (18). If texts are static and thus historic, then it is appropriate to leave their cataloging and indexing to librarians or even museum personnel. (The most extreme example of the library as museum is the Special Collections, where the physical properties of texts become so valorized that protocols of museums are literally followed.) The problem with a librarian monitoring "records of language" is the generalist approach that is used in devising schemes that will equivalently accommodate particle physics, cookbooks, and Zukofsky's

A. Such a system becomes extremely unwieldy: "Our ineptitude in getting at the record is largely caused by the artificiality of systems of indexing. When data of any sort are placed in storage, they are filed alphabetically or numerically, and information is found (when it is) by tracing it down from subclass to subclass. It can be in only one place, unless duplicates are used; one has to have rules as to which path will locate it, and the rules are cumbersome. Having found one item, moreover, one has to emerge from the system and re-enter on a new path" (Bush 101). Any such scheme must insist on the primacy of hypotactic relations.

Historically, the counterbalance to this hyper-hierarchy was that textual objects could be browsed in the stacks. A reader did not have to follow the system in any way and could always wander at will in the shelving areas for books. With the electronic medium, such browsing is no longer a physical activity. Nor could it be a physical activity. As the number of files extends into the many millions, the idea of such browsing becomes untenable. Hence, the retrieving system must accommodate this activity.

If the electronic text is mutable, then a theory of mutability must replace theory of the "embalming" of the text. If the "information age" exemplifies changes in the nature of information, then for literary purposes, what has occurred is the implosion of the indexing and distribution mechanism onto the text itself, as well as the collapsing of textual data with document metadata. Determinations of the relevancy of metadata will vary significantly by discipline. Literary materials may pose the most exciting possibilities of any field because of the complex and associative relations within texts that have become evident even in the print medium.

In the introduction to his *Selected Poems: 1963–1973*, David Antin, for example, invokes a number of approaches that evade the traditional rigidity of the text. Some of these poems, resulting from "found materials and [a] salvaging job" (18), were based on other texts that Antin happened to find at hand: "I took one of the books . . . propped it up near my typewriter and proceeded to flip the pages, reading a line and a line there, and then I got tired of it and started flipping through another book . . . and I realized I was enjoying it. . . . Then I put some paper in the typewriter and I began typing what I was reading, and it became a little game—no more than one line from a page. Sometimes only a phrase. Sometimes nothing. And I never went back. I read and typed relentlessly forward, quickly making up these little songs, till I was through" (16–17).

In the same introduction, Antin documents other techniques he used to compose poems. *Meditations* was created from word lists, including lists of words that high school students found difficult to spell. Another sequence was based on the footnotes to a text by *Epictetus*. In this case, Antin simply read the notes in sequence, extracting poetic materials from each footnote.

William Burroughs offers directions for a similar inversion of intended textual devices, in this case through using a tape recorder. Writing in a style promulgatory of the compositional process he describes, he explains:

> A tape recorder can play back back fast   slow or backwards   you can learn to do these things   record a sentence and speed it up   now try imitating your accelerated voice   play a sentence backwards and learn to unsay what you just said . . . such exercises bring you a liberation from old association locks   try inching tape   this sound is produced by taking a recorded text for the best results a text spoken in a loud clear voice and rubbing the tape back forth across the head . . . take any text speed it up slow it down run it backwards inch it and you will hear words that were not in the original recording new words made by the machine   different people will scan out different words of course but some of the words are quite clearly there and anyone can hear them words which were not in the original tape but which are in many cases relevant to the original text as if the words themselves had been interrogated and forced to reveal their hidden meanings it is interesting to record these words words literally made by the machine itself. (Odier 161)

Using the example of the machine, Burroughs pushes the technological features of the instrument beyond its intended limits to open material areas that result from the superimposition of the information system upon the text.

Not only is the textual apparatus used against its intended purpose in these cases, but the "literary" in such situations emerges from an inversion of what might be thought of as the logical use of textual order. Thus every technology may be seen as opening new textualities through an engagement with its material context. Extended to the electronic text's relation to its technology, the possibilities are immense.

Any classification system can only be expected to perform as designed. The Web was designed as a system of internal links. This internal order may never be effectively overridden; in fact, if written properly, one effective link should be all a person needs to begin the series of connections that yields relevant sources. Hypertext for the Web consists of hyperlinks. Important to this terminology is the prefix "hyper-," defined commonly as "over, beyond, over much, and above measure," from the Greek *uper* through Old English *ofer*. Charles Bernstein, for example, has referred to Brecht's theatre as "hyperabsorptive," meaning that Brecht wished his theatre goers to be involved in the plot of a given play but "over"-involved in it as well, that is, also engaged in critiquing it.[16] Bernstein comments that Brecht "doubles the attention of the spectator" by doing so. I would extend the use of "hyper" in "hyperabsorptive" to suggest that the spectator's double empowerment leads to exhaustion: not only is the spectator of the play exhausted, but the spectator's role of spectator is exhausted by the process of Brecht's play. The

Oxford English Dictionary (OED) provides an interesting assortment of examples of the use of the prefix "hyper." Thomas Castle's 1831 "A hyperbarbarous technology that no Athenian ear could have born," Shelley's 1820 "Scorched by Hell's hyperequatorial climate," and the 1866 *London Review* use of "that which is hyperpathetic, which is really too deep for tears," give some sense of the historical uses of the prefix. If anyone would argue that I am hyperetymologizing, I would point to the Internet itself. What is "hyper" about the Internet? Here are some facts, drawn from one set of available Web statistics:

Growth of the Web

Month	No. of Web Sites	Percentage Growth
6/93	130	—
12/93	623	479%
6/94	2,738	439%
12/94	10,022	366%
6/95	23,500	235%
1/96	100,000	425%
6/96	230,000 (est)	230%
1/97	650,000 (est)	283%
1/00	800,000,000	N/A

Sources: 6/93–1/97, "Matthew Gray of the Massachusetts Institute of Technology" (http://www.mit.edu/people/mkgray/net, 5 May 2000); 1/00, *World Almanac and Book of Facts,* 2000, accessed through Lexis-Nexis, 5 May 2000.

Clearly, the Web is growing at a frenzied pace, increasing by 600–800 percent in some years. This is a staggering rate of growth, supported as well by the growth of domains. By December 1996, about 627,000 Internet domain names had been registered, and by September 1999, over 10 million had been registered (*World Almanac*). One estimate gives the number of domains in May 2000 as nearly 15.7 million (http://www.domainstats.com)—and there are many possible Web sites within each domain. How many people are out there? According to the *World Almanac*, in 1994, 3 million people (most of them in the U.S.) made use of it. The number of U.S. users as of May 1998 was 57,037,000,[17] one out of five persons in the U.S. By mid-1999, close to 200 million people around the world were using the Internet, and it is estimated that by 2005, 1 billion people may be connected. In this regard, the *World Almanac* suggests that traffic on the Internet doubles every nine to twelve months. Finally, in terms of speed of transaction, the time required for an electronic signal to travel round-trip from MIT to McMurdo, Antarctica, is 640 milliseconds,[18] an unbelievable speed indeed!

These are all staggering statistics, the hyperbole of which has not been overlooked by the advertising industry; hyperbole that dominates almost every aspect of Web discourse. One must ask, what kind of rhetoric is this? Clearly, referring to the earlier Library of Congress example, it is not about the knowledge contained in the Library of Congress but about its volume. Who would want to transmit that much data and why? What thirst for power is it supposed to awaken? This is a very "hyper" rhetoric. Clearly, "hyper" is an appropriate prefix for the Internet. And think of contemporary uses of the prefix—"hyperacidic," "hyperactive," "hyperbolic," and "hyperexcitable"—all relatively familiar uses of the term. These varied terms lead to the conclusion that "hyper" is associated with extremism, manic activity, and disorder. Hypertext can thus be seen as being *disordered* by hyperlinks, destroying classification by the innate hyperactivity of its imbedded leaps.

This disorder extends to words themselves. Once a word assumes the status of a link word, it is forever changed. The action the word performs, or is capable of performing, changes the word irrevocably.[19] As Robin Blaser writes in a passage that could also be used to describe the link word:

> It is the interchange the form took
> like walking in and out of a star
> the words are left over   collapsed
> into themselves in the movement
>
> between visible and invisible
>   (Blaser 125)

Words and movement, then, become coexistent—and assume paramount importance. A fixed word is one that loses its ability to shift; in a text as large and as continuously re-constituted as the Web, the line between "visible and invisible" is a crucial one. Words that move enact the dynamism that has always characterized such a fluidity. Words further become mines for the hyperactivity inherent in links. It is writing that propels words into such an "interchange."

A well-written link is one that follows a natural digressive side thought or astonishes with brazen and quick abruptness of thought. "Hyper-" expresses an unhealthy agitation. Hypertexts are not just texts "beyond texts"; they are not merely texts that are linked to others. Considering the sense of agitation, disturbance, obsessive instability inherent in any use of the word "hypertext," we encounter a clear indication of what the character of a true Web-based writing would be.[20]

One of the truly unfortunate propositions to be heard in hypertextual circles is the tendency to believe that the Web links everything in the world. To write hypertext from such a perspective would only continue the "stockpile" of dead objects that is at the heart of institutions obsessed, as Baudrillard expresses it, with "linear and accumulative culture." (An all-inclusive approach to hypertext simply creates multiple linearities.) A similar misuse occurs when you stumble across a Web page that is an interminable scroll. To select a link in the middle of the page you must laboriously move your cursor past dozens of unwanted options. These points of online textual "form" are not minor ones: "accumulation" is not the objective of effective Web structure. Writing that is conscious of its internal order is writing that preserves its effectiveness against orders of institutionalization. Such writing is an engagement not just with the linear flow of words but a working with forms and relations of classification. As Robin Blaser writes:

> . . . I know nothing of form
> that is my own doing   all out
> of one's self   our words were
> the form we entered, turning intelligible
> and strange   at the point of
> a pencil.
>   (124)

An imbedded link is not something definable by <a href="url">link</a> but is a feature of writing itself; links will continue to embrace both print and electronic technology. With HTML and other forms of hypertextual writing, links are simply magnified. Texts continue to engage their own internal dynamics but literally (or is it figuratively?) have other texts superimposed or imbedded in them. Because imbedded links are not a feature unique to HTML documents but are an extension of the act of writing, it is crucial to understand the importance of internal orders. Though it runs contrary to common perception, libraries have survived as an institution in part because of the success of the internal orders of books. That is, the tension between the library's external order and the internal orders of books makes the library a success. The internal orders of books contain and supersede external orders though their status as writing. If the Internet is to provide new locations for texts, its status as a form as *writing* must not be overlooked. When HTML is written, it should not be mistaken as simply a vehicle for the presentation of texts, just as verse form is not, externally viewed, simply a vehicle for the presentation of text. (There is much published poetry that will attest to the uninteresting results of such an approach.) Instead, each word, each link written, is a re-inscription of form, a hyperinscription, an opportunity to keep Ramses *both* in and out of his crypt—in a place of action rather than one of decay.

3
Home, Haunt, Page

Home: The Page as Medium

> Back East had stopped being back home when home was out,
> West.
> —Lyn Hejinian, *My Life*

> Some day your Web address will be everything.
> —Television ad, Digital Equipment Corp., 1995

> By location, e.g., where
> or here—or what words in
> time make of things. Space,
> they say, and think a several
> dimensioned locus.
> —Robert Creeley, *Collected Poems*

In the incessant anarchic activity of the Web, the only "resting" place
that can be found is the home page. The idea of a home page is a curious
one. Almost everyone by now has been exposed to this locution. The home
page is a place you go on the Internet; a medium among the media of the
Net; a footing or a frame. Children are aware of the home page for the latest
Disney promotion. Home pages are as specific to individual commercial
films as movie posters once were. Corporations, entertainment conglomer-
ates, and political insurgents equally own home pages. Home pages are subject
to attack and counter attack; they are as much "home" as nations are. Take
for example the fact that one response to the bombing of the Chinese Em-
bassy in Belgrade by NATO/U.S. forces on 8 May 1999 was the defacement
of the White House home page. Virtual statehood can be also be seen as a
harbinger of political statehood. Thus the media excitement about the United
Nations Resolution to award Palestine the top level domain suffix "PS,"
such denominations being normally reserved for political entities.[1] The home
page can mean many things to many people, but its importance as a ground
is inescapable. What *does* a "home page" do? What are its attributes? How is
it *home*?

Purpose of the Page

> This life of wandering makes a three days' residence in one
> place seem like home.
> —Nathaniel Hawthorne, *Passages*

Unlike a book issued by Doubleday, a paper submitted to a scholarly jour-
nal, or a bibliographic entry in a library catalog, there is no authorized style
for a home page. Such a page could contain anything from a thousand links
to a single, unannotated photographic image of a miniature dachshund. Per-
sonal home pages constitute a category of their own. People use these to
present a persona to the world, for anything from job-hunting to romance.
The presentations of such personae can be idiosyncratically ironic or so punc-
tilious about personal facts that it becomes unbearable. (I once read a home
page giving an extensive account of how being an adoptee as a child led to
the love of cats.)

The class of home page discussed in this chapter might more properly be
called an "institutional home page." This institutional (or corporate or as-
sociation) home page exists to serve the needs of a group of people or body
composed of related interests and an agreed upon mission. This sense of
institutional or corporate identity has gray areas, as Robert Creeley sug-
gests: "There's a question of the corporate vis-a-vis the *common*. Latin would
argue that the corporate is the imagination of a body, that may or may not
have conjunction with other bodies" (Clark 90). In the case of the World
Wide Web, of course, the corporate achieves quite a different meaning, for
the point is that all "bodies" are conjoined. The difficulty is in establishing
identity in this environment. The contrast between a corporate and per-
sonal home page must be made, however. The institutional home page (called
"home page" hereafter) is driven by its political, social, or cultural mission.
These home pages are ubiquitous on the Internet. Though there is no stan-
dard format or prescribed means of presentation for its layout and content,
specific features of the home page have emerged as generally present. Thus,
a group starting a new home page must either incorporate these features or
consciously decide to ignore them. They do, in this manner, become ad hoc
standards.

> Baffling combustions are everywhere! we hunger and
>   taste
> And go to the movies   then run home drenched in flame
> To the grace of the make-believe bed
>   (Berrigan 54)

The idea of welcome suggests an architectural interpretation of the home
page. Where is the "home" in it? ("Home" is a word that causes some prob-
lems. Like "sunshine" or "country," "home" dissolves into an uncomfortable

generality. In the popular song by John Denver, for example, West Virginia is invoked in the most maudlin terms.) Does the home page function like the front door to a house or a lobby of a high-rise? The home page is an entrance, but how is it a "home"? Indeed, the use of the word "home" as opposed to "house" is curious, since the former suggests an environment offering security and happiness, whereas the latter is related to the verb "to hide." "House" would probably be more accurate, that is, a building for human occupation other than that of ordinary dwelling, or a building for the entertainment of the public. This usage is in line with uses such as ale-house, coffee-house, eating-house, public house, or charnel house and also resonates with "publishing house." In this sense, the home page would be an "information house," "data house," or "electronic file" house, if the architectural model were to be pursued.

It Must Locate

Some definitions of "home" round out dimensions of what is implied by a "home page." These include, according to the OED, 2nd ed.: "a valued place regarded as a refuge or place of origin"; a "headquarters" or "home base"; and "the place where something is discovered, founded, developed, or promoted . . . a source." These concepts suggest a position, in electronic space, which the particular page argues. (Not irrelevant is the definition "an institution where people are cared for. For example, *a home for the elderly.*") A home page locates a specific point, however defined, in online space.

Home Is a Technology

Home on the keyboard derives from the technology of the typewriter. For touch typists, the "home row" on a standard keyboard consists of the keys A, S, D, F, J, K, L, and ;. What is suggested by this "home" row? First, that in a technology, "home"—the "security and happiness" it gives—is characterized by discomfort. What could be more alienating than ASDFJKL;? ASDFJKL; is the starting point for entering text via the machine. (To be consistent, then, pages should not be named "home" pages on the World Wide Web but "ASDFJKL;" pages.) What is the reason that ASDFJKL; were chosen as the home keys on the typewriter, rather than, for example, ABCDEFGHIJ or HAWDYFOLKS? *The Cambridge Encyclopedia of Language* points out that this was to slow down the typist's speed to avoid jamming the keys of early typewriters. It goes on to point out a number of design flaws in the typewriter keyboard: "Some letter separations are motivated by the need to avoid key jamming. But there is no simple principle. The second line has a largely alphabetical arrangement. The top line, according to one story, contains the letters of the word *typewriter,* so that salesmen could find them easily when demonstrating their machines" (Crystal 192). Many of the developments in Internet technologies have been founded on equally capricious ground, the home page among them.

Home Is Navigational

Even more curiously, *home is column one position one* on a computer terminal screen. This fact has numerous ramifications. "Home" is a part of every document; it is its very beginning ("home home" or "control home") and the beginning of each line ("home left" or "home"). "Home" suggests a beginning place, a resting place, a source, a place you can retreat to. Yet as a point of entry, "home" binds you to the linearity that a Web orientation seeks to avoid. "Home" is a point of stasis in a dynamic textual environment.

Home Must Explain What Is "There"

A home page must explain what you can expect to find by visiting it. Though this might be presented as a mapping, in usual practice, such an explanation takes the form of a narrative or, more specifically, an annotation. (Though the comparison with a commentary might also be explored.) Explaining what is "there," whether the choice is narrative, annotation, or commentary, presents the page with the prejudice of its authors. There is no way to "explain" what is on the page; any attempt to do so simply adds a layer of language that must also be interpreted. Nevertheless, alternatives to this composition of explanation exist: symbolic "buttons" or maps. These graphical alternatives, however, equally present value judgments. (Why are certain colors chosen for certain buttons? Where is the visual center of a map placed? How is it "framed"?)

Home Evokes the Maudlin

A number of locutions suggest home as maudlin. Common are such phrases as "home is where the heart is." In this maxim, "home" is also uncomfortable because it assumes that one can *expect* comfort "there." (Most people know from their own childhoods that this is a difficult expectation to have fulfilled.) As William Burroughs has noted: "any sort of nonsense that the parents suffer from—any neuroses or confusions—are immediately passed on to the helpless child. Everyone seems to consider that parents have every right to inflict on their children any sort of pernicious nonsense from which they themselves suffer, and which was passed on to them in turn by their parents, so that the whole human race is crippled in childhood, and this is done by the family." Interestingly, a possible solution to this problem, Burroughs suggests, amounts to the creation of an alternative "home": "the children [could be] removed from their biologic parents at birth, and brought up in sort of state nurseries." This, however, would still not be a solution, he concludes, because "you have to consider what sort of training and environment they have in the state nurseries" (Odier 119-20).

A tenuous though interesting connection may also be made to the phrase "Magdalen home" (as in "Mary the Magdalene"), a place of charity for those who have strayed from the approved social path; that is, a refuge and home for the reformation of prostitutes. It was named after (Mary) of Magdala (a town on the Sea of Galilee), Mary Magdalen(e). The Magdalen(e) is often known as a "disciple" of Christ, though obviously excluded by gender from being an apostle. She is also Mary, "out of whom went seven devils" (Luke 8.2) and commonly believed to be the unnamed "sinner" (Luke 7.37) who washed the feet of Jesus with her hair. She is viewed in Western hagiography, in the words of the *OED*, 2nd ed., as "a harlot restored to purity and elevated to saintship by repentance and faith." Mary's fervor in repentance (this scene in the source text is intense and graphic) suggests an extreme longing for home. Adopted through French, the vernacular form of Magdalen is maudlin.

(Interestingly, Magdalen is still pronounced "maudlin" in the U.K., for example, when used for the names of Magdalen College, Oxford, and Magdalene College, Cambridge.) It is interesting then, that the appellation of Magdalen, the one who repented and came back to the fold, also carries the sense of overly sentimental emotional expression. This Magdalen who, according to John, was the first to believe in Christ's resurrection ends up being associated with the most effusive in emotional expression. A magdalen home is an interesting euphemism—and not foreign to contemporary usage. "Home" is often used to indicate comfort when realistically none is to be expected (for example, a "home for the elderly").

Most informative, perhaps, is the experience that is not uncommon for Alzheimer's patients who, sitting in the home they have lived in for thirty or fifty years, will suddenly declare, "I want to go home." All the caregiver can do is to say, "In another half hour" or "We have to get the car fixed first," counting that the patient will forget in the short term. This sense of home as always being somewhere just beyond our present position is crucial.

Structure of the Page

> Their abodes were equipped with every modern home comfort.
> —James Joyce, *Ulysses*

Scrolling versus Framing
The first decision in the design of any page is whether it will be scroll or frame based. In the former case, the sections of text to which the home page provides access are really (and literally) continuous sections in one long scrolling document.
1. → 2. → 3. → 4. → 5. → 6.
In the frame approach to home page design, the "page" (each unit of information) is not meant to occupy much more than a single screen.[2] The sequence then is composed of discrete parts (or lexia). Once a choice is made, the reader progresses into an array of other lexia to be chosen. These lexia are not necessarily symmetrical, nor are they unidirectional.

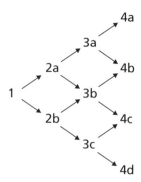

Frame-based reading differs substantially from scroll-based reading. The reader is not allowed the choice of simply sitting on the "down scroll" button. The frame approach to screen design rests on the fundamental tenet that choices must be made by the reader: each choice has a consequence and each consequence prescribes a separate path.

The choice of a scroll versus a frame approach is not a neutral decision. (One might say it is "neural" instead, because the actual "wiring" of the information transmissions is at the core of this decision. Neural messages do not scroll down a linear chain of command but spread or radiate according to local application.) The structure of the page determines the conceptual framework and underlying navigational frame of the site. Speak of "authorial intentions"! The reader's activity within the site is determined by this fundamental choice.

What is an order? A home page is an explicit presentation of order. It is composed of specific "textual" elements: wallpaper (background), graphics, surface writing, and links.

Wallpaper

Wallpaper, when used, can provide essential information about a site. (The term "wallpaper" also suggests an architectural model.) When used, wallpaper tends to loom extremely large. The CIA home page, http://www.odci.gov/cia, is an excellent example of this, the CIA graphic repeating multiple assertions of the power of an official seal. (This URL is no longer functional.) Of course, many sites may choose not to use wallpaper. Using wallpaper can add busyness to a design, and it can also, depending on the size of the background graphic, necessitate additional load time for a page. Although the lack of wallpaper cannot necessarily be interpreted, use of such ambient writing of the page can provide interesting background about the intentions, design principles, and conception of a site.

Graphics

Graphics on a home page declare the intellectual space circumscribed by the page, further the assumptions of the page, and suggest where the page will lead the reader. Whether to entertain, provide information, or contribute aesthetic elements, graphics should be read for what they say. Graphics can be design elements or may also be hot (clickable). Tone and ideological position are established by the content of graphics, their size, and their position on the page. (A CIA seal, http://www.odci.gov/cia, says one thing, whereas an image of a pieced together corpse, http://sunsite.unc.edu/otis/synergy/corpse.html, says another.) One often-used approach is to place clickable corporate (or noncorporate) logos on the screen, as if the logo were more meaningful than any writing could be. (See Prose and Contexts Online, http://www.io.org/~dalopes, for a positive use of such an approach.)

Writing

Surface writing is writing that would constitute the entire message of the page should the reader not follow any links. This is important writing! Some pages try to spell it all out while they've got the reader's attention. Others take a more eclectic approach and do not say much—or rely on clickable images or symbols in the frame. On pages that use writing, tone and ideological position are established by the same features as with any writing. Thus, it is necessary to consider point of view, intended audience, diction, rhetorical devices, sentence style and syntax, and types of figurative language to make conclusions about such writing. This surface writing may give a sense of the mission of the home page in question. (Such a statement of mission is usually presented on the home page or as an "about" link from it.) Of greatest importance are the ideological assumptions of a page: Does the site buy into the vocabulary of the Internet? (Is the prefix "cyber" used? Does it refer to readers as "surfers"? WWW Poet's Park, for example, subtitles its site "Your resting spot on the superhighway" and offers a link, at the bottom of their page, called "Surf to shore!")[3] Is the site service oriented? Does the site promote consumption of products? The language, even if not stating a purpose, must be read for its specific underlying motives.

Rationale

The reason for a home page is to curate links. Links determine where the reader can go from the home page. Without links there is no hypertextual movement from a page. Links can be represented textually (highlighted words in surface writing), graphically (as "buttons" or clickable images), or as both. Since many users in the world still read the Web from an ASCII browser, it has been common to make allowances for those readers in the graphical design of a home page. There are really only two choices in this case: repeat button bar choices as a duplicate row of text links or provide a separate page for ASCII users. The former approach is more prevalent.

Haunt: The Internet Itself

"Mrs. Heathcliff," I said earnestly, "you must excuse me for troubling you. I presume, because, with that face, I'm sure you cannot help being good-hearted. Do point out some landmarks by which I may know my way home. I have no more idea how to get there than you would have how to get to London."
—Emily Brontë, *Wuthering Heights*

So, to my fond faith, poor Pip, in this strange sweetness of his lunacy, brings heavenly vouchers of all our heavenly homes.
—Herman Melville, *Moby Dick*

As habitations, some hospitable, some quite extravagant: language, dwelling, being.
—Hank Lazer, *3 of 10*

A History in Case Studies

Any home page communicates through a variety of visual and semantic devices. For the following case study, home pages were visited and are described below. This is study of the state of the Web through an inventory of significant pages as they appeared from February 1996 through November 1997, a period crucial in the development of Web conventions. (Indeed, some aspects of these pages seem primitive by present day standards; however, it is useful to note where we were at that decisive point, what mechanics were used, and how these worked to represent the idea of "home" in the home page. The development of this concept has been crucial to our sense of the Web home page.) Categories assigned in this inventory are not meant to typify the structure of an entire site; these categories reflect the impact of each site's home page on the reader.

Architecture-Based

The White House
http://www.whitehouse.gov, 22 November 1997
Main image: The White House
Main links: graphical (image map)
Structure: touristic

A graphic of a gold plate announces "Welcome to the White House." Several labeled presidential seals ("Executive Branch," "The First Family," "Tours," "What's New," "Publications," "Comments") border an image of the White House, fronted by flowers and a fountain. Clearly this page is seen as a public image opportunity. Subtitled, "An Interactive Citizens' Handbook," it seems conscious of the effects that might accomplish this goal. For example, "Tours" offers a graphic of a printed ticket and buttons, leading to "three virtual tours that you may take." These are lavish. ("The Oval Office," for example, provides a 206,000 byte color image.)

The Library of Congress
http://www.loc.gov, 22 November 1997
Main image: Library of Congress
Main links: textual
Structure: departmental

The Library of Congress home page contains one significant graphic, a sketch of the Library's neoclassical architecture and landmark dome. Much is suggested by the focus on architecture. Because Washington is a city where social order is expressed by architecture, it is not surprising that the national library would extend this metaphor into Web space. In the words of one of its screens, "Symbols are history encoded in visual shorthand. Eighteenth-century Euro-Americans invented or adopted emblems—images accompanied by a motto—and personifications—allegorical figures—to express their political needs. They used them as propaganda tools to draw together the country's diverse peoples (who spoke many languages) in order to promote national political union." The Library of Congress site even includes an entry in "Electronic Exhibits" called "psychology of the unconscious uses capitol in advertisement," a 1900 Uneeda Biscuit Advertisement. This observation reminds us that such symbols continue to be used to promote similar themes, now in Web space.

Geography-Based

European Laboratory for Particle Physics
http://www.cern.ch, 22 November 1997
Main image: geographic
Main links: textual
Structure: topical

The home page for the European Laboratory for Particle Physics (CERN) is particularly relevant because CERN is the birthplace of the World Wide Web. (The Web's official information is now on a distributed set of machines collectively addressed by http://www.w3.org.) Interesting from the point of view of a site "explaining" an institution's identity, the meaning for the acronym CERN (Conseil Europeen pour la Recherche Nucleaire) is not immediately obvious. This site is highly geographic; under general information, literal directions are given for visitors arriving by plane, by car, or, for example, by train: "From the Geneva railway station at Cornavin, take the bus marked: '9 CERN' (about 20 minutes, stops at the CERN reception building)." General areas of information (about the laboratory, about physics, other subjects) are fairly clear. The most striking feature of http://www.cern.ch as a home page is the very large photograph of the many buildings of the laboratory against the impressive rise of the snow-covered Swiss Alps. The page is also quite conscious of the laboratory's geographic split between Switzerland and France. In fact, the third and fourth links following the photograph are dedicated to the national home pages of each of these countries.

Los Alamos National Laboratory
http://www.lanl.gov/Public/Welcome.html, 22 November 1997
Main image: geographic
Main links: graphical
Structure: departmental

Bound in a blue square, the rugged New Mexico landscape is evoked in the home page for Los Alamos National Laboratory. The earth is tough, mangled, but strong. In the distance, furious clouds sweep upwards from a clear blue Southwestern sky. This landscape is bound by a graphic motif. A rocketing cube-shaped grid arcs in a half circle around the photo, looking banged up but much more powerful than anything else shown. The main links appear as a series of diamond shapes at the bottom of the blue box. One box, "Welcome," is yellow; the others are red. These shapes each offer a link to a specific department or program area within Los Alamos.

La France
http://web.urec.fr/france/france.html, 22 November 1997
Main image: buttons
Main links: graphical
Structure: departmental

The La France home page makes extraordinary use of graphics. The opening screen is dominated by a rectangular row of seven, metallic-looking buttons (a "home row" of typewriter keys?). Scrolling down from this screen is a large map of France. Most selections are presented in the reader's choice of French or English. France is covered by region—and each one is done with great thoroughness. Corsica, for example, offers information in such categories as ports, beaches (the page offers an image of each of the 180 beaches profiled), weather, tourism, etc. (In a new design, this site is now at http://www.urec.cnrs.fr/annuaire, 3 May 2000.) La France follows the familiar theme of asserting the "logic" of political geography. This is seen in any number of sites, for example, such as The Virtual Tourist (http://www.vtourist.com/vt/ Nov. 22, 1997) where mouse clicks made on a world map bring up more detailed regional maps, themselves clickable.

Graphics-Based/Symbolic Orders

Central Intelligence Agency
http://www.odci.gov/cia, 22 November 1997
Main image: wallpaper/buttons
Main links: graphical
Structure: departmental

A striking use of wallpaper to reinforce authority, the Central Intelligence Agency Seal (an eagle's profile over a red compass) repeats across a white screen on the Central Intelligence Agency home page. Superimposed on these are six bold squares offering such choices as a "welcome", "public affairs," and "related intelligence community links." This is "intelligence that adds substantial value to the management of crises, the conduct of war, and the development of policy." (The CIA page, in a new design, is now located at http://www.cia.gov, 3 May 2000.)

Toy Story
http://www.toystory.com, 22 November 1997
Main image: graphics
Main links: graphical
Structure: character-based

The main images (not shown) in the home page for *Toy Story* are, appropriately, images of characters from the animated film. Each image is clickable and takes the reader to a home page for the character selected. These pages are richly illustrated and contain much information and also sound files relative to each character. Interestingly, this home page has taken the traditional movie poster and remediated it for the Web. The poster's strengths, its use of montage, iconography, animation, stills, and text, added to the Web's linking potential, makes it effective in electronic space.

Literary Sites

How do literary pages compare?[4] Literary pages are in an earlier stage of development (and are less well funded) than some of the sites described above. The above sites do, however, present a vocabulary and suggest a range of strategies used in the presentation of institutional identity on the Web. Literary sites vary as much as commercial sites. Graphics are key to sites such as Prose & Contexts Online (indeed, Fingerprinting Inkoperated, within the Prose & Contexts site is very rich graphically) and Subtext, an arrival on the Web contemporaneous with the above described pages. (Note: P&C is now defunct; Subtext no longer uses a graphical design.) Grist may be the site that makes the strongest statement. At the time of this study, it used a forceful graphic (with red lettering on a black background):

Grist On-Line
http://www.thing.net/~grist
Main image: graphical
Mail links: textual
Structure: table of contents

There is little by way of statement on the initial home page for Grist. (In fact, for the text-only reader, only one word, "Grist," appears on the screen.) P-Net (not pictured, now defunct) and the Electronic Poetry Center are less exclusively graphical. Instead, these sites place an emphasis on the home page's surface writing. Each does contain graphics, of course. P-Net's is a simple circular graphic, suggesting the kind of union it seeks to create among several literary participants. The Electronic Poetry Center's home page features a two-part graphic, combining both geographic and symbolic approaches to graphical design. Here, a Pleistocene buffalo plays on the name of its host city and the city's snow-swept, postindustrial character is represented in the transparent gif that serves as a heading for each page in the site. (Note: the banner discussed here is not the EPC's present banner.)

How to Haunt a Home Page
The knowledge is there, the bits and scraps, flickering on and off, turn about, winking on the storm, in league to fool me.
—Samuel Beckett, *Stories & Texts*

[San Francisco] is the home and the haunt of America's Beat generation and these are the Beatniks—or new barbarians.
—*San Francisco Daily Express*, 23 July 1958

The negative refusal of _Home_ is "homelessness," which most consider a form of victimization, not wishing to be *forced* into nomadology. But "homelessness" can in a sense be a virtue, an adventure—so it appears, at least, to the huge international movement of the squatters, our modern hobos.
—Hakim Bey, *Temporary Autonomous Zone*

A home page or a house page?[5] As we have seen, neither term is satisfactory. The architectural model fails as a name for this entry point, especially if you think that one inhabits a house or home (that is, dwells in, occupies as an abode, or resides in permanently or semipermanently).

A haunt might be a more accurate word. ("We talke here in the publike haunt of men" or "The favourite haunt of the wild strawberry is an up-lying meadow" or "He is gone from mortal haunts.")[6] A haunt is a place of frequent resort or habitation/habit. In addition, it is a regular feeding place of deer, game, and fowls; by extension, perhaps, a watering hole where one might quench the thirst for knowledge or information or entertainment (or increasingly, to placate the addiction of being a consumer). This geographic sense of "haunt" has resonance with Olson's use of this term in his "Talk at Cortland," in which he referred to a "haunt and habit" as difficult to achieve but "really what everybody's after and . . . all that counts" (*Muthologos* 2:4). In Olson's use there is, of course, an allusion to Gloucester, a place "habituated" by writer and reader in Olson's own work, a historical, cultural, visual, geological, and creative hub—what any home page would aspire to! (At this writing, the Cape Ann Chamber of Commerce's "Gloucester Home Page," http://www.cape-ann.com/cacc/gloucester.html, 3 May 2000, makes no mention of Olson.)

The home page is a singular (screen, place, subject) pitted against a multiple (World Wide Web, geography, object). Like any starting point, the home page presents a set of givens. The Internet is *not* infinite. Wherever you begin, you have specific and limited choices. (You may even have a directory of URLs beside you, but you are still limited. You cannot, for example, type random characters for a URL and very often get anywhere. It's like trying to get somewhere on a bus in Paris; you cannot just get on one that seems to be going in the right direction, particularly around Montparnasse.)

Depending on what I meant by here and me, and being, and there I never went looking for extravagant meanings, there I never much varied, only the here would sometimes seem to vary.

—Samuel Beckett, *Stories & Texts*

You must interpret the choices offered and act upon them. You also have specific and limited tools (the speed of your modem or type of connection, conventional and RAM memory, "peripherals" such as sound cards and video drivers, individual skill level). There are also environmental conditions to contend with (network traffic, servers that are down). Ultimately, however, a home page is an expression of ideology; the Internet is not about information but about *conditions of information*. Civic virtue for the Web citizen comes from questioning the relations that are engaged. The most successful navigational tool is a caustic wit. One must be able to see two sides of Dorothy's statement, "There's no place like home," if one is to get anywhere on the Web.

4
The Intermedial
A Treatise

Investigating the Medium

The "content" of any medium is like the juicy piece of meat
carried by the burglar to distract the watchdog of the mind.
—Marshall McLuhan, *Understanding Media*

Note how the 'medium' begins to define the form,
    as far as line length . . .
DOROTHY: This is just too slow for me boys . . .
BOZA: What is medium: is this a seance?
    —EPC Live, from the Electronic Poetry Center,
    20 Nov. 1995

Despite the level of technology upon which it depends, it is important to
emphasize that, principally, the Web is writing. It is presented as a series of
pages that are written. In addition, each page is also writing because it is
written in HTML. Considering the Web as a form of writing, the question
then arises: what are the particulars of its constitution as a medium? One of
the most interesting aspects to the Web is that it offers direct possibilities
for mixed media or intermedial writing. Intermedia has been a keen interest
of experimental writing in this century, from mixed works of prose and po-
etry to collages involving both text and images to works involving text, film,
and other art forms. It comes as no surprise that such investigations are also
relevant to a theory of the Web. Online intermedial prospects are even more
engaging when one thinks that the parts of a "page," though seeming to
constitute a whole, need not even necessarily be housed on the same conti-
nent.

The Page

Ay, ay, a scratch, a scratch; marry, 'tis enough.
Where is my page? Go, villain, fetch a surgeon.
    —Shakespeare, *Romeo and Juliet*

Though based on "pages," nothing could be further from the Web's ac-
tual constitution. The page, as displayed, is *a permeable surface composed of
parts*, a dysraphistic assembly that comprises a whole. The parts constitute
the page. They are not independent, and they are not interdependent. The

language of the "page" is the code that references parts relative only to their position in the field. (See the section titled "For Example, Code" later in this chapter.)

The knowledge that parts blend is key to understanding the relations between page and code. (There is not only a lack of substantiality in its presentation on a screen—i.e., paperless poems—but also that "one thing" is not what is transmitted. There is a control file at the source which, itself sent in packets, arrives to tell the host computer "where to put the furniture.")

Intermedia as Meshing Media

The fact remains that each medium indeed constitutes a "category of artistic composition." Thus, within a single "page," sound, video, graphics, writing—a composition of media marked by a distinctive style, form, or content—converge. The Web page is constructed of parts. These parts convene media.

The appropriate term for this is *intermedial*. The reason this term has not been considered for use with the Web is because the focus is generally on the *technology* of the media blending, not on the blending itself. We prefer to see fields of activity as media (cf. oils, acrylic, chalk) instead of genre (painting, sculpture, photography). The concept of medium itself might be enlarged to constitute greater wholes that would move from an avowed disposition replacing "discipline" with "medium." We could also limit ourselves to considering "form or content," which alone would allow these "extendible" "objects" (in all cases the reader is verb) distinctive materials working within inscribed areas of activity.

Media Descriptors

Medium	Indicator
Sound	.au, .wav, .ra, etc.
Image	.gif, .jpg, etc.
Video	.rm, .mpeg, .mov, etc.
Text	.html, .txt, etc.
Link	<a href="..."> etc.

This table of values suggests not only that there are indicators for formats (media) but that the hypermedial environment, beyond placing media within a tableau, "maps" them with distinctive (though varying) *extensions*. Because the electronic page *crosses media by definition*, such extensions are shorthand for the media to which they refer. (Of course you might argue that media and formats are at odds because a medium might be seen as a willful exploration of a format; however, the question itself proves the point.) Each extension is itself a field of activity, with its own particular characteristics, instrumentalities, conventions, and practices. Text contains media within itself, and media contain their own genres. Further, one can see the institutional genres that comprise text as subgenres. Thus any medium exists as both image and itself, that is, *the field is constituted by each medium's application of its own genres.*

Image as Its Own Exasperation

Central to the projection is the image, the image anchored on the tableau of the "page." Similarly, Emmanuel Hocquard writes the following in Section "32" of his *Theory of Tables:*

Question the word image

On a table arrange
the words which describe the image

Noting of course that "word" and "image," besides being words themselves, are appositional:

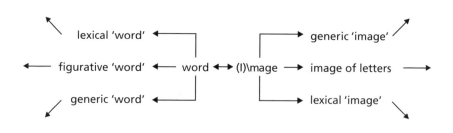

Thus Hocquard continues:

Question the words

The description of the image
is not an image

There (and also "there") is a transformation in the subsequent series of lines. The word "image" having collapsed into "word" now becomes "words." Also, with a sense of play that one also finds present in electronic image/text constitution on a screen, other transformations occur:

On a table arrange → The description of the image
The "table" or screen parallels the control file

the words which describe the image → is not an image
The "markup" is not the image

Finally,

The description dissolves the image
reopen the book with this

That is, if description = control file (HTML), then "interpretation" of control file = dissipation of "image." Note that image here is not the image referenced. In this case, it is the image as a field or "landscape"—in Stein's sense of landscape below. It is a field of *markup*.

Indeed, it is *the issue of the page* that is reopened.

For Example, Code

Hypertext Mark-up Language (HTML) presents a curious confusion between what is a page and what are its parts. For the page to work, the code cannot be viewed because the parts would overwhelm the page with their visual hyperactivity.

What is there to be viewed can only be viewed as image—a virtual economy within the frame of one that is restricted. The page is an assemblage within the physical area of a screen.

What appears on the screen is *not* the parts but the projection of the parts as a simulated whole.

They are not parts because there are no visible parts on the screen's page, only the projection of a whole. But where is the whole? In one sense it is located, beyond Projectivist determinations, in the physicality of the cathode ray tube—in the computer processing of code. What becomes important is not the success or failure of such a projection, not the way it fills the screen, but the activity or vectors associated with its acts of projection:

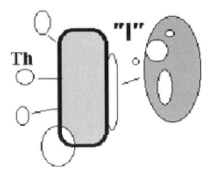

Display/Cognition

Image is a double-channel. It has a presence, on the one hand, that is graphical. But the graphical exists precisely in relation to a perceived *viewer*. Thus, the idea of a graphic cannot be separated from the idea of its public or audience. Hence the second qualification of the graphical, the character *projected to the public*, as by a person or an institution, especially as interpreted by the media.

Description Against Position

"I can look at a landscape without describing it" (Stein, *Stanzas* 76). The issue pits description against position. Code pushes semblance; semblance is visible but code is completely impenetrable. Yet code is readable. Of greatest importance is the conflict, a constant agitation, a flux, the

> By it by which by it
> As not which not which by it
> *(Stanzas* 76)

In Stein's "stanza" this conflict is itself verbal. The "which" and "by" are pivotal elements. They are not only dramatically the connectives of code but also the problem with the whole itself, which is itself verbal slippage.

Of course the myth of the electronic medium is that communication is involved—and that such intermedial links provide access:

> For it is in an accessible with it
> But which will but which will not it
> *(Stanzas* 76)

Again, the flux slips into its "which."

So the one unresolved point is how the parts accrue. Do the parts "add" to anything greater than their own consternation? Is there a poeisis in this infusion of media? Is this a "making"?

> Come to be not made not made one of it
> By that all can tell all call for in it
> That they can better call add
> Can in add none add it.
> *(Stanzas* 76)

and

> Forget questions
> about the formation of form
> in any empirical or ideal place
> loses the forms trying to write it out
> (Kuszai)

Are the parts that constitute the screen added to each other? The form is lost in its writing. The parts do not accrete; they are contiguous. In fact, in transmission the parts are actually split into *packets* and sent simultaneously. The data then ("can in add none add it," *Stanzas* 76) neither accrete nor form a whole: what is actually created is a series of partial overlays—superimpositions that, never stable, combine to present an apparent stable positioning of parts. The position cannot be described, only constituted. The apparency of these parts is contained within a single packet that is one of the parts. It is in no way "stable" or exterior to the code. Hence, there are no authorities to its issue.

The Electronic

Ultimately an electronic presentation in itself superimposes a genre on the medium under discussion. Any of the converging media might fail, but the presentation continues as a differently constituted whole. The presentations may vary according to different readers. (These are the interpretations by software of the referenced files—as well as by human interpreters of the transmitted "page.") The files constitute the body of the constituent text, and the reader's entry into it is a surgical maneuver. Retrieved items are then on par with the instruments of intrusion. The electronic reader is conscious of the .moz files, the hanging modem, the activity of receiving and re-piecing, a technology of mixed media and equipment of parts—akin to the medical practice of counting your instruments after a procedure to be sure you did not leave one inside the body.

5
Hypertext/Hyperpoeisis/Hyperpoetics

E-text as Medium

> If writing, as Plato suggested, is the head-on collision that results in a memory-numbing concussion, electronic texts release an underground text blast rendering all inhabitants of the planet amnesiac wanderers and nomads. Does "the nomadic" typify the new era of book-like textual emissions? Is this a good reading of Guattari, or is it merely delusional? Does the breakdown of the book signal the loss of authority? Wasn't the great concern about Gutenberg's press in the mid-fifteenth century that exclusive rights to interpretation of the Bible would be lost? Did this contribute to Luther's insistence that one get one's own copy and then talk to Him directly?
> —Loss Pequeño Glazier, *Tango*

Electronic writing is not simply the e-equivalent of paper writing, because writing that is electronic has different properties than writing that is on paper. Does a message carved into granite differ from one scratched into sand? One might be inclined to be slightly more taciturn in the former medium. The difference is in physical and material properties. The most interesting of these are not static properties (i.e., how many lines there are in the text or how many bytes it occupies) but properties that relate to the malleability of the electronic text. These are properties that inject the unpredictable into the work. Such a work always spins away from its author or reader the way a listserv by nature spirals uncontrollably off-topic. One's attitude toward it is analogous to some experiences of Web writing: if a page does not seem to display the way you intended, many times the only choice is just to live with it. In order to achieve a better understanding of the dynamics of Web-based hypertext, it is instructive to "read" such documents not as fixed documents of a specific but as electronic texts displayed and navigated through the medium of hypertext.

The Electronic Text

> What does not change / is the will to change.
> —Charles Olson, *Selected Writings*

As a physical object, the electronic text has certain specific qualities that distinguish it from a paper text:

1. It is searchable. Unlike a book, if you want to find the exact location where the word "utensil" is used in a thousand-page document, you can

get there instantly.

2. It is transmissible. Writing a letter on paper requires other steps to get it delivered to the person for whom it is intended; with e-mail, your message can arrive seconds after you type its closing exclamation point. (Or, seconds after you realize to your chagrin that you posted your intimate thoughts to an audience of 2,000 strangers.) With equal speed, you can send your *Poems on Various Subjects* to locations all over the globe. (The implication here is that the old system of publishing—the approbation phase, the editing phase, the stamping of metal into paper as if a seal of validity phase—are now gone.)[1]

3. The electronic text is nearly without physical size. You can carry the *OED* on CD-ROM in your dinner-jacket pocket or a copy of *The Work of Art in the Age of Mechanical Reproduction* on a floppy disk.

4. The electronic text manifests symptoms of being an "anti-text." It is often a text that you do not want. Its value is dependent upon signal-to-noise factors, delay times, "Not Found 404" messages (error messages that occur when you arrive at a non-existent Web page). There is often too much of it, and its excessiveness often limits your ability to spend time with the texts in which you are actually interested.

5. It can be manipulated. You can change the font. You can edit it. You can cut and paste it into a new document and submit it as a seminar response paper. It can be concordanced, analyzed for frequency of locutions, words can be counted, statistical studies may be performed, it can be cut to ribbons through collocation programs or be grepped down to a single character.

The electronic text acts as body, fulcrum, and as fertile crescent; its only constant is that it is likely to change for each instance in which it is viewed. It is a textual site with a momentum that can shift in any direction.

Defining Hypertext

REFERENCE
IS THE ONE
IMPOSSIBLE
THING
    To name it
    makes it
    what in it
    is
        —George Quasha, "Reference"

Someone once told me that if you have used a remote control, you have experienced hypertext. I suppose this is true, especially if there's also a newspaper draped across your shorts and you're reading the back of a bag of chips. But this is a rather extreme, decadent, and Homer Simpsonian definition. It is also a definition with a few clear drawbacks. For example, the range of materials that you can access via your remote is highly filtered, with the consistency and intellectual complexity of Spam—if we were to parallel television programming with U.S. gastronomy. Secondly, the reception is always clear. I would think that a "remote" metaphor would more accurately portray a remote connected to a shortwave radio. Here connections often fail, reception quality is less than perfect, sometimes things are there one minute and not the next, and "pages" can be evoked from the full circumference of the earth. An acceptable definition of hypertext would have to take into account a range of theoretical positions on this subject.

Hypertext is much broader than most would assume. For those who are struggling with HTML, it may come as a surprise that HTML-based hypertext is only one of the species in this genus. In a public talk at SUNY Buffalo in 2000, Jim Rosenberg described a range of hypertext systems, such as hypertexts of arbitrary structure, spatial hypertexts, set-based hypertexts, and knowledge-structuring hypertexts. The "alt.hypertext" FAQ[2] provides further examples, listing six types of hypertext systems. These include diverse systems. HyperWave, formerly Hyper-G, is "a sophisticated Web document management system for large information spaces." Microcosm provides "an open and extensible hypermedia system designed for managing and disseminating unstructured digitally encoded files." WebÞing's "holistic" hypertext is "an object-oriented hypertext system designed for collaborative authoring and implemented on the WWW. . . . Documents in WebÞing generate HTML links from other documents on-the-fly, relieving authors of the need to manage HTML links, and eliminating the problem of outdated or uncoordinated references." Xanadu, the system Ted Nelson wrote about in his ground-breaking book *Literary Machines*, pioneered an early—indeed the first—version of a Web system that was very different from the Web as we know it today.[3] Storyspace is a commercial product that describes itself as a "writing environment designed for the process of writing" and suggests that it is "especially well suited to working with large, complex, and challenging hypertexts" ("alt.hypertext"). (I would reword this last statement to reflect Eastgate's approach through mapping and its preference for links within a *controlled* universe.) Finally, of course, there is the World Wide Web, a popular system characterized by client-server architecture and running on the Internet. Of this broad array of systems, the two that we will be concerned with are Storyspace and the Web, because these are the most widely used for literary hypertext work.

If one were to define hypertext, how would it be done? First, we will consider some related definitions in order to cite the practice of hypertext. One must note that the line dividing hypertext and hypermedia is so indistinct that for most general purposes "hypertext" can be used to encompass both. Secondly, a distinction should be made between a hyperbook and a hypertext. Both employ hypertextual systems of linking, but the hyperbook consists of a stand-alone, presumably self-contained, universe of writings that are inter-referential. (Most of the publications of Eastgate systems, by this definition, would be called hyperbooks, even though Eastgate markets its products as hypertexts.) Thirdly, if a hyperbook (a reproduction of the package of a book) refers to its own limited universe of references, then our usage of the term "hypertext" by contrast should refer to a larger, uncontrolled universe. This "universe" is the Web. The network of documents that converge at the point of the link form the interwoven textual whole of the Web.[4] A further complication is that "Hypertext" refers to the dynamics of interlinking in both hyperbooks and hypertexts. The Electronic Labyrinth notes the same distinction as follows: "['hyperbook'] is distinct from the term 'hypertext,' which refers to the defining form of the work as a structure. An electronic book with hypertext features is a hyperbook. This distinction is not usually made in the literature; the two concepts being elided into one. We believe this lack of precision leads to sloppy arguments, though we acknowledge that it is sometimes desirable to use 'hypertext' in a more general sense" (Hyperbook).

Ted Nelson, who first coined the terms *hypertext* and *hypermedia*, wrote in *Literary Machines* that "as popularly conceived, [hypertext] is a series of text chunks connected by links which offer the reader different pathways" (section 0/2). It is useful to think in terms of these pathways, but an unresolved issue is the role of authorial control in the construction of such pathways.[5] Jakob Nielsen, author of *Hypertext and Hypermedia*, defines hypertext in his essay, "The Art of Navigating Through Hypertext": "Hypertext is non-sequential writing: a directed graph, where each node contains some amount of text or other information. . . . Hypertext should also make users feel that they can move freely through the information according to their own needs. This feeling is hard to define precisely but certainly implies short response times and low cognitive load when navigating" (Nielsen). If this were accurate, then the Web falls far short of delivering the "short response times" and "low cognitive load" called for. The Electronic Labyrinth defines hypertext as "the presentation of information as a linked network of nodes which readers are free to navigate in a non-linear fashion. It allows for multiple authors, a blurring of the author and reader functions, extended works with diffuse boundaries, and multiple reading paths" (Hypertext). The non-linearity of this definition is useful. What may be less than useful, however, is the insistence that the author and reader are blurred. This, I believe is one of the greatest myths about hypertext. The fact is, you can no more change most of the files you encounter than, as a film viewer, you can influence the father's fate in *Life Is Beautiful*, as much as we all may have liked that. The "alt.hypertext" FAQ emphasizes a layered sense of the Web, citing the *OED Additions Series* that texts "are interconnected in such a way that a reader of the material (as displayed at a computer terminal, etc.) can discontinue reading one document at certain points in order to consult other related matter" ("alt.hypertext"). This is a sound observation. Nevertheless, I would argue that it is a definition that can equally apply to a stack of magazines beside your reading chair.

Eastgate, a company that advertises itself with the blurb (quoted from Robert Coover from the *New York Times*), "The primary source for serious hypertext," is a proponent of hypertext distribution on magnetic and optical media. Eastgate states that "the World Wide Web is, of course, a huge and wonderful hypertext—a docuverse. Many sections of the Web, however, are not particularly hypertextual" ("Hypertext Resources"). This is of course a fair statement. But though Eastgate has pioneered visual mapping approaches to hypertext, their preference for closed hypertext universes transfers hypertextuality into what we might consider a laboratory setting. Granted that although the controlled environment typified by a laboratory can at times facilitate scientific breakthroughs in a given medium, such controlled environments are not intended to supplant the writing scene at large. The controlled environment of disk-based hypertext creates built-in limits, limits that seem strikingly out of step with the material and social context of contemporary hypertextual practice. Eastgate's publications are also sold following the commodity model of publishing's present power structure, a less than innovative economic model. Finally, Eastgate advocates something they have referred to as the "craft of hypertext" ("Hypertext Now"), an approach that may be compared to an argument sometimes made for poetry with a conservative ideological slant. ("Craft" not only meaning "skill" but having imbedded in it notions of artifice and even guile.) In this sense, there is an implication that hypertext should be genteel or proper, or at the minimum, well considered, a proposal that might be less than ideal for a publishing universe exploring a new paradigm.

Who Are the Masters of Hypertext?

> Here is
> where there
> is.
> —Robert Creeley, *Collected Poems*

If an adequate sense of hypertext cannot be achieved by way of definition, a survey of present practitioners may help further delineate the field. If you wanted to read work by hypertext practitioners, who would you read? I now refer to three notable sources from the mid to late nineties that present lists of prominent practitioners of hypertext. This is an important period for the emergence of a general consensus about hypertext, and these sources are highly respected and often cited. They are The Electronic Labyrinth, Scott Stebelman's "Hypertext and Hypermedia: A Select Bibliography," and the "Research on Hypertext" section of the Voice of the Shuttle's "Technology of Writing Page."[6]

The Electronic Labyrinth defines hypertext, listing as important hypertext practioners Ted Nelson, Michael Joyce, Jakob Nielsen, the InterMedia development team, Laurence Sterne, Paul Delany, and George Landow. Scott Stebelman offers the following as examples of what he calls "prominent writers of hypertext": Jay David Bolter, Jane Yellowlees Douglas, Michael Joyce, George Landow, Stuart Moulthrop, and Gregory L. Ulmer. The hypertext theorists who have a prominent individual entry in The Voice of the Shuttle's list of hypertext resources include J. Yellowlees Douglas, George P. Landow, Jerome McGann, Stuart Moulthrop, Ted Nelson, John Tolva, and John Unsworth. Which authors receive the most mentions? Comparing these resources, we arrive at the following table:

COMPARING "THE MASTERS"

Labyrinth	Stebelman	Voice of the Shuttle
3 REFERENCES		
George P. Landow	George P. Landow	George P. Landow
2 REFERENCES		
---	Jane Yellowlees Douglas	Jane Yellowlees Douglas
Michael Joyce	Michael Joyce	---
---	Stuart Moulthrop	Stuart Moulthrop
Ted Nelson	---	Ted Nelson
SINGLE REFERENCES		
---	Jay David Bolter	---
Paul Delaney	---	---
InterMedia Dev. Team	---	---
---	---	Jerome McGann
Jakob Nielsen	---	---
Laurence Sterne	---	---
---	---	John Tolva
---	---	John Unsworth
---	Gregory L. Ulmer	---

The lists from Electronic Labyrinth, Stebelman, and Voice of the Shuttle are surprisingly different in who they cite as prominent practitioners in the field. The results are even more surprising given that these lists are all slanted toward academic hypertext. Of these fourteen authors, nine appear only once. Among authors listed only once are Jay David Bolter, Jerome McGann, and Gregory Ulmer, a fact that is quite surprising for different reasons for each author. Jay David Bolter, a co-developer of Storyspace, should be more widely recognizable as one of hypertext theory's best-selling authors. Gregory Ulmer is a highly regarded theorist and literary critic who brings penetrating philosophical insights into the conversation. Jerome McGann brings the tradition of textual criticism to electronic textual theory and has pioneered crucial ground through such works as his "Radiant Textuality" and "The Rationale of Hypertext," and through his Rossetti Archive at the University of Virginia.

It is interesting to examine the five authors who were mentioned by more than one source. Only one hypertextual theorist, George Landow, is listed by all three sources, and four authors are listed in two sources. Of the five authors receiving two references or more, three are Eastgate authors. Of the remaining two, one, Landow, is associated with Intermedia, and one, Nelson, with Xanadu. Nelson may have received a greater number of references because of his pioneering efforts rather than for his influence in the practice of hypertext today. Overall, these results suggest that the general perception of what hypertext is, manifests a penchant for an Eastgate vision—a vision that, though instructive, is not at the front lines of the hypertextual public sphere of the Web.

While searching for a definition of "hypertext," we might ask the following: Can a sense of hypertext be garnered from the people who seem to be prominent in the field? Although each practitioner certainly would have a definition of his or her own making, it is interesting to consider a document by the hypertext practitioner who was the front-runner in the above comparison. Of interest particularly is the "Landow's Overview Types" page at The Electronic Labyrinth.[7] In this document Landow gives examples of six types of overviews that can be useful in hypertext:

1. The Graphic Concept Map organizes ideas, authors, terms, or other concepts in a hub and spoke pattern. This illustrates the influence peripheral concepts have on the concept in the centre.

2. The Vector Flow Chart presents directed lines connecting nodes, representing "lines of influence or causal connection." The length of the lines may be used as a measure of the strength or importance of the influence.

3. Timelines allow for concise chronological organization.

4. Natural Object overviews consist of anchors superimposed on pictures, maps, technical diagrams, etc.

5. Outlines "add a graphic component to text by breaking up the flow that characterizes discursive prose."

6. Source text may act as its own overview in networks that are dominated by a central node or nodes. Landow's example is a poem with hypertext commentary. ("Landow's")

Though such suggestions are certainly sound, I submit that most of them simply take conventional storyboarding techniques and make them electronic—hardly making use of the potentials of hypertext.[8] It seems reasonable to say that his approach is not centered on exploring innovation in the medium.

I would like to suggest that the most useful way to consider hypertext is not as a generic medium (a compositional medium that instantiates a number of genres) but as a delivery medium; and that each particular form of practice is the exemplar of an underlying ideology. In one sense, what a hypertext is about is how it is made and what it does. The above lists suggest that hypertext is widely misunderstood; further, the practitioners listed above not only practice similarly but also represent only a small spectrum of the practice of hypertext that is possible. The omission of many other important practitioners in the author lists above points to a profound need for a richer understanding of the range of practice possible within the medium.

Certainly some of the medium's earliest practitioners explored alternative models. These were scientists, mathematicians, and cyberneticists—including Vannevar Bush, Norman Wieners, and John von Neumann (famous for his work with the ECP, Electronic Computer Project)—and their work often compared the computer network to the human nervous system. (The human body as a network certainly resonates with the concept of the Web as a body of writing distributed across a network.) This is a model that has some interesting correlations, given some of the senses of the prefix "hyper" in "hypertext."[9] Though these thinkers paved the way, it was not until Bolter and others that the general concept of hypertext reached its present boundaries.

"La Vie en Prose"

> Prose may carry a load of ill-defined matter like a ship. But poetry is the machine which drives it, pruned to a perfect economy. As in all machines its movement is intrinsic, undulant, a physical more than a literary character. In a poem this movement is distinguished in each case by the character of the speech from which it arises.
> —William Carlos Williams, *Collected Poems*

What are some of the limits of the present dominant paradigm for digital writing? The most striking of these is an equating of hypertext with prose. A problem with this perspective is that a focus on the narrative or "story" or even alternative or permuted versions of stories can obfuscate the malleability, permeability, and materiality of the medium. Thinking of writing this way is like having a seance with an overly chatty guest at the table; such a session simply entails abrupt leaps from one anecdote to the next. Such a lack of focus on the materials of the medium also seems to perpetuate existing textual power structures and to efface any hope for the "death of the author." This concentration on prose is quite clear in three of the widest known hypertext theorists: David Jay Bolter, Michael Joyce, and George Landow.

In *Writing Space*, for example, Bolter constantly equates "writing" with prose. Speaking of *Writing Space*, he says, "We will consider the computer as a conceptual writing space: the nature of the electronic book and the styles of fiction and non-fiction appropriate to it" (11). His book has many statements like the following: "Writing in topics is not a replacement for writing with words: the writer must eventually attend to the details of his or her prose" (17). And "Hypertext shows how programming and conventional prose writing can combine in the space provided by the computer" (27). Clearly there is no attempt to see writing's "other" side, poetry, in Bolter's view. Landow's *Hypertext* contains an entire section called "Reconfiguring Narrative," in which he discusses plot, "narrative beginnings and endings," and Michael Joyce's fiction work *Afternoon*; however, Landow does not address any relation between hypertext and poetry. Further, if one were "reconfiguring narrative," it would be useful to consider John Ashbery's *Three Poems*, Robin Blaser's *Image Nation*, any text by Gertrude Stein, or Robert Duncan's *H.D. Book*, along with other works. Michael Joyce's omission of a discussion of poetry may be the most striking, because the last third of his book *Of Two Minds* is devoted to what he calls "Hypertext Poetics." This section has chapters on the multiple novel and hypertext narrative, clearly marking his sense of the poetics of hypertext as being prose based. Joyce even concludes a section called "Hypertext Poetics" with the chapter "A Feel for Prose: Interstitial Links and the Contours of Hypertext." Could one be accused here of seeing the world through prose-colored glasses? Could contemporary innovative poetry practice—or even Gertrude Stein, Jackson Mac Low, or Robin Blaser—be so unrelated that it does not emerge once in these three major works of hypertext theory? It seems to me that these hypertext theorists are ignoring some relevant information.

The omissions mentioned above represent a practice that seems widespread, even among writings by hypertext poets. Hypertext poets tend to position their practice in relation to hypertext fiction because it is hypertext, too. This perspective reveals an astonishing oversight, because classic hypertext fiction practice (like postmodern theory) is an extension of print. By contrast, print innovative poetry actually investigates the dynamics of linking, metonymy, process, and disjunctive poetics, which are key to hypertext poetry. Though poets who call themselves hypertext poets frequently mention the canonical classic hypertext writers, they rarely seem to mention the tradition of innovative practice that has put poetry in the perfect position to inform digital practice; though they often seem to evoke postmodern theory, postmodern poetry is surprisingly overlooked.

"Prose & Versus"

> Poetry in [the] vocal and intellectual sense is an ancient art or technology: older than the computer, older than print, older than writing and indeed, though some may find this surprising, much older than prose.
>
> —Robert Pinsky, *Sounds of Poetry*

Models cannot be drawn from prose alone. Robert Duncan, for one, explored this area in the "Nights and Days" section of his *The H.D. Book.* "Nights and Days" serves as the proving ground upon which Duncan's own poetics of the open field were developed, and it may provide information about a multi-genred poetic for hypertext. *The H.D. Book* is not merely argumentative; the text being not only a "defense . . . offense" of this poetic project but also an enactment of the process of the poetics it pursues. The process of writing is the project of "The H.D. Book"; its modus operandi is the progressive and continuous movement toward "opening" and away from closure. "I seek now in working upon the later draft of the book not to correct the original," Duncan writes, "but to live again in its form and content, leaving in successive layers record of reformations and digressions as they come to me" ("H.D. II" 7, 53). (This image is not unlike the experience of layering document files as you open on your computer desktop; the movement toward "opening" evokes open-ended hypertext, such as the Web.) The notions of reinscription and digression pursue a fundamental tenet of what a writer does in this "open" terrain: "I had gleaned from some reference to a dictionary that the word *verse*, our verse in poetry, like our prose in poetry, was *backwards* and *forwards*, as a man ploughing goes along one line and returns. *Prose*, forward in the row or line; then 'turning to begin another line' (as now I find in the O.E.D.) *versus*." To this Duncan adds, "But in verse now, we *return* to begin another line. We do not reach the end or margin" ("H.D. II" 8, 75).

Significant to "The H.D. Book" is the idea of verse and prose sharing a primary connection. In fact, it is not an interconnectedness but a similitude of emergence the two share, as in the undefinable similitude of night and day, the two "selves" on opposite sides of a boundary or border. There is a similar need to have the influence of some "versus" in the hypertextual medium. Given the metaphor of Duncan's plow, it is obvious that the field of hypertext might benefit from a turning by some poet-plough-persons.

Could the medium of prose possibly be sufficient? The nature of the Web suggests, in fact, that it accommodates a mix of genres and media.

Indeed, the multi-media appearance of the Web presents itself like a pile-up of many innovative arts practices: mail art, installation art, happenings, visual poetry, and mixed media compositions, among them. It furthers—or perhaps consummates—the degradation of the sacred-object status of the book undertaken by Fluxus, certain British small presses of the seventies, and in conceptual projects like Allen Fisher's Edible Press, where each publication was a food object, perishable in the most literal sense. (Thus it was not a case of "publish or perish" but of publishing a perishable.) In the Fluxus work, *How to Explain Pictures to a Dead Hare*, for example, Joseph Beuys walked around the gallery for about two hours with his head covered with honey and gold leaf and with one shoe soled with felt and the other iron. The concept of a piece of art as an "action" is particularly compelling in the light of JavaScript, animated GIFs, and other text-manipulating programs that are often as much about staging an event as about the event's content—how I often feel waiting for the server to respond.

What is the future of digital writing? If we take the text's ability to be active as a criterion, then hypertext might be considered a "still life with apples" as compared to an Edible Press poem painted on an apple. That is, we have to be critical about what really characterizes digital writing and what simply qualifies as a longing for the past. Placing earlier technologies into a new medium (linking, for example) is simply remediation, and hypertext may be a preliminary, and necessary, step backward as we stumble into the future. We need to ask ourselves what is the actual advance of the new medium, in order to define writing that will put that medium to task. The basic defining feature of hypertext, its ability to link, is operationally identical to the codex with its footnotes, index, table of contents, *see also*'s, lists of prior publications, parenthetical asides, and numerous other devices of multilinearity. As Marie-Laure Ryan notes, "Through its structured network of choices, hypertext stands halfway between texts that impose a strictly sequential reading order (traditional novels) and texts with a totally free mode of access (encyclopedias, texts written on cards that can be shuffled)"(7). Though she continues to argue that hypertext should be classified as "the embryo of an electronic genre," I feel it is equally sustainable to argue that its primary kinship is to the codex. Following this reasoning, it would be very dangerous to look at link node hypertexts as harbingers of new textuality. At the very most they are the Photorealism of digital writing, a last attempt to render the perfect oil painting before moving on to the real potentialities of the new medium.

Our need, then, is to find new paths through the digital forest. To find work that, like innovative poetry itself, questions and investigates the materiality of the electronic medium. Outstanding work has been done in this area, specifically the work of John Cayley in his Indra's Net/programmatology project, Jim Rosenberg in his Integrams, Eduardo Kac in his holographic work, Miekal And in his Flash and MOO experiments, the work I have done in "Mouseover," "Bromeliads," and other works, and in the kinetic works of various e-poetry practitioners. Further, one can argue that poetry, not prose, is the arena for this medium to be explored. The "strictly sequential reading order" that Ryan identifies as the limiting factor to hypertext is opposed to the more granular approach that poetry offers, with its acutely sensitive literal/lexical surface. As Jim Rosenberg notes, "It is very exciting to me that as poets we have much more freedom to work this way than the fiction writers, since our approach to words is already so 'granular' anyway" ("Re: Update"). A true digital text is one that is highly sensitive in every grain of its surface. This practically defines innovative poetry, the ability for any word or character to be part of the action of the text. Thus, poetry, it can be argued, has already been on the scene and may be uniquely qualified to serve as the site for emergent forms of digital textuality.

Who are the masters of hypertext? Though we may now have a good idea of who might be included in such a group, we may have fallen far short of the digital Valhalla. This question, also addressed later in this book when authority is considered, might not be as important as putting hypertext in a proper context. As Jennifer Ley notes in the introduction to *Riding the Meridian—Lit (art) ure*: "Only a year ago, web writers were comfortable calling html-code-intensive works hypertext. But now that term seems lacking, incapable of describing the myriad technical approaches now available and the creative changes which working in a web-specific medium has wrought."[10] Thus, I would argue that the task ahead is one of placing hypertext in the correct context, of working toward a more useful definition of e-writing, and of establishing a newly envisioned canon of e-literature. Such resources would usefully help to locate the future for new poetries in digital media and would position us to engage a broader understanding of digitally based emerging literature.

6
Coding Writing, Reading Code

Grep: A Grammar

> The working through of any real process will contain a sequential logic according to its own particular, essential dynamic. The character of that dynamic, which it acquires only in that exact and self-same process, becomes its own definition.
> —Johanna Drucker, "Process Note"

> Larger productions, such as poems, are like completed machines. Any individual sentence might be a piston. It will not get you down the road by itself, but you could not move the vehicle without it.
> —Ron Silliman, *New Sentence*

If you are writing ASCII in the C-shell along the forbidding but captivating coast of UNIX, the grep command will be an essential tool at your side.[1] Though grep is typically used for file maintenance, of interest here are other uses of grep, especially its use as a writing *method*. Such an innovative use of grep is a concept that would probably leave many UNIX programmers scratching their CPUs. Yet this vision of grep makes particular sense if we can begin to move from a view of writing as the production of something static (a codex or file) to a more dynamic or fluid concept, that is the *action* of production (process). From this perspective, it is the procedure or algorithm that counts, the output being simply one by-product of that activity. This is not an easy position to argue because so many of our assumptions about textuality rely on a traditional "fixed" literary object. What exactly is a grep and how can it have relevance to the production of text?

Grep is one of numerous related programs, including ed (a line editor) and sed (a "stream of text" editor), along with its sibling utilities, egrep and fgrep. Such programs process input text and produce output, according to user-specified modifiers. At its lowest level, grep is a "find" command. In the words of a UNIX guidebook: "Use grep to search for text in files, or in the standard input, then display each line matched on the standard output" (Topham 70). More specifically, grep filters text according to given patterns: "Grep searches files for a pattern and prints all lines that contain that pattern" (Heath 312). Grep commands, though often considered counterintuitive, are quite simple. For example, to search for lines that contain the word "halibut" in a file called "fish," you would enter "grep halibut fish" at the command line. If the source file "fish" contained only the following

three lines:
    smoked salmon sings
    sad halibut sags
    grand carpe diem
Then the output of "grep halibut fish" would be "sad halibut sags." Therefore, grep will use the pattern word as a filter to return lines (in this case only one) that contain that word.

One could argue that this command is only useful for locating text strings; however, grep allows greater possibilities because it is a rigorous text processing procedure. In this sense, "rigorous" is not meant to be confused with difficulty of use. (The popular impression of UNIX as an unforgiving and inhospitable system, especially for infrequent users, is accurate. That is not the point.) "Rigor" is used here to refer to literalness that characterizes these processes. Unlike many GUI and "user-friendly" programs that attempt to interpret or second guess the user's needs, grep does specifically what the user instructs, and it treats the text as a purely material element of that operation. Unlike Microsoft Word, for example, it does not pop up with questions like, "Are you sure?" or "Can I help you write your letter?" It assumes you know what you want and will, like the "algorithm" invoked by the magician's assistant in "Fantasia," follow your instructions literally and to the letter. Such a rigor bespeaks a direct relation to the electronic text, a fearful symmetry, indeed.[2]

Such materiality is evident in how concretely the language elements of grep are addressed: "literal strings," "strings," "regular expressions," and "compound expressions" are among the way language is viewed in the world of UNIX. (Grep patterns are constructed from "regular expressions," which are "ordinary" non-binary characters, such as digits, letters, and various characters used as operators, the fundamental "materials" of writing.) Materiality is also foregrounded by the intensified rigor of program grammar employed to specify grep activities. Such a grammar, once invoked, sets into motion a determinate process of textual production. Thus one writes instructions for the *process*, and the output text is simply a by-product. As Johanna Drucker has written on other process work, "It is occurring then carries through whatever growth is appropriate to the logic of its own development. . . . That becomes the logic of its own development, the way grammar becomes an absolute fact of language: because the words are such powerful objects they command relation—or is it more simple, even, they are the units and any sequence of units becomes a structure" (Drucker, "Process" 264–65). The grammar of grep is literal and precise.

More specifically, grep's user-determined modifiers allow more precise text filtering processes. For example, let us say we have searched a file called "ocean" for lines that contain the word "fish" by entering:
    grep fish ocean
at the command line. Let us say the output of this grep was:

jellyfish, cuttlefish, crayfish
my wistful fish
fish sticks wish
fisherman, fishy, slips

Let us now suppose that one wanted more specific results, such as lines containing *only* the word "fish" itself (not lines containing "fishy," "fisherman," "crayfish," etc.). One would then issue the command "grep -w fish ocean." This will restrict the output to occurrences of the whole word "fish" only. The result would be as follows:

my wistful fish
fish sticks wish

The brief qualifier or flag, "-w," is one of a number of very specific operators performing highly literal "interpretations" of the source text. Thus grep offers a range of powerfully subtle ways to filter, refine, and determine the operation. For example, "grep -i halibut fish" would retrieve both "halibut" and "Halibut." Whereas, "grep -l hal* fish/*" would retrieve anything beginning with the letters "hal" in any file in the directory "fish" and would only output filenames of occurrences, not actual lines of text. The shorthand for some of these possibilities is expressed by "grep [-bchilnsv] pattern file(s)," an arcane-looking proposal, yet one that lays the range of possibilities for these rigorous procedures; it is one that also seems to invoke Ron Silliman's assertion that "structure is metaphor, content permission, syntax force" (*New* 57).

It is interesting to note that grep emphasizes the line as the basic unit of input. This could be called a "phrasiform as opposed to word form" conception, as Johanna Drucker has written on another procedural investigation ("Process" 264). To conceive of the basic unit as the line could be seen as having special relevance to poetry. For UNIX, there are historical reasons for this; namely that grep is descended from ed, an editor that displays text on a line-by-line basis (rather than on a complete screen). Such a concept evokes the use of teletypes instead of terminals, and it dates from a time when a key concern was keeping the amount of data transmitted to a minimum so that communication lines would stay open and costs be kept down. The mechanics of the teletype medium, like the medium of International Code of Signals explored by Hannah Weiner in works such as *Code Poems*, offer potential objectifications of language, thus providing access to its materiality. Such explorations provide, in Charles Bernstein's words, a "radical reaffirmation of a commitment to writing as a specific kind of object making, an investigation rather than an aestheticization" ("Making" 286). The mechanics of grep provide a medium with consistent properties; this fact is important for a production of writing that emphasizes its material qualities.

The second reason grep has greater possibilities than being merely a search tool is that it treats the text *as a file* and operates on the text at a non-represented (or more material) level. One must image a dual world: The first level, the visible or tangible level (surface), presents interpreted or represented objects (pages) on the level of interpretation (via the Web browser or through Windows). "Location" here can be points within individual documents or points within documents on different servers. The second level is the non-displayed. On this more chthonic level, objects are uninterpreted (files) and exist as the material surface at the location where writing "takes place" (through the editor). One might think of this as an intangible or invisible place, but it is *not* invisible; it is as present as the representations of browsers. In fact it might be *more* tangible because these are files composed entirely of "real" text ("regular expressions") with no control characters.

For one engaged in the production of representation, grep is a simple tool and would not generally be thought of as a text production engine. Similarly, someone painting portraits of judges for display in a courthouse might not think of a can with a hole in it as a painting utensil (as Jackson Pollack did). Like Pollack's paint can and many other UNIX utilities, the grep command is a solid conduit for text with strictly defined rules and properties, rigorous in its execution of procedure. Like the hole in Pollack's paint can, a grep offers an opening into the materiality of the words that constitute the electronic text file.

Most important, a grep is a procedure. Like the procedures of Oulipo participants, John Cage, Jackson Mac Low, or procedures such as those suggested in Charles Bernstein's poetry "Experiments" list (see chapter 7), a grep is a formal method or program for parsing or altering machine-readable text according to a fairly basic procedure. Grep tells the machine: "Check the first line of text. If that line of text contains x, output that line; if there is a subsequent line of text, check that one and repeat the procedure; otherwise, stop." The simplicity of this procedure makes it seem merely utilitarian. But its ability to unadornedly incise text makes it a valuable member of any inventory of text-altering programs.

Grep Poetry: Some Experiments

What possibilities might there be for grep and poetry? To answer this question, one must consider actual examples of the grep procedure used in the production of texts. The reader is therefore referred to the online appendices to this book, available at http://epc.buffalo.edu/authors/glazier/dp, where Appendix I presents a number of exhibits of grep-generated texts. To give a sense of the possibilities for such experiments, descriptions of the procedures used to produce these texts are listed below.

A Grep of "Methods for Reading and Performing Asymmetries" (Exhibit I in the online Appendix I)

The source text for this work consists of Jackson Mac Low's "Methods for Reading and Performing Asymmetries" as it appears in *Representative Works: 1938–1985.* (Lines were kept consistent with the original to allow comparison with the published text, echoing grep's natural emphasis on the line.) The UNIX grep command was used to produce blocks of text from the individual words in the title, "Methods for Reading and Performing Asymmetries," with the omission of "for" and "and." Thus the first section collocates all lines containing the word "method," the second "reading," and so on. (The title is also generated as the first line of each of the output sections because this title begins each section of the source text.) Use of the grep was a way to examine a procedural work through a procedure. The date of generation was 5 August 1997.

"The Fishtail" and "Grep on 'Y'" (Exhibits II and III in the online Appendix I)
These two works were both derived from writings of Hawthorne and Melville, with an emphasis on Melville's letters to Hawthorne.[3] Parts of the multi-section poem "The Fishtail" were generated through the grep procedure: (1) In section "M," "Shakespeare" was used as a pattern word to generate the indented text from the source text "Mosses from an Old Manse." (2) The epigraph to Section H is a grep of the pattern word "church" on the source text *Moby Dick*. (The output was reformatted for paragraph style). (3) A grep of the impulse-chance selected pattern words "manse," "book," "house," and "mosses" from the source text "Mosses from an Old Manse," generated the section "Manse/Mosses." (This section also treats the source HTML file as a literal text, allowing HTML coding to result from the grep.) (4) Finally, "from Melville's Letters to Hawthorne" is a grep on the twelve surviving letters from Melville to Hawthorne.[4] Pattern words for this grep, impulse-chance selected, were "gable," "book," "mount," "gray," "dard," "shore," "house," and "pit." Except for the reformatting into paragraph format noted above, no post-grep alterations were performed on the output. Given the extent to which their literary interchange affected the writing of these authors, collocation of their words through the grep procedure seemed a natural way to explore the interrelation of these texts. The date of generation was 2 March 1997.

"Ego non baptiso te in nomine: A grep on Y" (Exhibit III)
This is a very simple grep, using a single pattern word consisting of one character, "Y." The source text consists of the twelve surviving letters from Melville to Hawthorne. "Y" was selected as a pattern word due to its vocalic kinship with the personal pronoun "I." (The letter "I" itself could not be used due to the inordinate amount of output it would have produced.) The "I" is very important to these letters; as correspondence these writings are the "I" speaking. Further, this correspondence has to do with Melville's "I" reaching out to another literary "I." Thus a grep on the "Y" sibilant of the "I" seems to offer an intriguing resonance. No post-execution editing was performed. The date of generation was 2 March 1997.

"Clear Eyd Fox Quickn Brown Hoax" (Exhibit IV)
The fourth grep experiment documented here is "'Clear Eyd Fox Quickn Brown Hoax': A Grep of the 1995 Poetics Logs." This 221-line grep uses the 1995 archive of the SUNY-Buffalo Poetics electronic discussion list (listserv) as the source text, a large corpus from which to draw (nearly 300,000 lines).[5] The procedure for this work is somewhat more complicated than the grep works mentioned above, because the volume of grep output required substantial editorial attention. As with all procedural works, it is crucial that editorial decisions are documented. They are presented here as details of this procedure.

"Clear Eyd Fox Quickn Brown Hoax," the input phrase for this procedure, is my own variation of the typewriter repairman's stock phrase, "a quick brown fox jumped over the lazy moon," using the impulse-altered words as pattern words. For the first Web version of this work, HTML was used to display the output files. For the print version, word wrap was determined by Netscape's default display parameters. (Internal truncation of title words was also guided by Netscape's pixel width on a standard monitor.)

PROCEDURE

The UNIX grep command was used to parse the Poetics log files for 1995. Thus, every word in this text was written by persons posting to Poetics (one or more of the approximately 200 subscribers to Poetics at the time). The input string was altered in some cases ("browning" for "brown," for example, as detailed below) to keep the output within the 3- to 100-line range that was deemed optimal for this composition.

TEXT PREPARATION AND IMAGES

Each section represents the unedited output for the grep returns on the indicated expression with two exceptions: (1) The "clear" section was truncated at 41 lines due to an excessive length. (2) Recurrent repetitions of e-mail subject lines ("Life," "re: Life," "re: re: Life," etc.) were trimmed so that results would not be skewed toward discussion-list threads. Images were a crucial component to the Web version of this work. For images, Alta Vista was used to search the Web, based on search phrases identical or similar to the grep pattern word. The first usable (nonproprietary) image encountered was downloaded and incorporated into the installation.

Details about the input phrases are as follows:

Title Word	Grep Pattern Word	Alta Vista Search Phrase (for Images)
clear	clear	clear images
eyd	eyed	eye image
fox	fox	fox
quickn	quicken	quick images
brown	browning	brown
hoax	hoax	hoax images

How did these variations occur? First, a grep pattern word was tried that was as close to the title word as possible. (For example, using "eyd" results would have been null if the grep pattern word had not been expanded to "eyed." For images, "search word" + "images" was first tried (to force the results to contain image files). If this did not work, "search word" + "image" was tried. As a last resort, if nothing could otherwise be found, the search word on its own was tried, even though it meant looking through hundreds of hits. Interestingly, "fox" was the most difficult word to search because of numerous movie and sports hits containing proprietary material. "Clear Eyd Fox Quickn Brown Hoax" was designed as a procedural reflection on the Poetics electronic discussion list. The Poetics list is considered by some the nation's premier electronic discussion list for innovative poetries. During the early years of this list, postings were marked by an extraordinary vitality of writing, due partly to the novelty of the medium at the time. "Clear Eyd Fox Quickn Brown Hoax" intends to condense this voluminous textual corpus into a form that might give a readable experience of its textual vigor. Grep seemed a promising method for distilling an entire year of interactive writing on this list. This grep creates a topography of textual themes and topics for the year. This is presented in the form of a collaborative assemblage drawn from postings by the subscribers to the list at the time. The date of generation of "Clear Eyd Fox Quickn Brown Hoax" was 12 November 1996.

Such examples begin to show the range and diversity grep adds to the field of writing. Grep stands as the harbinger of an approach to textuality that allows computer generation of text to be a valuable tool for the poet. Indeed, a plethora of possible text generation tools come to mind, including Internet browser searches on given terms, text analysis operations on specific words (indexing, concordancing, and stylistics), the adaptation of OCR errors for text generation (for example, my "Eclout" in the online Appendix

II), or the use of custom text generation programs and macros for creating acrostics, diastics, and other textual permutations (for example, Travesty, discussed in chapter 7). Indeed, the possibilities for program-assisted composition of poetry have only just begun to be explored, even though procedure, in varying forms, has always been part of poetry.

ABC's of Coding

Whenever I design a chip, the first thing I want to do is look at it under a microscope—not because I think I can learn something new by looking at it but because I am always fascinated by how a pattern can create reality.
   —W. Daniel Hillis, *Pattern on the Stone*

Writing a "href=" is writing.
   —Loss Pequeño Glazier, "An Online Defense"

There is something that comes home to one now and perpetually,
It is not what is printed or preached or discussed . . . . it eludes discussion and print,
It is not to be put in a book . . . . it is not in this book,
It is for you whoever you are . . . . it is no farther from you than your hearing and sight are from you. . . .
   —Walt Whitman, *Leaves of Grass*

Code's Syntax

   The poet/programmer: Is there such an identity? It is informative to consider an approach to writing code that treats the source code as a fundamental part of the meaning-making structure, not as secondary to another "purpose" (checking if you are a valid user, totaling a column, maintaining a list of subscribers, formatting a document).[6] What does code amount to? What does it mean for code to follow style? Jim Marchand, in a 1996 posting to the Humanist Discussion list, comments: "I go back to the days before languages, even to the days when one had to slap switches, so I remember the good old days (of Eliza and the like) when aesthetics in programming meant parsimony or at best elegance. If my program required less space than yours and did roughly the same thing, mine was better than yours" (Marchand). Marchand suggests that there are a number of books on programming style, "mostly on avoiding go-to's and loops and being economical," and he comments on the fairly prevalent practice of copying relevant pieces of code from other programmers into one's own program:[7] "I half the time do not know what goes on in the black box of the module, but what the hey? No need to reinvent the wheel. Since I am using someone else's art object, I cannot be accused of bad aesthetics. Programming nowadays is folk art" (Marchand). Marchand's view of programming as a popular art is quite insightful. Certainly, the wide circulation of snippets of JavaScript and HTML through the Web, written fragments copied and pasted at will, would support that suggestion.

The ability for "writing" to circulate in this manner also marks its relation to poetry, as if the JavaScript fragments were tropes or passages in an oral poetry corpus, freely incorporated from one recitation to the next (and just like oral poetry, subject to permutation each time it is passed on). Further, a relation between code and poetry is suggested by the attention to space and compression of language that has been mentioned. Don Wilkins, posting earlier to the same discussion list, states this connection even more strongly: "In a sense code resembles classical poetry. The requirements of meter (poetry) and syntax (code) pose both limitations and challenges for the good poet/programmer to adhere to and overcome in the process of writing a great poem/program. Also, in code there are many conventional approaches followed by the experts, just as there are certain elements of style followed by good writers" (Wilkins).

Clearly, style is relevant to the production of a text/program. For one thing, a text/program that ignores style can be difficult to read or work with. (For example, if there are no comment lines or procedural notes, if the file consists of a single endless line, or if the file is overpowered by spurious control characters, it becomes difficult to circulate, re-use, or debug.) Moreover, the poem/program and its style are so interrelated that it is difficult to draw a clear line between them. According to the *New Princeton Encyclopedia of Poetry and Poetics*: "How are we to distinguish between what a poem says and the language in which it says it? On the one hand, there is no such thing as a 'content' utterly separable from words; on the other hand, something can be said about the words, which does not refer directly to the content" (Bennett 1225). These comments hold up equally well when we are discussing the code and the content of the work in both basic and subtle ways. In terms of basics, sloppiness in coding can have direct repercussions. For example, failing to code correctly may allow the page you are creating to display on the browser on which you view it but may cause it to fail on different kinds of browsers in different configurations.[8]

On more subtle levels, how does the structure in which you think influence what is expressed by interpreted code? For example, in architectural terms, a cathedral and an igloo both realize not just structure but systems of thought. Yet, though each implies a quite different structure, structure and expressed form are equally integral. In terms of the digital, consider the following excerpt of code.[9] (It is drawn from a larger section of similar lines.)

```
| <a href="http://epc.buffalo.edu/authors">Authors</a>
| <a href="http://epc.buffalo.edu/e-poetry">E-Poetry</a>
| <a href="http://epc.buffalo.edu/books">Books</a>
```

These lines of code appear almost like a Whitmanesque catalog stanza (see Whitman epigraph above), the concatenation symbol acting as a repeated lexeme invoking variations on a string. As code, it is a vertical arrangement of horizontal lines and makes sense in this presentation: the connecting unit (the concatenation symbol) and link mechanism (<a href="http://) appears first in each case, making these lines easy to read. Further, the vertical alignment of repeated elements creates a parallelism that not only reaffirms structural similarities but highlights difference. This is a classic use of anaphora, a "technique of coordination and replacement allowing for, and even emphasizing, juxtaposition" (Dupriez 39). This anaphoric structure (more accurately symploce, because the lines also end identically), helps prevent coding errors by reaffirming structural similarities while highlighting contrasting targets (or destinations).[10] This type of juxtaposition is "A natural means . . . of creating accumulations of analogical, antithetical, or heterogeneous elements" (Dupriez 39). That is, this process is a compositional activity engaging the material properties of the medium. Not only does this code employ technique that is clearly literary, it also makes good sense because this technique helps make the code accurate.

This example of code is further interesting because, when interpreted by the browser, the vertical arrangement of lines actually displays, not vertically, but on one horizontal line. The concatenation symbols then appear not as initial repeated beginnings of lines but as *medial* markers of difference, the lines of code that begin with concatenation symbols now concatenated into a single horizontal line:
    | Authors | Mags | Small Presses
Thus, the visual structure of the code is like a frame that, when interpreted by the browser, is turned on its side, giving the interpreted text horizontal stability drawn from vertical order. This stability is not apparent in the displayed text but, I would argue, is a structural component of the order that is made manifest. This visual ordering builds that section of the page by projecting an internal order into an external implementation. The vertical series of images turns into a horizontal one yet remains structurally the same. If one considers Johanna Drucker's observation that "writing is not only an instance of language—it is also an image" (*Figuring* 61), then one sees an even more powerful view of this code: it consists of images that make writ-

ing in HTML; and the image/pattern it makes in HTML becomes writing when interpreted by the browser. In this sense, code is an exoskeleton that transposes into endoskeleton; it provides a material and visual writing scheme that enriches itself when interpreted. It is writing per se and provides a way to write along two axes of visible language, an interesting project indeed.

These relations are also suggested by the literal meaning of "mark-up." According to *The American Heritage Dictionary, Third Edition*, mark-up is "detailed stylistic instructions written on a manuscript to be typeset." Yet in the case of HTML, mark-up is not just a set of instructions that are executed and discarded because mark-up remains a structural part of the writing. Considering that an HTML document consists of data (the "information" of the page), the code (the mark-up and other meta-language that presents that data), and the interpreted document (the combination of data and code as viewed through a browser program), a number of interesting inter-relations are present in HTML. Just as content is not separable from words, these three parts of the text can neither be entirely disentangled.

The Elements of HTML

What can be communicated through any literary production depends on which codes are shared with its audience.
—Ron Silliman, *New Sentence*

Following are brief observations on some elementary considerations of points of HTML mark-up style with similar material ramifications.

Observing Boundaries
A comment line is a line viewable in the mark-up but coded so that it will not be displayed on the browser. Carefully placed comment lines allow one to mark important regions of the HTML document, separate one class of text from the next, or create a reference point in the HTML document. To separate classes:

apples
<!-- --- -->
oranges

To mark different regions:

<!-- Part Two -- -->
The next day the code-master awoke early. "Brackets," she thought.

Mimetic Value
Displayed features (the <hr> in this example, which displays in the browser as a horizontal line) may be mimed by comment lines to produce a visual

analog in the code:

```
<hr>
<!-- ---------------------------------------------------------------- -->
```

Documentation

As has been noted, documentation is essential in any procedural work. Such documentation or annotation takes on a special value when placed within mark-up, because it literally occurs within the work that is documented, collocated at specific points of relevance.

```
<!-- This version of this file generated 25 Aug 2000--------------- -->
<!-- based on the source text, Hache Te Eme Ele--------------- -->
<!-- a seventeenth century transl. from the Nahuatl--------------- -->
```

Labels

Labels, short HTML comments used for identifying regions of mark-up, are crucial components of HTML. Labels are used in the first line of a document where it is standard practice to name the document. (This prevents errors while working, for many sites have numerous files of the same name, index.html, default.htm, accueil.htm, etc., that can sometimes be confused.)

```
<!-- EPC HOME PAGE -->
```

The title field also provides an important label. This displays in the top bar of the browser version of the document and is a writing area of the document that is often overlooked.

```
<head>
<title>Electronic Poetry Center Home Page</title>
</head>
```

To Suspend

It is possible to change code while preserving the version one is superseding. To do this one may leave the previous coding in comment lines to easily reinstate previous code when desired:

```
<!-- font color="black" -- Greetings Comrade! -- /font -->
<font color="red">Happy May Day!</font>
```

An experienced reader of HTML, if reading code along with the browser version of a document, will concurrently be able to read the commented version, effectively gaining access to more than one version of the same text.

Visual Dynamics

The potential for visual interleaving of text and mark-up is great indeed.

Because all blank space is compressed when the code is interpreted, one can put generous amounts of space between characters without affecting the document. Thus, many HTML layout possibilities present themselves. Such a situation provides the poetic license to spread writing all over the page, even when writing prose. One can spread words apart logically, categorically, or at a whim. One can also create a "map" or grid through the use of white space, to provide metaphoric or material arrangements of writing or for mnemonic purposes.

```
                      <center>
                                        One <br>
                      </center>
        Events        that take        space            are largely
<!--                                    =======
        -->
        events        that take        place
                                                          as largely
                                    misunderstood
                not                        senseless.
                      <center>
                                        Two <br>
                      </center>
```

One might think of Charles Olson who, in *The Maximus Poems* referred to the American as "a complex of occasions, / themselves a geometry / of spatial nature" (185), a phrase that might also describe the global citizen of the third millennium.[11] This statement also describes the kind of writing Olson was investigating. Thinking of visual dynamics, this statement makes even more tangible sense in digital space, a medium typified by flexible and infinitely extensible alphabetic geometries.

Lineation by Material of Writing
     Interlineation is a highly effective way of alternating text and code. This layering provides clarity at the code-level reading, accuracy (because markup can be more easily maintained), and the ability to read verbal text on its own level; for example:

Locally administered resources include the electronic poetry journal
<a href="http://epc.buffalo.edu/rift">RIF/T</a>,
the rich audio art of
<a href="http://epc.buffalo.edu/linebreak">LINEbreak</a>,
the online performance space
<a href="http://epc.buffalo.edu/epclive">EPClive</a>,
the full-text, electronic editions of

<a href="http://epc.buffalo.edu/biblioteca">Biblioteca</a>,
and the archive, calendar, and files associated with the
<a href="http://epc.buffalo.edu/poetics">Poetics</a>
discussion list and Poetics at Buffalo program.<p>

Naming
There is great potential for the names of files to add to a document's
textuality. File names should participate in meaning-making by reflecting
the subject and some sense of version of the file.

<img src="./images/cactus-snow3a.jpg">

Alternatives to Images
A useful space for writing is available if you identify alternatives to im-
ages in the image "alt" tag. That is, what will the reader see while the image
is loading? This will be all the reader sees if the viewing browser is configured
not to display images.

<img src="http://epc.buffalo.edu/images/drawings/eclipse.gif"
alt="Where the sun don't shine">

Special Characters
The possibilities for surface textuality discussed thus far do not include
some situations where the resistance of coding, or its disruptive penetration
into text, give code a more arcane look. For example, symbols add an inter-
esting twist to writing as represented in code. Copyright, for example:

<font size=3> All EPC text, graphics, and sound © the
authors. </font>

Diacritics present more of a challenge. This is a situation of which many
English speakers might not be aware. The disruptions that code imposes in
these cases are not minor. The lyrical opening to Rimbaud's poem begin-
ning, "Ô Saisons, Ô Chateaux," for example, is as follows:
Ô saisons, ô châteaux,
quelle âme est sans défauts?
(*Collected* 228)
("Oh seasons, Oh palaces, what heart is without flaw?" trans. Glazier.)
The above lines would be turned into a stutter of typography in HTML:

Ô saisons, ô châteaux,
quelle âme est sans défauts?

And a line with the simple clarity of the opening line to "Aube" by Rimbaud,

"J'ai embrassé l'aube d'été" (*Collected* 268) ("I embraced the summer down," trans. Glazier), would transmogrify into the following:

J'ai embrassé l'aube d'été.

For "d'été" to have to appear as "d'été;" is no small matter. Not only does this five-character phrase now expand to nineteen characters, an increase of 380 percent, but the interruption, except to an experienced eye, nearly obliterates the chance for this phrase to seem meaningful in HTML. (Other languages, it should be noted, present even greater HTML reading problems.) This is an issue that demonstrates the linguistic slippage of code.

Such difficulties noted, one can nonetheless inspect these examples and observe that there is a consistent pattern to diacritics as represented in HTML: Most special characters are prefixed by the & character and close with the ; character. Thus, an é (e with acute accent) becomes "é"; the ô (o with a circumflex) becomes "ô"; and the Spanish ñ would become "ñ"[12] (Spanish characters such as ¡ and ¿, however, require the more arcane "¡" and "¿"). This is simple enough to follow but shows the bias of HTML against non-English characters. (As a further example of this, the mnemonics themselves for these codes are based on English.) Thus, materiality for a non-English language includes the presence of characters that appear unwieldy. This occurs in English for special characters, such as & ("&"), > (">"), and others. The strangeness of such text can add an opportunity for additional play, though it may not always be welcome.[13]

Is such an attention to detail necessary? Will one's code always be "read"? The answer to this last question is that, of course, it will not always be read, just as poems may not always be "read." Nevertheless, it is not about whether a reader will fathom the intricacies of your code. Rather, the issue here is that HTML coding has material dimensions and that writing, as an act, means working within such dimensions. Therefore such "writing" of HTML is an engagement with the materiality of the medium. As to whether the details matter, it is certain that every aspect of code has a ramification, some of which often cannot be anticipated. One must be alert because what one commits to code may become reality. Take, for example, the image "alt" tag mentioned above. The text one types into this area is not only what a viewer reads when waiting for a page to load but is also sound, because image alt tags are how Web users who are blind "hear" images. If you add to such unanticipated circumstances the innumerable variants that different browser configurations pose to code, one can see each detail explodes into numerous possibilities, making code writing a field of intricate twists and turns.

Writing/Coding

> Words,
> > where they are not
> added to the real
> > > but compose it. . . .
> > > > —Robin Blaser, *The Holy Forest*

> peace be
> photon
> twist
> cork aground
> > > —Joan Retallack, *Afterrimages*

The closeness between writing and coding is rarely acknowledged. Indeed, such activities are often seen as antithetical, reinforcing the long-standing divide between science and art. As David Gelernter writes: "We are rarely willing to see machine beauty, no longer put machines . . . in the art we make, refuse to acknowledge . . . the intellectual and spiritual closeness of art and science" (16). This reference to "machine beauty" is even more striking when one considers that a program is often referred to as a "virtual machine." One's word-processing program, for example, is not an object in one's computer but a series of lines of instructions intermingled with numerous other lines of data, instructions, and utilities; yet it has the appearance of being its own machine, something that gets a certain job done. Such a machine's performance is enhanced by effective design; specifically, it must be well *written*. Code that works is not necessarily well written, but well-written code delivers something greater than the machine itself, a certain intangible excellence in execution, or interface, or performance. It is code that has not only been written but that has been written with alacrity and cohesion. This type of writing applies equally to traditional text as to writing on the Web.

Well-written code explores the inter-relations that the code-writing dynamic makes possible. It includes attention to housekeeping concerns, such as not letting lines run off screen, keeping clear breaks between blocks, and keeping a clean slate of any stray control characters. Importantly, there are no rights and wrongs; an informed view of coding does not emphasize adherence to rules but encourages the poet/programmer to invent, clone, adapt, or appropriate styles *based on the writing's content and/or activity*, that is, in relation to specific concerns present in the writing. W. Daniel Hillis has noted that "a skilled programmer is like a poet who can put into words those ideas that others find inexpressible" (40). This suggests that coding is not merely a task of converting one type of writing into another, but a way of thinking and *making* the written word. In this way, style in HTML opens up architectural, metalinguistic, and conceptual spaces for poetic improvisation. Such a detailed concern with the mechanics of code not only renders a more considered text but also is in itself writing.

Because code is words, or consists of word-like typographic fragments that interact with words, code is integral to the text being rendered. The tableau of coding crosses between the visible and invisible, between the active and passive, between meta-text and readable text: it is a form of interweaving of material, typographic, and narrative or subject elements. As Bennett points out about poetic style in general: "Observation of any text . . . but especially of a closely woven 'aesthetic' text, reveals how the meaning of words depends upon the contexts created by the other words in the text. Meaning entails correlation, every word bearing the pressure of all the other words" (1226).

Though there are many times when code plays a merely utilitarian role within the textual environment (for example, rendering a phrase in italics as a convention), there are other far more interesting interactions. One must not underestimate that the code has entered the field of writing, that code consists of "words" too, and that all textual elements coexist here, as in other forms of writing, with a near explosive friction of adjacency. As Charles Hartman comments: "How do words mean when we put them into new contexts? Under what conditions does the meaning web tear apart? What meanings can words make (or can we make of them) when we disturb their normal relation to each other? These are questions that any poet can be seen as asking; and from this point of view, someone experimenting with computer poetry is continuing an age-old project" (*Virtual* 104). Exploring the material possibilities of these meaning (or textual) webs is a project that is a natural extension of innovative poetic practice. One need only cite any of numerous pointers, etymological plays, language derivations, or unreadable text in Charles Olson or Rachel Blau DuPlessis or Susan Howe to see a similar interweaving. The dynamic relation of such parts to other parts is what Olson called the "field" of writing. It is, like HTML, a place "where all the syllables and all the lines must be managed in their relations to each other"[14]—here extended to include typographic and metatypographic characters (*Selected* 20). Olson calls the elements of poetry "objects" (an idea strikingly resonant with the object-oriented programming paradigm). How do these work? "Every element in an open poem (the syllable, the line, as well as the image, the sound, the sense) must be taken up as participants in the kinetic of the poem just as solidly as we are accustomed to take what we call the objects of reality" (*Selected* 20). What could be more kinetic, indeed, than writing that must be projected to be read and that is, at its core, the product of numerous dynamic renderings?

If one were to start with the statement that "code resembles classical poetry" (Wilkins), then considering its material possibilities, one would need to follow through to suggest that code also affirms the possibilities of innovative poetries. Code is akin to innovative poetry in the physicality of its interweaving of text, metatext, and erased text. What better opportunity to explore the dynamics of innovative writing than to design writing in HTML? Writing is the project of the screen and the projection[15] of a textual field onto a browser, always with variable results.

The poetry of code departs from code as style through the play of its parts. In fact, one can apply Ezra Pound's "means"— phanopoeia, melopoeia, and logopoeia—to code. The fact that HTML is extremely primitive as a layout language forces the writer to be inventive—engage the material—in order to attain wished-for results. Is there such a thing as a poet/programmer? One must argue that there is, since programming follows the practice of exploring the interrelations of words that poets have pursued all along. The poet/programmer can guide through casting shadows from comment lines and arrangements of non-alphabetic characters into repetitive sequences; induce correlation by arranging <p>'s and
's as visual tropes and for rhythmic qualities; set up conceptual frames and supporting structures. The interpreted text is itself a simulation of associations. Code is a scene of poeisis, as real as ink or an awl in the hands that guide its impression into the pliant but invisible grooves of the magnetic medium.

A How to Read

ys at en.
· counter st.   ..uorio'
.ctual width laborio   ..··s in its actu·
e odd angles an act Milton in the r?
nstituent dyschords   nresent of ·
ring the script indi·   ⁴acks pro g.
.eak. Houses ·   ··lumn.
ıngles of

fish

From *(Go) Fish* (Glazier)

Reading code is reading what renders the text.
—Martin Spinelli, "Communication
Technology"

The reader's position is tricky though because he ends up alternately in the neck of the spiral spring inside the steel coil and somewhere outside of it but in any case himself performs a spiral movement with a certain amount of dexterity acrobatically gifted readers can despite the contortions intertwinings dislocations and tactically split attention which are necessary from time to time follow both spiral texts viz text spirals at the same time.
—Oskar Pastior, "Poempoems"

Dream of reading through a passage so narrow that its walls threaten to press into fossils the broken bones of a breath. . . .
—Christain Bök, *Crystallography*

Scholars such as Jerome McGann, Johanna Drucker, Marjorie Perloff, and Cary Nelson have argued convincingly, we have noted, about the significance of material and production contexts to the "reading" of a literary work. The physical construction of a text (typography, illustrations, and layout), its social context, how the work negotiates its medium, what material dynamics are set into motion, how production influences the work itself—all contribute to the "reading" of a text. Material qualities have equal significance in electronic space.

Accordingly, if one considers the Web, it is apparent that the material dimensions of Web documents can have important implications for how they are read. These dimensions clearly inform the context of the content of a page. For example, a work such as "Mouseover" (see next section) purposely teases textuality from such Web under-workings as HTML, JavaScript, sound capabilities, and source code. A recognition of such qualities might cause us to re-examine how we read (or teach reading) within the universe of Web documents. What specific factors of writing must be considered in order to mine the subtleties, strategies, and rhetorical implications of a Web-based document? Given the sheer volume of possible features and the fact that new configurations are appearing daily, it would not be possible to create a definitive list. However, in order to suggest the range of implications of these textual features, it is helpful to identify a sample of textual elements that add meaning to the writing in Web pages. Among many possibilities, the following might be considered a checklist of elements important to a list-in-progress for considerations of how to read the Web.

Compositional Considerations

Title Bar

Is there any content in the title bar? Title bars are represented more significantly on a Mac than on a PC, but on either platform, this writing "area" can be an expressive one, framing "real," alternate, or intended identities for Web documents.

Canvas Size/Re-size

What is the "size" of the writing field? Are there scroll bars? Scroll bars should be tested to appraise how much the canvas extends in either direction. The canvas size reveals certain specifics about the readerly parameters of the page. If the page scrolls down, is it essentially an electronic version of a paper document? If the page scrolls to the side, is it poor design, or is there a reason or context for the reader to have to make such an awkward movement to read from side to side? Does the author/programmer seem to take into account the fact that many readers only read what is visible without scrolling? Does there seem to be ample content for the canvas size? If you change the shape of your browser window, does the text formatting maintain its integrity? Or does it somehow lose cohesiveness, the layout seeming to deconstruct? Canvas size is as relevant to the meaning of the page as are the dimensions of a Pollock or Monet is to its alleged subject. In the very least, the sense of scale must be considered.

Design Components

What do we make of the use of color, font size, and layout? Is the background color so close to the text color that text is difficult to read? Is type inordinately small or large? Must you resort to extreme measures, like cutting and pasting into a new document, in order to read the text? Does the page use white or light type on a dark background, thus making printing impossible for many readers? Was this a consideration of their design? What is the page's "gimic threshold"? Does it parody its own possibilities by overusing or employing meaningless animated gifs, ticker tapes, blinking text, and other such elements? Such elements necessitate extra download time and are quite onerous for some users. Is the visual and conceptual drain that these features impose worth the demand on the reader?

Images

What is the relation of the image on the page to the "real" size of the image? Is the image size shown at 100 percent, or is it a link via a compressed (postage stamp) representation? Does it pre-load with an alternative ("lowsrc=") version of the image? If it is a link to other versions of the image, does the page image consist of a section of the larger image, or is it a miniature of the full image? These factors describe the designer's conception of image. Further, what is the relation of image to text? Is the image merely illustrative, or does it express something inexpressible by text? Are the images original, from a stock library, or commercially produced?

Structure of Site/Local Mobility

What do the file and directory names in the URL box tell you about the structure of the site? Do the names of files and directories indicate structure or content of the pages? If you erase portions of the URL, do you gain access to lists of files that might give you other indicators about the content of the pages? What do URLs say about the content of a given page or the attitude of the designer to the subject of the page? (For example, what difference in attitude/content is expressed by a URL ending in "docs/ephemeral" as opposed to one ending in "docs/flaky"?

Referenced URLs

Where do the links point? Are they internal or do they go to outside sites? (Many browser versions allow you to place your cursor over a link and read the referenced URL in the status bar.) Numerous internal links indicate depth, or abundant content, local to the site. Numerous external links indicate shallowness, or sparse site content. In this latter case, the page may serve more as a filter, anthology, or gateway to Web resources. Does it articulate its editorial criteria or objectives? What do referenced URLs tell you about the material selected? (For example, if many are ".com" sites, it might be commercially oriented. If many of the referenced URLs are long or have tildes (~) in their paths, the page may connect to pages low in the destination site's hierarchy, such as student web pages. Such information can be useful in getting an immediate idea of the composition of the site.)

Dynamic Features

Hypertextual Features

What kind of hypertext is this? Is it simple link-node hypertext? Are there any hidden links or links that are conditional? How much text is present on the page? (I like to make the distinction between what I call a "document" page and a "menu" page, the former being largely a work in itself and the latter largely like a traffic policeman, directing users along other routes. Of course, these are just generalizations of how a page can be constituted; pages really exist on a continuum between these two extremes.) How many links are there? If there are few links, does following these reveal depth? If there are many links, do the links appear to branch shallowly (links branch to a small universe of pages), or do they branch widely (links branch to a large universe of pages)? Are many of these links to a single page? Depth and diversity of links and amount of content are crucial considerations in evaluating a hypertext's composition. These features offer a wealth of information about such writing.

Auto-movement

When you view the page does it re-load or are there auto-navigational features such as client pull at work? What does the purpose of this feature seem to be? Considering that some browsers will crash under auto-load and that some readers will not wait long enough for the feature to work, are the risks of such auto-movement worthwhile? What about readers who find this feature annoying?

Windowing

When you click on links, do they open into the same window, or do they spawn multiple browser windows? What about when the spawned window has no scroll bars and the whole page in that window is not viewable? What is the significance to the work of the burden of multiple-presentations that windowing introduces? For many readers, especially those with low-end equipment, this is extremely frustrating. Does this seem consistent with the site, or does the feature seem unplanned?

Client-side Programming

What is the function of JavaScript and other client-side programming on the page? Is there scrolling text in the bottom bar of the screen? Does any text appear in the bottom bar or elsewhere on the page when you move your mouse? Do any portions of the text change, or do any dialog boxes appear? What does the purpose of such programming seem to be? Does it provide alternate readings or variant meanings to the main text of the page, or does such programming seem to be merely incidental? Does any of this programming employ randomization or otherwise contextual generation of text to create conditional dimensions to the page?

Under the Surface

Hidden Links

If one runs the cursor all over the screen, does the arrow turn into a hand? Are there any non-apparent links? Do such links appear to be unintentional, or does access to these links seem to be intentionally obscured?

Coding

View the source HTML of the page, the text that underlies the page's presentation.[16] Is there any meaningful writing in commented sections? Are any interesting "arguments" presented through the hypotaxis, parataxis, or other structural features of the code? What does the structure and style of the HTML tell you about the document? Do the layout qualities of the HTML seem consistent with or at odds with the page? What might this mean?

Collateral Text/Alt Image Tags

Turn off your browser's ability to display images.[17] Then reload the page. If you have done this successfully, footprints or outlines will replace actual images, and text will now be visible within those footprints. Is there any meaningful "hidden" text present in these image "alt" tags? If this text reads "Image," then the designer overlooked this area or chose not to consider the needs of users who cannot receive images. If text is present, differences in alternative text, say "distinguished gentleman" versus "old man" may provide additional information about the designer's relation to the subject of the page.

"Meta Name" Tags

"Meta name" tags are tags created by the designer to describe the content of the Web page for indexing services, such as Yahoo, Lycos, and so forth. These tags appear in the <head> area, viewable through the document source option of your browser. Such descriptions can give key indications about what the designer thinks of, or hopes to express, through the page. Two such tags of interest are "keyword" and "description." These appear as follow in the source code of a document:

<meta name="keywords" content="poetry, poetics, writing, electronic, kinetic, programmable, animated, media, literature, writing, academic">
<meta name="description" content="The home page of the
Electronic Poetry Center, an edited site devoted to the presentation of full-text resources for innovative writing.">

The keyword area presents a series of descriptive words separated by commas. Obviously, these statements can reveal information about how the designer views the site, what the designer would like to be known for, who the designer seeks to attract. The description area presents a succinct statement of the site, obviously also very much of interest.

The factors I have described in this section are not simply meaningless physical features of the page. Whether intentionally or not, such features indicate specific rhetorical and ideological strategies employed to realize the text. As should be apparent by now, my argument is that making the text happen is never an innocuous affair. (The writer cannot just tell you a story; the writer, by definition, is trying to convince you of a viewpoint.) Each decision that is made, whether to strap the patient in with frames and etherize them with scrolling banner text in the status bar, is critical. Whether to degrade readers with pop-up advertising windows, to infuriate them by making them click through dozens of pages until they arrive at the phone number of the plumbing emergencies hotline, is central. Every decision one makes in making a page involves as much grappling as two sumo wrestlers trying to force each other out of a raised earth ring of signification.

In many cases of course, examinations of these areas may turn up no information, irrelevant material, or simply indicate that the page was created with many of the defaults of any given program. Nevertheless, there will be a large number of documents and works where an investigation of these features will prove richly rewarding. Indeed, the reading suggestions presented here may contribute to the definition of close reading in the future. Though electronic writing is relatively young, it will not be long until the sophistication of writer/programmers reaches the point that these writing "dimensions" will be increasingly capitalized upon for expanding richness of subtlety, expression, and irony. These dimensions are a crucial part of the rhetoric of these electronic pages; they cannot be overlooked. Knowledge of these areas is of course essential for any successful "reading" of e-poetry, as much as knowledge of iambs, trochees, anapests, and dactyls is for accentual-syllabic verse.

What is the right way to build a set of tools to read the writing on the Web? As Espen Aarseth has suggested, "There is of course no 'proper' way to approach the digital media, and most mistakes we make at this still early stage will probably prove to be useful lessons later on" (in Ryan 32). We must watch for our mistakes in such readings of digital media, learning from them as we go. What cautions should we heed? About digital media writing, or ergodic art, as he terms it, Aarseth notes, "The worst kind of mistake an aesthetic theory of ergodic art can make is to assume that there is only one type with which to be concerned, e.g., 'the electronic text,' 'electronic literature,' etc., with a single set of properties" (quoted in Ryan 34). Accordingly, this list of criteria can remain useful as long as we keep it flexible, open, and multiple in the forms of digital writing it hopes to describe. Similarly, it must adapt new forms as they emerge and adjust how criteria are interpreted, depending on emergent technologies that contextualize digital writing.

Sidebar: On Mouseover. Reading "Mouseover Essay in JavaScript"

> For instance one could just as easily take the TURK POEM and make an AEROPLANE and vice versa the possibility of such transformations lies less on the nominal level and more in the material consistency even in this particular case it is quite easy one folds the turk poem according to the pattern for making an aeroplane and ends up with an admittedly highly simple but airworthy aeroplane.
> —Oskar Pastior, "Poempoems"

> random access mem-O-rees
> Single engine aer-O-plane
> —Joan Retallack, *Afterrimages*

Coding writing and reading code suggest the possibility of deeper engagements with digital media. Such forms of writing and reading extend traditional literary skills of critical inquiry into a new context. How does one *read* in e-media? How does one evaluate the workings of divergent technical elements? How does one unravel those particular strands of code that allow an informed interaction with a digital text? This sidebar provides an example of one reading of a specific digital text, "Mouseover Essay in JavaScript." This text, named for the computer input device that is the key to its reading, was first published in 1998 in the *Electronic Book Review*.[18] Readers are encouraged to view the Web version of this work in conjunction with this sidebar.

Rationale

"Mouseover Essay in JavaScript" was created in JavaScript for several reasons. This is a dynamic work, requiring programmability. Also, because the work was to be published at a host site *(Electronic Book Review)* and not on the author's server, it was decided that the mounting and maintenance of CGI or other scripts would not be practical. The work needed to contain its own program and launch executables, not from the host server, but from the client where it would be read. JavaScript was a suitable program for this purpose. JavaScript was also deemed the most appropriate program for expressing a specific tension between alternative modalities of reading the given piece. This was especially true in the context of what "Mouseover" set out to accomplish.

The structure of "Mouseover" is designed to facilitate alternate readings.[19] The home page of this work consists of a Web page located at a single URL. This page is longer than a typical screen, so the customary scroll bar allows the reader to read the bottom of the page (downward movement). "Mouseover" is composed of four panels, plus a narrow, wide, title banner at the top. (Boundaries between these panels are not necessarily distinguishable.) Each of these panels will display one of three different textual variants ("readings"), providing a kind of lateral movement within each panel. As the title of "Mouseover" announces, these frames become active/hidden depending on the user's intentional (or accidental) positioning of the mouse. The first "reading" of each panel could be called the "native" or pre-mouse iteration; once touched it never returns (though a savvy reader will suspect that reloading the page may restore it). The two remaining readings for each panel will display, depending on whether the mouse is positioned within the panel (the mouse "on" position) or outside the panel (the mouse "off" position). That is, the second reading appears when the mouse touches the reading area; and the third one appears after it has touched the panel then moves away.

Mouseover: An Analysis

The title banner for "Mouseover" introduces the dynamics of shifting readings in an obvious manner—and not without humor. The banner's presentation of the title is unstable, as is its subtitle. For example, following is the pre-mouse reading of the title panel:

Mouseover
Refreshing to see Letters again.

The title "Mouseover" (printed in red letters) immediately declares that this is a Mouseover work, something many readers will understand. (If they do not, trial and error will make this dynamic understandable.) The suggestion is also made that it is now "refreshing to see letters again," as if we had somehow lost our view of something, typography or writing, perhaps. If the reader moves the mouse so that it is on the banner, the banner changes into the following:

Mooseover
Other terms Letters again.

The title, subtitle, and image all change, not only dramatizing the instability of the text but also asserting the power of the reader to alter the text. The vocalic play between the names of the obviously unrelated animals, mouse and moose, introduces humor and playfulness. But the panel is no more stable in this position. The third possibility arises once the mouse has touched the title panel but is no longer positioned over it. This third reading appears as follows:

Mouseover
Other terms might be

That is, the banner does not return to the "native" reading but instead displays a third iteration (the "colonized" or "mouse off" version). The title reverts to the original title (though not the original color), but the subtitle takes on a third reading. The graphic of the moose is now replaced by the graphic of a computer mouse. There is humor in this particular series of frames, of course. The idea is that such a shifting series of frames may induce a mood of giddiness. The alternation between "Mouseover" and "Mooseover" presents a slapstick animal substitution based purely on an internal off rhyme. The play on the animal after which the computer's pointing device is named thematizes the instrument of control over the text. The changes in the subtitle form a poem of shifting two or three line couplets, hinting that the "refresh" button might be a way to view these works. Such changes also dramatize text tentatively stable against an usually unavoidably moving mouse.

The dynamic of "Mouseover" is enacted in its title banner. Once readers begin reading the four main panels of the text and employ the mouse to induce its various possible changes, they recognize the reading strategy that allows them to navigate the many possible renderings provided by these combinations. The three readings in each panel can be viewed laterally within a panel, vertically, or diagonally across panels, with effective use of the mouse. Panels occasionally include images within the frame. (These images sometimes evoke the theme of colonization.) In order to explore the possibilities of reading this work, the contents of the first two of the four main "text" panels will be introduced here. Though a close reading of the entire text is out of scope for this book, some thoughts about how one would contextualize the different texts here are given.

Structure of Mouseover
Panel 1, in its pre-mouse state, presents the image of a Mesoamerican pyramid set amid tropical greenery:

In its "mouse on" position, it reads:

own. From the graphical exclamation point, the next possibility that arises

is of course the double exclamation point. Then the triple exclamation, and

on and on, until you get to such an extension of exclamation that the

narrator, in an oral parallel, could thrown himself under a train and it would not match the machine version of the story.

Thus at a certain point, there is no longer a need even for the *story*. But of

And in its "mouse on" position, it reads:

The way (back to that wrestling image) there is a moment before the

competition begins, where one wrestler crouches on all fours and the

opponent kneels next to him. On the textual level, take the exclamation

point as an instance. Is there such a thing as an exclamation point in oral

"telling"? No, the story simply exclaims. It is a physical action. But once

the instrument is involved, the graphical symbol takes on a status of its

Investigated here is the issue of where a text actually begins, the first reading picking up at the end of a sentence. An apparent "beginning" for the narrative occurs in the "mouse off" (third) position, but only grammatically, as the narrative semantically seems still not at its beginning. The text in the "mouse on" position does seem to continue the passage in the "mouse off" position but knowing this does not give us any key to the narrative.

Panel 2 addresses another conundrum of the work. In its pre-mouse position it presents text in the format of a poem:

What is a text if you can't have certainty? That's the point of all

writing, isn't it? To nail down your points, spell them out so there

can be no doubt. "Publication" means posting them on the public

board in the town square. The intellect is made to engage. Ergo

rhetoric—and why that word will never be the name of a rap group—

because it has meaning and because *meaning*, like language, is inviolable.

In its "mouse on" position, the panel continues the poem structure with a new sentence but with no continuation of thought:

You have spoken of the computer as a step *back*. I wonder if you'd clarify?

I think it's actually rather clearer in this passage:
The sea is a scroll but also a typewriter knob

"Yup. 'Found' poems lever this issue wide open"

That's why the button on the right that slides in its track

The cans didn't have labels. They were simply metal

Though the preceding panel concludes with an open sentence, and the third ("mouse off") frame begins with the end of a sentence, they do not connect:

course you know this. You are well established in this "field"

You have detailed in your writing, most notably in your "Occlusions"

essay, rather concise history of the writing machine, including the cut-ups

of Burroughs and Olson's sense of the typewriter as a scripting mechanism.

In this vein—and I know this also resonates with your spin on "the buffer"

in your poem "Direct Contact" which you read here in Manhattan not long

Also introduced in this frame is a shift in discourse, as the lines in this panel mimic the interview style without observing any of its typographical "boundaries" or giving any clues about where this interview fits. The discourse shift not only highlights the polymedial environment of this work but also echoes the physical shifts that are occurring on screen. In addition, the "cut up" technique discussed in this passage is also mimicked by the Mouseover effect.

Looking at these two panels and the six frames that constitute them, it is difficult to pin down a narrative. To make any sense of "Mouseover," one must look toward the content of each fragment and the relation of these fragments to each other in their shifting interplay. We have only looked at reading various iterations within a given panel; there are also, of course, readings that cross panels. These alternative readings offer multiple possibilities and constitute numerous textual variants. Variant readings are obviously a concern of this "essay" in JavaScript.

"Reading" Mouseover

Clearly, the "meaning" that one might guess at would have to take into account the instability of any given reading. It also depends on how "heavy-handed" the reader is, because the text that is displayed is a direct result of the physical actions of the reader. Physicality of text is also an investigation of this work. One aspect of this physicality is that the first version disappears the moment you touch it. This creates a minor panic as it is very difficult, mouse in hand, not to touch some of these areas, especially as one's hand generally goes where the eye is focused. It is important that this is a "physical" work and that physical interaction with the work determines its content.

In addition to these JavaScript dynamics and the hypertextual apparatus alluded to above, "Mouseover" makes use of other textual features. These include links to Real Audio sound bites, accessible at various points through an icon that resembles a small horn. These files contain simple sound effects and semantic elements to supplement or parody various textual elements. These performed lines include the following:

1. I wonder what the reload button would do? (Bell sound.)
2. Neither a clarinet nor a clarion call but homemade mescal. (Clarinet sound.)
3. A clock is not a closet. Nor is it a barn. (Tick sound.)
4. A forest is just a field on stilts. (Clarinet sound.)
5. The problem is you can't reload the frames—without waiting for a reload of the script. (Bell sound.)

Some of these, obviously, are comments on the physical activity involved in "reading" this work, including more clues about the reload button.

A final feature of interest is the blinking parenthetical statement at the bottom of "Mouseover" that reads: "A document source is writing, too." This is an obvious call for the reader to use the reveal codes feature of the browser to view the source code for "Mouseover," an essential step in reading this work. As an exploration of the interrelation between code and writing, the source code of this document not only makes important statements through its layout but also includes sections of writing to which the non-code-viewing reader will not otherwise have access. Indeed, it is a way of saying that if you do not read the code, you are not reading the full work.

Likewise, it is essential for the reader to use the "reveal codes" feature of this book accessible in the online Appendix III, where the full source code of Mouseover can be read. Do not think you have "read" this section without consulting its source.

7
E-poetries
A Lab Book of Digital Practice, 1970-2001

> A poem is a small (or large)
> machine made of words.
> —William Carlos Williams, *Collected Poems*

> Poetry is a simple art where everything resides in the execution.
> —François Le Lionnais, quoted in Queneau's
> *Oulipo Laboratory*

> Numbers are something to work against, a form to transform
> as number-generated writing takes on its own life, spawning
> more numbers, other ratios.
> —Michele Leggott, *Reading Zukofsky's "80 Flowers"*

E-poetries, innovative poetries written in relation to computer media, are key to any assessment of late-twentieth-century formally innovative poetry. What has been brought to the public view since 1970 in American e-poetries is a somewhat motley corpus of works scattered across various platforms and media.[1] This state is not surprising considering the disarray that accompanies any shift in writing technology, a situation exacerbated by competition between computer corporations more interested in market share than in the integrity of their software. Nonetheless, e-poetries, which show characteristics of Futurism's concern with the machine, the procedures of Oulipo, the multi-media events of Fluxus, and the material innovations of contemporary meta-semantic innovative poetries, substantively demonstrate that we are well past wondering *when* an electronic poetry will appear: e-poetry has arrived. Indeed, e-poetry affirms that it is *the poet* who is at the front lines of writing in the electronic medium. This chapter is a lab book that presents a typography and analysis of key movements in this new terrain with attention to its significant works and relevant documentary materials.

Early Procedural Poetries

The terrain of e-poetries was first entered with poets investigating the significance of procedure in the generation of poetry texts. This early stage in the evolution of e-poetries, of course, does not require a computer at all. A program simply executes an algorithm, or set of instructions; a set of fixed instructions that spell out a process for generating a work shares a lot in common with a computer program. Procedural works or programmed poetry, then, significantly introduces the algorithmic method to contemporary poetry.

Emmett Williams was an early practitioner of programmed poetry, a concrete poet who worked in numerous media, and one of the founders of Fluxus (along with Jackson Mac Low, George Brecht, Dick Higgins, and Robert Filliou). Though an American, his strongest affinity has been with the European connections of Fluxus, especially the concrete, avant-garde, and performance traditions in Germany (where he has continued to live). "Fluxus . . . with its emphasis on the merging of art and life, on intermedia, and on an ironic relation to the products of consumer culture" might be seen as a significant predecessor to Web writing, especially in its concern with multiple media (Rothenberg and Joris 2:17). Fluxus artists eschewed the idea of the finely crafted "art object" that was static, and they opted instead to make Flux-boxes or Flux-kits, as has been mentioned, boxes that contained instructions for the generation of a work that would be different each time. Procedural works by Williams push the premonitions of Fluxus even further. He produced writing that operated within constraints such as permutation, repetition, minimalism, and adherence to procedure. His *13 Variations* (Cologne: Galerie der Speigel), a poem generated from six words by Gertrude Stein, appeared in 1965. The following year he translated and edited Daniel Spoerri's *An Anecdoted Topography of Chance* (New York: Something Else, 1966), and in 1973, his *A Valentine for Noël: Four Variations on a Scheme* (Barton, VT: Something Else) appeared.

Williams employed his "Ultimate Poem" procedure as early as 1956. How does such a procedural poem begin? Williams explains this theory in 1973 in *A Valentine for Noël* as follows: "The rules of the game are simple: (1) Choose 26 words by chance operations—or however you please. (2) Substitute these 26 words for the 26 letters of the alphabet, to form an alphabet-of-words. (3) Choose a word or phrase (a word or phrase *not* included in the alphabet-of-words) to serve as the title of the poem. (4) For the letters in the title word or phrase substitute the corresponding words from the alphabet-of-words. This operation generates line one of the poem" (quoted in Rothenberg and Joris 2:213). Such a method can easily be seen in terms of programming. It employs standard programming elements such as the array (the "alphabet-of-words"), the algorithm (the simple substitution procedure), and input and output "files" (the alphabet-of-words and the finished poem, respectively). Technically, this "game" is a program that can be executed by hand or easily written for machine execution. The results, such as Williams's "What" (Rothenberg and Joris 2:214), witness the "pure products" (borrowing a phrase from William Carlos Williams) of such a procedure. Such a procedure can work from any alphabet-of-letters and allows an engaging method to re-view language. Using Williams's procedure and title, for example, to generate a poem from my own alphabet of letters would result in the following:

what
Into dew up lark

mango dove lark flight
thrush song into
white shadow
even up dot certain

(Rothenberg and Joris 2:214)

One can immediately begin to see the alphabet-of-words that forms the array for this production or "performance." At a glance it is clear that w = "into," h = "dew," a = "up," and t = "lark"; thus "into" reveals that i = "mango," because the first line in the first stanza ("into") is composed of "mango dove lark flight." Such a use of procedure is a key to programmed poetry. Williams defined an early practice that still has immense resonance.

Before looking at computer-aided works, we must position this activity in relation to the procedural works of the critically important French endeavor, Oulipo. Oulipo is an acronym for Ouvroir de Littérature Potentielle (Workshop for Potential Literature), a workshop founded in 1960 by novelist/mathematician Raymond Queneau and poet/chess master François Le Lionnais to explore the possibilities of incorporating mathematical structures into literary creation. The goal of Oulipo is to investigate "artificial restriction in literature," a term that means "a constraining method or system or rule that is capable of precise definition" (Queneau et al. ix–x). In terms of restriction, the Oulipian sees "not limitations but *potentiality*, an apparent paradox that tends to disappear when such methods are actually put into practice: restriction then becomes the mother of literary invention" (x). It should be noted that this practice does eschew writing's aleatory potentialities, choosing instead to focus on the author's ability to overcome restriction. In this sense, such restriction does not problemmatize authorial intention to the same extent as other procedural practices do. Nonetheless, Oulipian invention provides a rigorous investigation of the program as a generative agent in the literary work, and its methods provide a useful reference point for considering algorithmic generation of poetry.

In poetry practice in the United States, Jackson Mac Low's use of chance-operational and deterministic methods is extraordinarily interesting.[2] Widely considered the most important experimental poet of his time, Mac Low has since 1954 often used chance and deterministic methods. After June 1989, some have been computer automated.[3] (Mac Low's reading-through system probably influenced John Cage's very significant "mesostic writing-through" text-selection procedures, begun in the late 1960s.)

Though the focus here is on Mac Low's use of deterministic methods and computer programs, he has written in many other ways. These include traditional deliberate and "intuitive" writing, "liminal gathering" (the poems in *Twenties: 100 Poems* [New York: Roof, 1991], and the presently unpublished *154 Forties*), and several types of nonintentional writing other than chance-operational and deterministic methods, such as "impulse-chance" writing, and composing texts by using several systems in tandem, such as chance methods, deterministic methods, and revision or "mining" of the results of the latter (including some of *Barnesbook* and many of the poems in his ongoing poem series *Stein*). He has also composed musical and verbal-musical works in many different ways. The focus on one aspect of his work in this essay is not meant to underplay the diversity of his methods, his rationale for which has changed through the years. Mac Low has written, "I consider theories as mere scaffoldings that help artists make works and that they are subject to discard as often as helpful or necessary" ("Re: 'Aleatoric'"). However, a look at his deterministic methods for writing poetry is relevant to this survey: Mac Low calls these methods (as well as chance procedures) "nonintentional" in that "the author cannot predict what will be drawn from a source text, but 'deterministic'" in that the result (before revision, if any) will be the same every time the process is carried out correctly with the same source and "seed" texts (*Barnesbook* 47). (By contrast, chance systems give a different result each time.)

As to "seeds," Mac Low writes: "Most of these [diastic] methods use a 'seed' or 'index' word or phrase that is spelled out by reading through a source text to find words that have, successively, the seed's letters in corresponding places" (*Barnesbook* 47–48). The seed is an indexing tool, but more important, it is a linguistic element that becomes embedded in the text, stitching elements from the source text together to create a new work from those elements. Of Mac Low, Cage commented: "That way of working that he calls 'seed,' using a seed, is extraordinary because it means a letter is not only a letter but a place in the text. So a word is not only a word but is a series of letters in the proper places. When you work that way, it is so detailed. It's much more detailed than anything I would think of doing with words" (Retallack, *Musicage* 154).

Mac Low has employed two groups of deterministic methods, acrostic and diastic, both of which he mistakenly thought until the 1990s were kinds of chance operations, rather than deterministic ones. He now calls them acrostic reading-through text-selection and diastic reading-through text selection. Given the importance of Mac Low's work, a detailed survey of his major works would usefully inform our consideration of the field of digital poetics.

In writing the poems in *Stanzas for Iris Lezak* in May–October 1960, he read through source texts—whatever he happened to be reading at the time—drawing words, phrases, sentences, and so forth, which begin with the letters of the seeds. (Usually the seed was the source text's, and his poem's, title.) Often chance operations decided which linguistic unit(s) should be drawn from the source; however, in writing the numbered *Asymmetries* in October 1960–61 he used acrostic reading-through text selection as follows: "Usually an initial word was found in a text (or [rarely] in the environment) and words (or strings) having its letters as their initial letters were then found by reading along in the text (or by careful perception of the environment). After the first line, the initial letters of the words or strings of which acrostically 'spelled out' the first word, words beginning with the second and subsequent letters of the first word were found to begin the second and subsequent lines, and these words were spelled out in those lines" (*Representative* 106).

His "Daily Life" methods (1963–64) start with preparation of a sentence list of which each sentence corresponds to a letter and a number. This may be used either deterministically (with a seed word or phrase, as described below) or chance-operationally (with random digits or playing cards).

He devised and began using diastic reading-through text selection in January 1963 ("Diastic" = Gk. *dia*, through + *stichos*, verse line, on analogy with "acrostic"). In using it, one reads through a source text and takes into the target text (output) words, word fragments, phrases, or sentences (any linguistic unit from a single word to several pages) having the letters of a seed or index text in the positions they occupied in that text. Mac Low has been using diastic methods intermittently since 1963.

In 1964 he wrote *The Pronouns—A Collection of 40 Dances—For the Dancers* diastically, using as source text a pack of index cards on which were typed "ing" action phrases derived by chance operations from the Basic English List. The seed text for each poem was one of these phrases, which was then spelled out diastically by phrases found subsequently in the pack. The phrases were turned into sentences having as subjects "forty pronouns (and pronoun-like nouns) . . . the same pronoun throughout each poem" (Clay and Phillips 142).

Mac Low composed the "PFR-3 Poems" on a computerized programmable film reader (PFR-3), a group of devices including a minicomputer, at Information International in Los Angeles in 1969 as part of the Art and Technology Program of the Los Angeles County Museum of Art. From lists of words, phrases, or sentences entered by Mac Low, the computer selected and permuted items, showing resulting lines or line groups on a monitor and printing out every tenth line or group.

In making "A Vocabulary for Custer LaRue" (1978), he drew words by chance operations from a list of 202 words spelled solely with the letters of that name. He made similar lists for each of his "Vocabularies," most of which are large word-drawings, drawing and placing words from the lists by various methods. For the room-sized "Vocabulary for Annie Brigitte Gilles Tardos" the list included 5,000 items, groups of which were output from a computer and incorporated by hand into sentences on wall-sized, oil-stick paintings. Other such sentences were typed, hand composed, and printed on colored transparent-acetate sheets placed over the room's windows.

He used a diastic method in 1976–77 to write *The Virginia Woolf Poems*

(1985), whose first section was "Ridiculous in Piccadilly": "After finding the title phrase . . . , I drew one word for each of its letters. Beginning with the phrase itself, I culled only words in which the letters occupied corresponding positions . . . "*r*idiculous P*i*ccadilly.// en*d* stai*n*/ book*c*ase,/ reass*u*ring brutal*l*y/ eatingho*u*se.// waitresse*s*,/" (*Virginia* n.p.).

In 1980–81 Mac Low wrote the last three works in *Bloomsday* (1984) "with the aid of systematic-chance [and deterministic] operations" (*Bloomsday* 11). In 1981–83 he used the "words-nd-ends variant" of diastic selection to draw out words and letter groups while reading through Ezra Pound's *Cantos* to compose *Words nd Ends from Ez* (1989). This work constitutes an important reading of Pound. Charles Bernstein notes that "Mac Low's 'objective' text-generating procedure foregrounds much of the 'free play' that remains the most salient feature of *The Cantos* by systemizing the Pound 'error' that Pound only quixotically pursued or permitted," a statement that indicates the critical potential of systematic works (*My* 165). Mac Low also used the words-nd-ends variant of diastic to write *Wörter nd Enden aus Goethe/Words nd Ends from Goethe* (produced as a Hörspiel for four speakers at Westdeutscher Rundfunk Köln in 1986).

Mac Low's "Pieces o' Six XXXII" (*Kurt Schwitters Almanach 1987* [Köln] 85–91; *Pieces o' Six* [1992] 168–75) was derived by "impulse-chance selection" from two books on Schwitters that include some of his writings, titles, and so forth. That poem became also "1st Merzgedicht in Memoriam Kurt Schwitters" (*42*, 1–5). After that Mac Low used random-number chance operations to draw linguistic units from it and its sources to make 29 more "Merz poems" (1987–89). In June 1989 Prof. Charles O. Hartman of Connecticut College, New London, sent him Diastext, a computer program automating an early diastic method that Mac Low largely abandoned after 1963 and that used the whole source text as the seed text. Later in 1989 Hartman sent him Diastex2, 3, and 4, which allow the use of a seed other than the source text, producing output less repetitious than that of Diastext, and Travesty, a program by Hugh Kenner and Joseph O'Rourke that selects words from source texts by a complex method utilizing, as Kenner explains, "English letter-combination frequencies . . . to produce random text that mimics the frequencies found in a sample" (*42*, ix). Travesty was first published in *Byte* magazine in 1984 (see discussion below of Hartman and Kenner's *Sentences*). Mac Low used Diastext, Diastex4, and/or Travesty to make the last twelve Merzgedicht. He also used a deterministic letter-to-pitch-class "translation" procedure to turn the "22nd Merzgedicht" into a ten-page musical score printed at the end of the book.

The source texts of the four poems in *Barnesbook* (1996, written 1989) were chance-operationally selected and mixed sentences from five works by Djuna Barnes, different sentences and mixes for each poem. Each mix was run through Diastext and the output was revised, slightly for the first three, extensively for the last.

His poem-series-in-progress, *Stein* (begun mid-April 1998) uses substantial passages from works by Gertrude Stein as source texts and others, from paragraphs to several pages, as seed texts.[4] Mac Low's meticulous use of interwoven methods is remarkable. For example, "See Them Together (Stein 59)" is composed of "Nine strophes in which the number of lines/sentences in successive strophes comprise the ascending and truncatedly descending Lucas sequence 1, 3, 4, 7, 11, 18, 11, 7, followed by a one-line coda" (Mac Low, *See*). Its source is a section of Stein's "Pink Melon Joy" selected by chance operations utilizing the Rand Corporation's random-digit table. Mac Low notes, "The order of the source passage's paragraphs was newly randomized by random-digit chance operations, then long paragraphs were broken into shorter ones, the new ones were given random numbers, and the whole series of numbered paragraphs was randomized again. After that the reordered passage was run through Diastex5, Prof. Charles O. Hartman's most recent automation of one of my diastic text-selection procedures, using as 'seed' a paragraph from Stein's *Long Gay Book*" (Mac Low, *See*).

As explained above, the "seed" is a text "spelled out" with words having the seed-words' letters in corresponding positions. To reach the final poem Mac Low modified the procedure's output by turning it into normative sentences, which became verse lines that were grouped into strophes by the number sequence. (Some poems in the *Stein* series are syntactically normalized; others are not.) "See Them Together" shows the rich complexity and levels of intricacy attainable through methodical use of such systems.

Mac Low's work, then, can be seen as opening numerous fields of activity and as developing these to produce extended, well-conceived, literary works. His consistent, methodical exploration of deterministic approaches to text generation is singular and immensely informative to the field of digital poetics.

Recent Procedural and Computer-Generated Works

Procedural poetry has been undertaken by numerous groups of poets interested in innovative poetries. Such an interest in method can be seen in Louis Zukofsky's *80 Flowers* and John Cage's *Roaratorio*, five mesostic *Writings Through Finnegans Wake*, and many other poems. It has also been evident in other recent innovative practices, including Ron Silliman's use of the Fibonnaci series in *Tjanting* and Lyn Hejinian's use of a specific number of textual units for her autobiographical long poem *My Life*. (Subsequent editions affirmed the centrality of procedure. The first edition contained 37 sections, one for each year of her age at the time, with each section containing 37 sentences. For the second edition, eight years later, she not only increased the number of sections to 45, but also added eight sentences to each one. Thus, though it meant altering her text, more important was the consistency of the procedure to an accurate second edition. Accordingly, *My Life*'s third edition will contain sixty sections of sixty sentences.) Marjorie

Perloff discusses these works, as well as those of the French group Oulipo, in "The Return of the (Numerical) Repressed," a chapter of her *Radical Artifice*. Her discussion of the difference between predetermined poetic form and predetermined procedure is very useful. In discussing the latter in the context of George Perec's *Life: A User's Manual*, she also introduces the interesting notion of "deliberate imperfection" or "Lucretian clinamen—an error or bend" (*Radical* 144).

The issue of the clinamen does foreground the complication of the fact that the author is part of the process from beginning to end and that the design of any such project can never be "neutral." Even with computer-generated texts, though the program determines the generated text, the programmer chooses the input data and the procedure to be used. John Cage comments: "If I used chance, the question then would be formed in such a way that my choice would be evident. At some point in that task, I would have to express my choice" (Retallack, *Musicage* 156). Mac Low also makes this point: "The very devising of methods must involve the author's taste at certain points, even if as many decisions as possible are made by asking questions to be answered by an objectively hazardous oracle or by employing deterministic . . . nonintentional procedures" (*Barnesbook* 51). For many writers who employ procedure, the output provides significant additional opportunities for authorial engagement. Mac Low comments: "The fact that Charles O. Hartman has automated some of my diastic text-selection methods seems to free me to interact with his programs' outputs in other ways than those required by my 'nucleic' methods [writing freely between procedurally given 'nucleus words'] . . . Nonintentional operations and intuition seem to be made for each other!" (*Barnesbook* 51–52). He also notes that "in writing the poems in the 'Stein' series—from April 1998 on—I work closely but intuitively with [a] procedure's output to make the final sentences of the poem" (Mac Low, "Re: My Article").

Clearly, there is no suggestion that a program will ever do everything; rather, a program realizes one textual event in the exploration of the material possibilities of the work at hand. As Mac Low continues, "Like the seemingly senseless [Zen] *koan*, the products of nonintentional selective or generative procedures may stimulate intuition to leaps it might never otherwise dare. . . . [T]he obscurely manifold resources of the individual mind, when called upon directly as well as obliquely, produce a 'richer' poetry" (52). Thus a deterministically produced text may be developed in concert with any number of other methods, including varying degrees of authorial intervention, rule-guided and/or intentional, to produce the final work. Given the potential for alteration of such a text, the author must decide how to annotate the process of writing the text. Such an annotation must make clear what constituted the procedure, what deviations were made from it, and/or how the output was edited. Deviations can be documented in a footnote or endnote or using internal annotation typical of programs and HTML mark-up. In these cases, comment lines are used to provide metatextual information. The degree to which a deviation is known or described is entirely up to the writer, but the annotation offers additional "writing" space that can be effectively employed.

A significant publishing event in computer-generated writing was the appearance in 1995 of *Sentences*, a poem series by Charles O. Hartman and Hugh Kenner. In the words of Kenner, "A deterministic process (a chain of computer programs) generated *Sentences* with minimal human interference, after crucial human decisions" (Hartman and Kenner 77). *Sentences* was made by sending the 3,250-word source text *Sentences for Analysis and Parsing at the Thayer Street Grammar School* (Providence, c. 1870), probably by Samuel S. Green, through Travesty fourteen times, each time specifying a different "order" of Travesty (roughly, the number of characters in its initial sequence). Each Travesty was run through Diastext to produce the fourteen poems. The "human decisions" were the choice of the source texts, the programs to send it through, and the elimination of "nonwords" in the Travesties. As Kenner explains: "You supply Travesty with an 'Order'; if the order is 4, it seeks out every occurrence of the initial 4-character sequence and records the character that comes after. It then chooses at random from its notepad one character to append, moves forward one place, repeats the whole process" (Hartman and Kenner 77).

In Kenner's description of the process, one can see the close parallels with the procedures of Emmett Williams, Oulipo, and others. However, though using a computer, Hartman and Kenner's partially deterministic process may be less disciplined than its non-automated predecessors because the authors intervene in the generation of the text in several ways, as explained in Kenner's detailed afterword to the book. Interestingly, the final step for the output file is to run it through a second program, Diastext, a program by Hartman that performs a machine-execution of one of Mac Low's earliest methods for diastic writing. (This is a system that uses the whole source text as its seed, a method Mac Low himself seldom employed after early 1963, as explained above.) It seems curious that *Sentences* was ultimately produced for paper publication, as was Hartman's *Virtual Muse: Experiments in Computer Poetry* (1996).

Virtual Muse is written in the mode of a personal essay and recounts Hartman's philosophical and aesthetic experiences using computers to generate poetry, especially the MacProse program. The introduction to his book gives a loose but interesting history of computerized poetry and the volume also includes numerous poetry texts generated by Hartman. The book's limitation may be its attempt to graft an already outmoded ideal of modernist style onto computerized poetry; the book employs the computer as a form of innovative practice, but the resultant text appears contrary to innovative practice. This bias is illuminated by Thomas Disch's statement about Hartman's book used in the book's Web advertising. He writes that Hartman "writes graceful, jargon-free prose on a subject that often—especially in the hands of the 'language poets' and their apologists—inspires only cant and obfuscation. Hartman is the Amerigo Vespucci of a whole new intellectual territory, and Virtual Muse is a map worth studying" (Disch). Disch's out-of-context disparagement of Language Poetry leads one to believe that a subtext does exist for this undertaking, as do comments Hartman makes.[5] For example, Hartman writes that "by actually programming the computer to help to select and manipulate words, we can probe, even more intimately than with hypertext, into the poet's and reader's relation to language" (*Virtual* 5). With this statement Hartman seems to suggest that there might be some universal relation to language, an idealized position to write from. Nonetheless *Virtual Muse* offers an extensive treatment of this subject. *Sentences* and *Virtual Muse* are two of about one dozen cataloged works in this genre published worldwide since the 1970s;[6] they are certainly the two most relevant to this study because they are the major works in English and because of their authors' careful explanations of methodology.

Finally, computer-less procedures such as those used variously above (programs that can be run without a machine) continue to be of interest to contemporary poets. Particularly of note are Charles Bernstein's "Experiments" page at the Electronic Poetry Center, a resource compiled in 1996 (based on an earlier version by Bernadette Mayer).[7] "Experiments" lists over 60 experiments, including homolinguistic, homophonic, and lexical translation, acrostic chance, "Tzara's hat," "Burrough's Fold in" and other cut-ups, substitution procedures, serial sentences, alphabet poems, alliteration, doubling, collaboration, attention, counting, list, chronology, and other writing exercises. Bernadette Mayer also maintains a long list of poetry-generating situations, propositions, and possibilities in "Bernadette Mayer's Writing Experiments," also available on the Web, as indicated in the preceding note.

Electronic Formats

What for example—of file formats?
in the ship's hulk—deserting rats?
java pipo pipes up download—frases
Adobe Acrobat™—dances with elvis . . .
—Loss Pequeño Glazier, *Uniform*

Though some of the works previously mentioned use programming to produce texts, it is interesting to note that in most cases the final output is circulated in the codex format. (Significant exceptions to this do exist. For example, Jackson Mac Low is presently publishing a number of his "Stein" works on the Web; he and numerous other poets have also circulated a number of works on audio CD.) Many other authors are, however, presently writing directly for the monitor. Works designed for or delivered via the computer monitor seem destined to provide a significant addition to the future corpus of e-poetry, floppy disks, CD-Roms, and Web-based productions among these. A significant body of writing already appears on these formats.

Magnetic Media

Two important publishers of literary and related magnetic media publications are Voyager and Eastgate Systems.[8] Voyager is the more commercial of these, publishing a wide array of titles in all disciplines, with a handful of interesting but important literary titles, such as *The Beat Experience* (New York: Voyager, 1995), *Understanding McLuhan* (New York: Voyager, 1996), and *Poetry in Motion* edited by Ron Mann (New York: Voyager, 1994). *Poetry in Motion* includes works by Ted Berrigan, Charles Bukowski, William S. Burrows, John Cage, Robert Creeley, the Four Horsemen, Allen Ginsberg, Michael McClure, Anne Waldman, and others. The production of *Poetry in Motion* is excellent; it provides a well-heeled exemplar of hypertextual and multi-media employed for the straightforward presentation of works by, and commentaries on, literary authors. One drawback is of course that the volume of the material provided is limited by the capacity of a CD-ROM. Further Voyager's use of technology, though a skillful demonstration of a conservative economy of multimedia, by no means provides any far-reaching lessons in innovative applications of technology.

Eastgate Systems, in the business of marketing hypertext on magnetic media, is probably best known for the much-lauded interactive fiction titles it has published, including *Afternoon, A Story* by Michael Joyce, and Stuart Moulthrop's *Victory Garden. Afternoon* is widely regarded as "the first commercial literary hypertext" (Koskimaa).[9] Robert Coover called *Afternoon* "a graceful and provocative work . . . utterly essential to an understanding of this new art form" (Coover). This quote typifies Eastgate's efforts, for, according to its Web page, it considers itself the publisher of "serious hypertext, fiction and non-fiction."[10] Eastgate's emphasis is on what it calls the "craft" of hypertext; this "craft" is achieved in the Eastgate model through a careful control of links and the use of visual structures to map paths. (Eastgate also describes itself as a creator of new hypertext technologies; it has in part made its name from the marketing of the hypertext-authoring tool Storyspace, a program that facilitates such an approach to hypertext authoring.) Eastgate's catalog is a carefully curated list of what they consider "serious" hypertext or, in the case of *Twilight*, writing characterized by "extraordinary beauty and fragility and intelligence" (Maso). Their list includes work by Deena Larsen, Michael Joyce, Stuart Moulthrop, and J. Yellowlees Douglas, as well as David Kolb's *Socrates in the Labyrinth*. Samples of *Victory Garden* and Deena Larsen's *Marble Springs* are available at the Eastgate Web site. In the poetry category, Eastgate lists Robert Kendall's *A Life Set for Two*, Judith Kerman's *Mothering*, Deena Larsen's *Marble Springs*, and Rob

Swigart's *Directions*. Of special note are the important works by Jim Rosenberg, *Intergrams* and *The Barrier Frames Diffractions Through*. Unfortunately, some of these are only available for the Macintosh platform (running under HyperCard), a clear limitation for the reception of this work.[11] Rosenberg's poetic texts explore the possibilities for a theoretically based poetic expression. Michael Joyce has commented that Rosenberg creates "new poetic textuality that is quite literally not reproducible in this older one" ("Nonce" 593). Of greatest note is the work of Rosenberg, whose poems, indeed, are not reproducible in the previous medium; they are multi-layered, dense, interrelated webs that provide a linguistic depth not often seen in any other hypertextual undertakings. In Joyce's words: "His poems flicker and focus from a dark sea of blurred and overprinted language as the mouse moves over their surfaces, clearing suddenly into discernable patches, like the backs of golden carp rising briefly to sunlight in a dark pool or floating into focus like the fortune-cookie scraps of text of the old prognostic eightballs. No sooner do they snap into clarity than with the least movement they are lost again and again as soon as they are gained" ("Nonce" 593). Rosenberg's investigation of hypertext as syntax may be one of the most valuable investigations currently under way in hypertext poetry.

A significant CD publishing event occurred in 1995 with the appearance of the special multimedia *The Little Magazine, Volume 21* (subtitled "The Egg of Thought Becoming Human"). This publication, edited by graduate students in the English Department, SUNY Albany, is of course dwarfed by the much larger operations of Voyager and Eastgate. This CD-ROM, however, must be recognized for its outstanding and wide-ranging explorations of the multimedia environment; in fact, this issue of *The Little Magazine* clearly marked the cutting edge of experimental poetry's engagement with digital technology. Importantly, there is a marked anti-business tone to this volume as its poetics manage to be non-elitist, non-commercial, experimental, and daring at the same time. It is clear that language is being explored in this volume, language seen through the prism of the experimental. Norman Weinstein explains: "*The Little Magazine*, Volume 21 is worlds removed from . . . genteel and oh-so tasteful literary atmospheres . . . promoting instead cutting-edge writing calling forth novel uses of digital technology. Simply stated, this is writing taking risks, displayed with audio and visual art of a very high order" (60). Weinstein suggests that "limitless plasticity" of the words in *The Little Magazine* show that "digital media offer equally fluid and mutable forms of audio/visual data to amplify the ever-changing nature of literary experience" (61). The list of authors included in this CD-ROM is impressive; it includes Charles Bernstein, Lee Ann Brown, Nathaniel Tarn, Jackson Mac Low, Anne Tardos, Nathaniel Mackey, and Robert Grenier, among its list of over seventy contributors. This experimentation was continued by *The Little Magazine, Volume 22, Gravitational Intrigue: An Anthology of Emergent Hypermedia*, an excellent anthology that includes such notables as Stuart Moulthrop, the Critical Arts Ensemble, Eduardo Kac, Christy Sheffield Sanford, Mark Amerika, Tabetha Dunn, and Komninos Zervos.

New Media Poetries

The term "New Media poetries" refers to poetries that do not employ the medium of the book (or more properly the codex): this includes holo-gram pieces,[12] works in programmable media, and video or non-print works. (Due to their relation to procedural poetries, works in programmable media are examined separately here.) Eduardo Kac defines "New Media Poetry" in his introduction to the *Visible Language* issue on New Media Poetry as po-etry that "pushes language into dimensions of verbal experience not seen thus far" ("Introduction" 99). In addition, Kac explains that "the work of [such poets] takes language beyond the confines of the printed page and explores a new syntax made of linear and non-linear animation, hyperlinks, interactivity, real-time text generation, spatio-temporal discontinuities, self-similarity, synthetic spaces, immateriality, diagrammatic relations, visual tempo, multiple simultaneities, and many other innovative procedures" ("In-troduction" 99). Kac's work provides a good introduction to new media poetry. On his Web site (http://www.ekac.org, 1 March 1999), he divides his own work into the following categories: "Performances," "Mixed Media" (works in photography, artist's books, graffiti, and public installations), "Holopoetry" (the word projected into the fourth dimension), "Telecom-munications Events" (work using telephones, videotext, fax, live TV, satellites, slow-scan TV, computers, videophones, and modems"), "Multimedia" (hypertext, digital video, looped animations, VRML), "Interactive Works" (telepresence, biological, and telematic event-installations), and his projects "The Erratum Series" and "Telepresence Art" (the Ornitorrinco Project). Kac's Web site is also an important resource for new media poetry. It pro-vides not only numerous examples of Kac's holopoems, performances, telecommunications, and visual works but also a wealth of documentary ma-terial including interviews and essays, such as "Recent Experiments in Holopoetry and Computer Holopoetry," "On the Notion of Art as a Visual Dialogue," "Holopoetry, Hypertext, Hyperpoetry," and "Telepresence Art."

Kac's poetic works push textuality into other realms of experience. A good example of this lies in Kac's considerable oeuvre of holopoems, holo-textual works displayed in three-dimensional space, works that change according to time and the viewer's position in relation to the text. Kac explains that the holopoem is "a spatio-temporal event: it evokes thought processes and not their result" ("Holopoetry" 186). The holopoem "Adhuc" (shown from six different points of view on Kac's Web page), for instance, is "an example of the complex discontinuities that structure the syntax of . . . holopoems" ("Holopoetry: Complete"). In it, letters and words seem to drift into the distance, superimposed on each other, eerily suspended in a spherical mist, or atmosphere, the color of which varies from red, green, yellow, and blue, depending on the viewer's position. Words that are readable include "whenever," "ever" and "or never," reaffirming the temporal nature of the piece and the fact that the text is not fixed. About "Adhuc" Kac notes that "all the words refer to time in varying ways, contributing to an overall vagueness that could resist assessment at first sight. The muddled interference patterns that blend with the words help to create an atmosphere of uncertainty, not only concerning the visibility of the words but also about the meanings they produce" ("Recent"). Kac has also noted that "the complex technology of 'holographic art' erases its author and its referent; what matters is that it works, not that it points to something outside itself. Its contents seem strangely unmotivated, strangely out of key with the technical sophistication of its mechanisms . . ." ("Photonic"), an observation that informs a reading of this piece.

"Astray in Deimos" (three views of which are shown on Kac's Web page) illustrate other aspects unique to holopoetry: "fluidity of the verbal sign and semantic interpolation, i.e., mutability of the actual topology of words in space leading to changes in meaning" (Kac, "Holopoetry"). The letters in this work appear as hand-scratched representations of three-dimensional block letters, varying in darkness and readability, on a luminous green circle. (This circle is superimposed on a half-blue, half-red tie-die appearing backdrop.) The letters have a kind of empty solidity (solid because they are three-dimensional but empty because they are transparent), and they seem to refuse to express lexical meaning, though the words "eerie mist" seem to emerge at times. Other works evoke a wide array of qualities. "Havoc" is like a vortex, or galaxy, the text spinning into waves of unreadability as they spiral in brilliant flares of color. "Zero," by contrast, presents rigid, solid letters, boldly determining a three-dimensional axis, askew against black space. Of "Zero" Kac comments, "words grow or shrink, or turn and break . . . to express the drama of an identity crisis in a future world. Rotations, fusions and other actions make the words emphasize their relations and meanings in space. The multiplicity of 'Selfs' that would be inexorable with the proliferation of cloning is the ultimate theme of the poem, but for a more attentive reader the answer for the enigma could be found in words residing in other words" ("Recent"). Such works explore completely new textual possibilities and relations, and clearly define new relations between technology and writing.

Web-based/Networked E-poetry Libraries

The Web is a powerful tool for the circulation of poetry. Although there are millions of poetry sites on the Web (Alta Vista lists 3,257,560 Web sites for "poetry,"[13] a few more sites than one might reasonably be able to peruse), the sites profiled in this section are sites that show a "larger" vision. These are sites providing a substantial body of work from multiple authors and/or sites advocating a larger literary project. This excludes single-author sites and sites for most individual magazines. This is not intended to be a definitive list but a list that provides various exemplia of interesting, innovative, and visionary poetry web building, as available at this writing.

Grist On-Line Magazine (GOL), appearing in October 1993, was one of the first poetry sites that appeared on the Internet.[14] GOL reincarnated an earlier venture, the print magazine *Grist*, which appeared from 1964 to 1969, a similarly vibrant period in alternative publishing. The print version of *Grist* included such poets as d.a. levy, Ted Berrigan, and Ron Padgett, poets associated with the era of the mimeo magazine. GOL set out to be more than just a magazine, however; for it consciously sought to create an archive for both earlier and current work and to issue a number of works as electronic chapbooks. The digital GOL presents work by numerous innovative writers including Ron Silliman, Jackson Mac Low (reprints), and Anne Tardos. Besides its online magazine, GOL has housed The Abington Book Shop, Cyanobacteria Publications, *Anabasis, Room Temperature*, and Light & Dust Poets. The last of these is another site that bears some comment.

Light & Dust Poets presents a valuable library of online texts through its main index.[15] This index begins with a list of authors and works by author, followed by a list of other resources. The author pages include a great diversity of poets, such as bpNichol, Michael McClure, Larry Eigner, Robert Grenier, Alexi Kruchonykh, d.a. levy, Jackson Mac Low, David UU, and many others. (An excellent selection of Kruchonykh's visual works are presented here.) Young's site also has included "Group Efforts," *Kaldron* (a visual poetry magazine), the International Shadows Project Retrospectives, a selection of author pages, pages for specific movements (Lettriste, Australian visual poets, Chicano), some criticism, "Multiple Views," and reviews. Some of the anthologies compile personal selections rather than representative lists. It is crucial to note that numerous resources, particularly essays, reviews, commentary, and visual poetry at this site can only be accessed from this secondary list. (This is not necessarily obvious.) The d.a. levy section, for example, is an excellent resource and contains a number of complete books, many of them out-of-print and some published here for the first time.

Another distinguished effort is Luigi-Bob Drake's "CybpherAnthology of Discontiguous Literature,"[16] a component of his Burning Press Web site, an "in-process attempt to locate community(s) among various online writing projects" (Drake, "Burning"). Drake has created a communal resource by compiling materials from the following interesting electronic publishing efforts: Jake Berry's *The Experioddicist* magazine and online chapbooks; *Juxta Online*, edited by Ken Harris and Jim Leftwich; Tom Taylor's *Anabasis;* Peter Ganick's *Potepoetzine* and *Potepoettext* projects; and Kenneth Sherwood and my *RIF/T* magazine and electronic chapbooks. A terrific service that the site provides is a cumulative author index to the collective contents of these publications, providing a kind of "people's" *Readers Guide*. Other types of indexes and additional magazines may be provided in the future, but as it stands, this is a valuable resource. Further, Drake has a very clear vision of the purpose of this site. Emphasizing the "anthology"[17] in "Cybpher-Anthology," he points to other anthologies based on magazines (Clayton Eshelman's *A Caterpillar Anthology*, Cid Corman's *The Gist of Origin*, and Andrews and Bernstein's *The L=A=N=G=U=A=G=E Book*) and institutions (Black Mountain College and the NuYoRican Cafe) as being able to define communities of poets. These, he notes, stand in opposition to more traditional, canonizing anthologies. As to the importance of little magazines and their role in his site, Drake notes the following:

> Electronic & otherwise, [it] seems to me that zines, as active instruments of community(s), simultaneously structure and reflect socially constructed grouping . . . a shared culture being used here, provisionally, as a defining characteristic of community. Recognizing that, this project aims to collect & index a body of works which collectively may constitute such a culture/apparatus. That collection & distribution is here facilitated by online technologies, which suggests one possible . . . approach to the material: how, or to what extent, the underlying community formation is influenced by that technology. (Drake, "CybpherAnthology").

The CybpherAnthology is an effort that provides a considerable body of poetry texts. In addition to the CybpherAnthology, Drake's Burning Press site also includes the Wr-eye-tings Scratchpad (a "laboratory" for Web-based intermedia), Machine Made of Words (online visual literature and audio art), *TapRoot Reviews* (Drake's impressive series of reviews and annotated entries for literary small presses, Web sites, and ASCII publications), "InYrEar: Performance and Sound poetries," "Cleveland Poetries," and the invaluable Text Worx Toolshed, discussed later.

The Coach House Books Web site,[18] operating from Toronto, is an extraordinary project. Coach House has been one of the most important presses for innovative writing for many years. Rather than simply serving as a publisher's site, however, its Web site is pushing the possibilities of publishing and the Web. It makes full-text copies of some of its books available, including such important works as bpNichol's *Martyrology*, Steve McCaffery's *Carnival*, Darren Wershler-Henry's *Nicholodeon*, Victor Coleman's *Letter Drop*, Paul Dutton's *Aurealities*, and Alan Halsey and Karen Mac Cormack's *Fit to Print*. In addition, the Coach House Books site is undertaking a number of other projects. These include the "bpNichol Project" (destined to be a definitive repository of work by and information about bpNichol), bpNichol's *Borders*, "Digital Ephemera" (digital projects that will be available for a short time then disappear), the CHB "Earchives" (in conjunction with UbuWeb's Sound Poetry resources, an effort to make a wide selection of Canadian sound poetry available), "Print Ephemera" (bringing back on-screen Coach House's postcards, posters, and other ephemera from the 1960s and '70s), and "Post2Cards" (a facility with which the user can send an e-mail postcard to others). The Coach House site also includes a link to Prose & Contexts, a site by the designer of the Coach House site. As well as providing links to a small number of allied small presses, Prose & Context's page offers links to a number of its literary and commercial projects. These include "Project X 1497–1999," a poetry-multimedia Web site exploring "discovery, technology and colonialism through Vasco da Gama" ("Prose & Contexts"), and "Sensory Deprivation," the online version of Damian Lopes's collection of visual poetry. These sites are designed to explore and challenge the medium of the Web, using frames, JavaScript, dynamic fonts, and style sheets, and are all worth considerable examination. It should be noted that good equipment and higher speed connections are preferable for viewing these materials.

Launched in 1996, Kenneth Goldsmith's Ubuweb: Visual, Concrete, and Sound Poetry (named after the Alfred Jarry's Pere Ubu character in *Ubu Roi*, the first absurdist drama) is a resource of immense importance in the 90s exploration of the Web's potential as a literary space.[19] Ubuweb, a far-reaching and excellently curated Web resource, has amassed more than 8,000 files totaling four gigabytes of experimental writing and performance. It contains the major sections, "Historical," "Contemporary," "Sound Poetry," "Papers," and "Found + Insane." These categories appear in a new, easy-to-use interface inaugurated in 2000. Ubu's "Papers" section offers crucial essays and bibliographies about concrete, visual, and experimental poetries, and Ubu's list of links (under the pull-down menu "Resources" then "Links") provides an insightful and eclectic selection of supplementary materials. The "Historical" section contains seminal authors such as Guillaume Apollinaire, John Cage, Henri Chopin, Augusto de Campos, Haroldo de Campos, Ian Hamilton Finlay, Philip Guston, Václav Havel, bpNichol, Kurt Schwitters, Emmett Williams, and Louis Zukofsky, as well as a section of "Early Visual Poetry 1506–1726." This section provides an excellent primer of experimental poetry.

In "Sound Poetry" the site provides a plethora of varied and compelling audio works by such poets/performers as Apollinaire, Cage, Augusto de Campos, Chopin, Jean Cocteau, Marcel Duchamp, Brion Gysin, Wyndham Lewis, Jackson Mac Low, F. T. Marinetti, Schwitters, Cecil Taylor, and Edwin Torres. Goldsmith's in-depth knowledge of the field, exhibited by the selections he makes in his historical and sound sections, gives him a unique qualification to make choices for his "Contemporary" section. Here you find Bruce Andrews, Susan Bee, Charles Bernstein, Jake Berry, John Cayley, Johanna Drucker, Dick Higgins, Peter Jaeger, Bill Luoma, Spencer Selby, Torres, Darren Wershler-Henry, Jody Zellen, Komninos Zervos, Janet Zweig, and others.

The contemporary section is the most interesting from the point of view of the impact of technology on textual practice, because works here almost certainly have been created with computers. (Though admittedly, a number of works were remediated, simply transferred print versions to screen format.) Cayley's "From the Shadoof Home Page" presents six different stills of program-generated work. Johanna Drucker provides four stunning visuals from "The History of The/My Wor(l)d." The texts presented in this section provide an extraordinary range of possibilities for poetry's dialog with digital media. Charles Bernstein provides two texts from "An Mosaic for Convergence" in this section. "Alphabeta" suggests that "many of the most radical features of hypertext were technologies made available by the invention of alphabetic writing and greatly facilitated by the development of printing and bookmaking" ("Alphabeta"). The text appears in a heavy, oversized type (the weight of the alphabetic) that is at odds with a gauze-like background leaping in a multi-colored fête of superimposed, brightly colored, though muted, alphabetic characters; it provides an on-screen visualization of the legacy of type.

Bernstein's other work, "Politics," argues that "For all the utopian promise of technological optimists, the answer is not in our machines but in our politics" ("Politics"). The text of this work consists only of this one cogent observation repeated over a gray background, as if the conciseness of this phrase makes the argument without needing any additional verbiage. Yet each letter in this repeated sentence has a different, often sharply differing color than the letter adjacent to it. The colors of the letters seem to appear in three intensities: some of the letters are a light color, such as silver gray, pink, or white; others are bold, primary colors like red or royal blue; and some of the letters are bright yellow, lime green, or turquoise. It is the juxtaposition of these colors, however, that gives "Politics" a tangible textual depth and almost gleeful sense of movement. These qualities seem to destabilize the idea of a writing "surface" while, at the same time, somehow giving the rather straightforward sentence a sense of cunning omnipresence. Bernstein, known for his work as a poet and essayist, has in fact published a number of visual and typographically oriented works throughout his career, including *Veil* (Madison, WI: Xexoxial Editions, 1987) and such typographically intense poems as "Liftoff" (from *Poetic Justice* [Baltimore: Pod Books, 1979]) and "Erosion Control Area (2)," recently published in *Experimental - Visual - Concrete* (K. David Jackson, Eric Vos, and Johanna Drucker, eds. [Amsterdam: Rodopi, 1996]). The use of color in these works gives us a glimpse of what we may have been missing in the principally black-and-white economy of paper publishing; this dimension points to the often under-acknowledged fact that color is a valuable contribution electronic writing makes via the Web.

Goldsmith also makes available important glimpses into the field of computer-created kinetic poetry, one which is integrally related to traditions of visual and experimental poetries, with Wershler-Henry's "Grain: A Prairie Poem" and my "*(Go) Fish.*" "Grain" begins with a single two-part frame on a white background. First, the larger area of the frame, then the smaller area slowly fill with numerous lower case *g*'s (the "grains" in this work). In its second phase, *g*'s stretch from the lower frame and cross the boundary between the two frames. This incursion generates gigantic *g*'s that explode like volcanoes issuing a rain of tiny *g*'s. "*(Go) Fish,*" opening with the comment that "there are more fish than people," provides a stream of fish formed of streaming text, punctuated by occasional graphics of fish, and single piscine nouns in various typographic styles, such as "cod," "roughy," and "herring." These works make tangible certain previously unexplored potentials of visual poetry and demonstrate motion, a potent quality that digital media make available to electronic poetry.

The Electronic Poetry Center (EPC) was one of the earliest sites to appear on the Web ("gopher space" at that time).[20] The EPC grew in tandem with the electronic poetry magazine *RIF/T,* which first appeared in Fall 1993. Once *RIF/T* was published, it became clear than an online repository for poetry was needed. From its inception in June 1994, the EPC was designed to serve as a gateway to resources in electronic poetry and poetics that were related to the interests of the SUNY Buffalo Poetics Program and to the innovative writing community at large. Its goal was, and continues to be, to serve as an archival, classification, and dissemination agency for the literary and critical output of this community. Praised for its extensive content and called by *Publishers Weekly* "one of the largest, most comprehensive poetry resources on the Web" (Reid), the EPC serves several million users a year in over eighty countries (including such widespread locations as Mauritius, Sri Lanka, Cyprus, and Estonia, as well as the major developed and developing nations). It houses numerous resources and also curates lists of selected links to other resources on the Web. EPC resources are organized into its main "author," "magazine," "books," and "sites" libraries. There are about 150 authors in its author list, including such luminaries as Robert Creeley, Charles Bernstein, Susan Howe, Steve McCaffery, Jackson Mac Low, Cecilia Vicuña, Michele Leggott, and others. Author pages are designed to present full texts (not excerpts of their work) along with bibliographic, critical, and biographical information about each writer. These are often supplemented with sound files, visual works, and/or other materials. Its magazine and book lists include electronic publications as well as information about often ephemeral and fugitive small-circulation print poetry resources. Materials contained in these categories make the EPC a library of original and secondary texts, a reference center, and a teaching resource. All materials are delivered electronically and free of charge via the Web. Extensive, highly curated lists of links are included in the magazine, books, sites, and links pages.

The EPC is not only a collection of resources but also operates with the goal of providing a site where the potentials of electronic "writing" are explored. To this end, the EPC hosts special projects, such as the audio art of LINEbreak (a series of half-hour programs of interviews with and performances by a range of innovative writers and artists),[21] and it provides a gallery, sound room, and other resources highlighting specific experiments with nonprint poetry. Additionally, through its "e-poetry" page, the EPC tries to identify key works in the medium. Here, as throughout the EPC, the genres of kinetic/visual poetries, audio art, and other experiments in the medium (such as the JavaScript "Mouseover") are explored. It is also developing a number of resources for programmable poetries, including texts, performances, and software. It is important to note that the EPC does not try to provide access to *all* poetry on the Web; rather, it selects the best examples within given parameters. A tenet of the EPC is that it is an *edited* site providing a collection of "authorized" primary texts; thus, texts housed at the Electronic Poetry Center are "definitive" texts inasmuch as, prior to posting, they have been approved by their producers. (This concern with accurate texts is atypical for much of the Web.) The EPC has set a standard for electronic poetry texts and has served as a national model for mining the possibilities of a true online archive on the Internet. In addition, through the Online Computer Library Center's[22] United States Department of Education–funded project CIRG (Cataloging Internet Resources Group), and the initiative of the University Libraries Central Technical Services Group, SUNY Buffalo, selected texts are cataloged and made available nationally and internationally through major bibliographic library databases. Latin American and French language author components to the EPC's lists are presently being planned.

Cross-Cultural E-Poetics

> Place a small pale-cream bowl (to signify abundance)
> on the table-top in front of you.
> —Maggie O'Sullivan, "Narcotic Properties"

When one considers what might constitute a typical Web page, for most people it is probably not too far-fetched to assume that the page that comes to mind is in English.[23] The fact is, though U.S. practice is typically the dominant force, present-day advances in the electronic media extend more widely, and cross more borders, than one might think. Further, as with literary, theoretical, and visual works, different cultures can take a new medium and apply it in diverse and engaging ways. Regarding the importance of such diversity, the hologram artist Eduardo Kac urges, we should look at a "larger context of 'experimental writing'"; by "larger context" Kac means, "Not only the multiplicity of forms, styles, and groups, but also the multiple traditions of distinct countries" ("Re: Back"). Indeed, it is all too rare that such multiple traditions are invoked in electronic poetics. There have been, however, some important moments in the development of an international e-poetic consciousness; it is a rewarding prospect to survey the diversity of approaches that form the "larger context" of the electronic medium, putting the "world" in World Wide Web.

One of the first of these moments was the "Assembling Alternatives" Conference, an international poetry conference/festival held at the University of New Hampshire, Durham (August 29–September 2, 1996). The topic of e-poetry was entertained through the inclusion of electronic media in the event. (Note that "assembling" has an echo here, "assembler" being "a computer program that translates," a portentous resonance.) Indeed, the panel was scheduled as a prominent event, a plenary session. Though this conference was not about electronic poetries, the organizers should be congratulated for recognizing that the formal issues about writing at the heart of experimental poetries are similar to those being explored by the literary electronic media. Caroline Bergvall, one of the poets present at the conference, made this affinity of interests strikingly clear in one of her comments: "When I talk about the performance of writing, I do not mean to favor staged live work exclusively. I use the term in a broader sense, to indicate an activity of writing which uses and is aware of the various kinds of media it can (and does) manifest itself through" ("Writing"). This was certainly one of first times that in a literary conference such a kinship of language concerns had been addressed.

Subsequent significant events have included the Performance Writing symposium at Dartington College, U.K. (April 9–14, 1996), and "In the Event of Text: Ephemeralities of Writing,"[24] the second international symposium on writing and performance (April 28–May 2, 1999), both organized in part by Caroline Bergvall. (Bergvall's essays, "What Do We Mean by Performance Writing" and "In the Event of Text: Ephemeralities of Writing" provide excellent additional information on topics related to these events.) "In the Event of Text" was a collaboration between the Utrecht School of the Arts, Netherlands, and the Dartington College of Arts, U.K.; it included artists from the United Kingdom, the Netherlands, Canada, Austria, Belgium, Denmark, Norway, and the United States. The goal of "In the Event of Text," in the words of its organizers, was to "explore, through work and discussion, the ways in which writing can be seen to function as a time-based, transient, ephemeral artform when played out in the context of different media and environments" with curated work focusing on "the disappearing text and contemporary live performance, the dispersal of written material through new interactive and sonic media, electronic writings, cybertext and hypertext, [and] the local sites of mobilised writing including poetic and book-based practices" (Allsopp). The conference investigated important intertextual areas and featured an exhibition, "The Chute of Language," curated by Cris Cheek and Sianed Jones, and a virtual cybertext collaboration initiated by the symposium's writer in residence John Cayley.

Two seminal conferences occurred under the important imprimatur of Digital Arts & Culture. Digital Arts & Culture 98 occurred in Bergen, Norway, in November 1998. This international conference was sponsored by the SKIKT Program of The Norwegian Research Council and the Cyber/

Media/Culture Project at the Department of Humanistic Informatics, University of Bergen. It aimed to provide a locus for the presentation and discussion of artistic and theoretical developments in digital arts, media, and culture. One of the goals of the conference was to strengthen "the links between the many different players and subfields within the rapidly expanding field of digital culture and aesthetic studies" ("DAC 98"). The conference has added international awareness to the growing digital arts movement and has helped to strengthen ties between participants from Norway, Sweden, Finland, Germany, Denmark, Slovenia, Russia, Uruguay, Australia, the United Kingdom, Canada, and the United States. The second of this series, Digital Arts & Culture 99 occurred in Atlanta, Georgia, in October 1999, co-sponsored by The School of Literature, Communication, and Culture, Georgia Institute of Technology, and the Department of Humanistic Informatics, University of Bergen, Norway. This conference, as one would expect, had much more of a U.S. presence, though it continued to strongly represent work being done in Europe and elsewhere. Nevertheless, for many of the U.S. participants, this was a first chance to gather and discuss digital writing in such a context and as such it was a very valuable event. Of the conference highlights were an address by N. Katherine Hayles, a roundtable on narrative with David Jay Bolter, Espen Aarseth, and others, an opening reading by John Cayley and me, and a keynote address by Robert Coover. DAC produced two subsequent conferences, DAC 2000 (Bergen, Norway, August 2000) and DAC 2001 (Providence, Rhode Island, 2001). At this writing, DAC is presently undergoing reorganization.

In the U.K., a variety of efforts have been under way. Most notable is the work of John Cayley, whose series of works in programmable media not only have forecasted the possibilities for digital writing but also have explored the subtleties of its manifold possibilities. Cayley's site, "Indra's Net or Hologography,"[25] includes substantial resources by and about Cayley. His section on "Programmatology" gives an overview of Cayley's view of the field of procedural and combinatorial practice, his "Catalogue" provides descriptions and exemplars of his many diverse textual projects, and "Theory/Practice" provides a number of his theoretical writings. Some of Cayley's works are also mentioned in the following chapter of this book. Digital textual practice in the United Kingdom emanates as parts of other larger efforts, some of them now associated with the remarkable "Performance Writing" program headed by Caroline Bergvall, in collaboration with the late Alaric Sumner and others at Dartington College. Both of these writers have made notable contributions to digital poetics. Ric Allsopp, one of the editors of *Performance Research* and also working at Dartington, has also curated digital text art. Artists and writers associated with the important U.K. magazine of digital culture, *Mute*, might be included in the field. Though Dartington and *Performance Research* are more strictly concerned with performance, and *Mute* is strongly engaged with new media design and production, numerous projects emanating from these groups have advanced significantly digital textual practice in the U.K. One of these projects is "*Performance Research On Line: New Media Work for CD-ROM*," a "*Performance Research* Supplement" to a special issue of *Performance Research*, edited by Ric Allsopp and Scott de Lahunta. The CD was produced, the editors explain, "to represent at least some aspect of contemporary work in the field in a digital form" ("*Performance*"). The CD features Simon Biggs, John Cayley, Joseph Hyde, Jane Prophet, and Louise K. Wilson and provides works selected for their "range through textual, visual and sonic approaches to work" ("*Performance*"), an excellent glimpse, indeed, of some current U.K. practitioners.

Also important in the U.K. are the efforts of Cris Cheek and Kirsten Lavers. Lavers's site, Things Not Worth Keeping (http://www.thingsnotworthkeeping.com/flames.html), mostly consisting of installation/performance works, is an important project. Works like their "Flames," where overlaid words flicker and reconfigure themselves through dual frames before congealing into dark pools, serve as an interesting exemplar of digital textual practice. Finally, it is important to mention TrAce, (http://trace.ntu.ac.uk) an "online writing community" that uses the Web to further writing through online chat meetings, online courses, and postings of opportunities for writers with specific focus on the impact of technology on artistic practice. TrAce also sponsors online journals, writers-in-residence, conferences, and Assemblage, the women's hypertext gallery compiled by the Canadian writer, Carolyn Guertin.

Continental practice has included numerous works in the French "generator poetry" movement, the A.L.A.M.O. group, and works by Philippe Bootz, Jean Pierre Balpe, and Tibor Papp, important practitioners of digital poetry. Probably the most extraordinary publishing event related to French practice is the issuance of the *DOC(K)S ALIRE* combined issue with CD-ROM, *(Soft) DOC(K)S[sous rature]* Series 3 nos. 13/14/15/16 (Fall 1997) and *aLire* 10, "Poesie & Informatique," discussed in the following chapter. Another special journal issue of importance, also with CD-ROM, is the electronic literature issue of the Flemish publication *Dietsche Warande & Belfort* (August 1999, no. 4), edited by Jan Baetens and Eric Vos. This special publication presents four articles in Dutch on digital poetry. One of these, "Zestien screenshots," also by Vos and Baetens, presents a catalog of digital practices (keyed to the issue's accompanying CD-ROM) through sample annotated screenshots, some of which are in color. The annotations include URLs for the work discussed. This is quite an interesting compilation that can be appreciated by any reader.

An excellent Web site has been created for the Oulipo movement. "Oulipo" includes a great deal of information about Oulipo in two sections, "Informations sur l'Oulipo" and "Interactivité, multimédia."[26] The "Information" section includes lists of members, bibliographies, some fundamental texts about OuLiPo and its activities, and more. In the "Interactive" section there are OuLiPo-related sound and image files, *Le petit Norbert pirate*, and a "What's New" section. A new project from France is the "Un bureau sur l'Atlantique" site,[27] recently constructed by the French editor, translator, and artist Juliette Valéry. The sponsoring organization, Un bureau sur l'Atlantique, founded by Emmanuel Hocquard in 1989, is a non-profit association (supported by the Centre National du Livre and the Centre de Poésie & Traduction at Fondation Royaumont) dedicated to advancing the knowledge of American contemporary poetry in France. This bilingual Web site, hosted by the Electronic Poetry Center, provides several lists of publications, including a catalog of the *Format Américain series*, information about Bureau activities, and work by Emmanuel Hocquard.

There have been numerous developments in Latin American countries. Kac describes this tradition of work in Brazil:

> Two fascinating directions of experimental poetry . . . are the pioneering interactive object-poems of Ferreira Gullar and his group in the late '50s and early '60s and the "Process/Poem" movement headed by Wlademir Dias-Pino in the late '60s and early '70s. Under the paralyzing environment of censorship imposed by a violent military dictatorship, Dias-Pino had the brilliant insights of (1) creating poems without words and, in a direct reaction against the stability of concrete poetry, of (2) giving priority to "process" over "structure." Dias-Pino was also very interested in the poetic use of computers. ("Re: Back")

An important gathering occurred in São Paulo, Brazil, in August 1999. In the words of its organizers, "Invenção: Thinking about the Next Millennium"[28] examined "the consequences of [the] convergence of art, science and technology on our sense of self and human identity, on consciousness, community and the city, as well as on learning and leisure" (Kac, "Invenção"). A key presence in theories of avant-garde Brazilian poetries is the late Philadelpho Menezes, author of numerous digital poems and of *Poetics & Visuality: A Trajectory of Contemporary Brazilian Poetry* (San Diego: San Diego State Univ. Press, 1994). Menezes is the subject of numerous tributes, including the VII International Biennial of Virtual Visual/Experimental Poetry (Mexico City, 2001) and an online tribute hosted by the EPC[29] and mirrored by the International Association of Word and Image Studies web site in the Netherlands. Other active Brazillian e-poets include Wilton Azevedo (Menezes's collaborator), Gisselle Beiguelman, and Lucio Agra, among others.

In Mexico, experimental poets assembled for a significant event, the Sixth Biennial of Experimental Poetry. The Sixth Biennial, organized by César Espinosa y Araceli Zúñiga, brought together participants from Mexico, numerous Latin American countries, the United States, and Germany. In addition to an exhibition at the El Chopo museum in Mexico City, the Sixth Biennial maintains a virtual gallery, the Sala Altamira,[30] as an extension of its events. Sala Altamira, curated by Juan José Díaz Infante, includes a rich collection of texts about digital and experimental poetry, along with details about the activities of the Biennial, and other resources. Also included is a link to the Light & Dust Poets Web site in the U.S., which hosted the "U.S. and Canadian Pages for The VI Biennial,"[31] a collection of contributions of visual work done in the experimental spirit of the Biennial (though not necessarily relating to the Mexican or Latin American experience). Also a part of the Biennial were conceptual works defining new forms of textuality presented and performed at Caja Dos/Artenativo, an experimental performance space in Mexico City directed by José Guadalupe Lopez and the late Armando Sarignana.

A final event taking place in April 2001 was E-Poetry 2001, sponsored by Just Buffalo Literary Center and the EPC, SUNY Buffalo. Billed as "the first convocation of digital poets and artists to focus on the state of the art of digital poetry" ("E-Poetry"), E-Poetry 2001 assembled 50 digital poets from 14 countries, including France, Germany, Slovenia, Canada, Brazil, Malaysia, Australia, the U.K., and the U.S. One of the goals of the event was to focus on e-poetry as a genre, with attention to its international context. By all accounts, the gathering succeeded in helping to crystallize a new sense of e-poetry as a plural, multi-faceted, and cross-cultural experience, foregrounding a range of practices defining the art.

It is clear these international and cross-cultural events bring writers working in different countries together and help realize the potential for international collaborations. What influence will European and Latin-American practice have, as these potent interpretations of the medium increasingly become available through the Web and contrast with some of the viewpoints in the U.S. now dominating the conversation? One cannot say for certain; however, the convergence of so many cultural perspectives will certainly produce an effect. A familiarity with diverse cultural practice must become more common, and we thank such poets as Caroline Bergvall, John Cayley, César Espinosa, Emmanuel Hocquard, Eduardo Kac, and Juan José Díaz Infante for their part in spreading these diverse perspectives. Indeed, one hopes the facility with which one can communicate electronically with geographically distant locations will make international collaborations increasingly common.

An Occlusion for the Millennium

> The writerly text is a perpetual present, upon which no consequent language . . . can be superimposed; the writerly text is ourselves writing, before the infinite play of the world . . . is traversed, intersected, stopped plasticized by some singular system . . . which reduces the plurality of entrances, the opening of networks, the infinity of languages.
> —Roland Barthes, *S/Z*

Me vi al cerrar los ojos:
espacio, espacio
donde estoy y no estoy.[32]
—Octavio Paz, "Libertad," from *Selected Poems*

The presence of so many different forces active in the digital field raises important questions about the international context of e-poetry. In the U.S. conversation, it does not seem uncommon for discussions to focus exclusively on U.S. practice. Some U.S. theorists would imply that U.S. practice is the most advanced (perhaps because it is perceived as dominant?)[33] or, if not going that far, the lack of mention of international efforts at minimum indicates a disinterest in e-poetry's larger context. Further, the dearth of foreign language portals for major Web sites, the paucity of references to the works of non-U.S. authors, and the near absence of works in any language other than English indicates a lack of scope, I would argue, on the part of U.S. practitioners. Even a site as notable as that of Eastgate Systems, to cite one example, which declares itself "the primary source for serious hypertext" (http://www.eastgate.com, 26 Nov. 1999), offers work only in English. Let us consider this fact. Is this to say that "serious" work does not exist in any other language or simply that such work does not merit being included in this "primary" index of material? Of course, analyzing Eastgate's claim in this manner is unduly harsh, and it should not be taken here as a criticism. Nevertheless, even if I withdraw these comments, the tinge of such a general U.S. bias is still perceptible. How does this occur? It is part of a general cultural perspective: it is not uncommon in the U.S. to hear phrases such as "the World Series," "the World Heavyweight Champion," "the world's greatest fajitas," and so forth, that further this insularity on a national level. This type of narrow position is present in literary practice as well.

This perspective is tied, in part, to the increasing disregard of other languages in the U.S. It is unfortunate that such a disregard extends to literary culture, a field that for many years has been open to works and criticism in other languages. Yet, given the speed of communication around the globe, especially to the immediately "adjacent" cultures of Europe, Latin America, and Canada, such a cultural myopia is even more astonishing. It is as if the lack of borders in communication seems to have caused practitioners to put up an accordingly thicker ideological wall, a virtual Berlin wall secured with barbed ASCII. What possible counter arguments are there for this monocultural stance? One might answer that there is enough going on in the U.S. to satisfy our needs here. But ironically, nothing could be further from the truth.

First, because the present developments in digital practice are truly international, digital practice should be sited within a global digital ecosystem. In fact, a literary phenomenon so truly international has not been seen since the Concrete Poetry movements of the 1950s through the 1970s, movements in which, similarly, the importance of material qualities of writing rose to a level that transcended national interests. During this period, numerous anthologies were issued as "international" anthologies, some of the original founders of these movements coming from nations as diverse as Brazil, Switzerland, Sweden, Germany, and the United Kingdom. Emmett Williams quotes Jonathan Williams as declaring, "If there is such a thing as a worldwide movement in the art of poetry, Concrete is it" and, of Concrete Poetry's origin, he writes, "The confused geography of its beginnings reflects the universality of its roots" (vii, vi).

Secondly, the international context must be acknowledged because some of the most important advances in the field are presently occurring outside the U.S. This is partly because many U.S. practitioners seem locked into the paradigm of hypertext for their vision of the digital future, a paradigm that has probably already ceased to be useful. In fact the discourse of hypertext and narrative is incredibly lopsided, seemingly oblivious to the multiple forms of digital practice, as documented in *Cybertext*, by the Norwegian scholar Espen Aarseth. If a nascent paradigm for poetry is to be cited, it is one of programmed poetries. In this regard, emerging literature has less to do with nationality than with the type of digital practice undertaken. Interesting work is not work that is merely remediated (e.g., print work transferred to the screen) but is work that engages the cogs and wheels of programming as writing. These are the practices, I would argue, from which new writing will emerge.

In the way that the Concrete Movements allowed strong national movements within a kind of international "intelligence," digital practice must be seen as a series of national practices that constitute an international web of interests, further interconnected by numerous collaborative sites, texts, Moo installations, and performances. Any vision that denies the power of these connections and the possibilities for these multiple practices to mutually inform one another will reduce any individual national practice to a mere outline of its own potential.

8
Future Tenses / Present Tensions
A Prospectus for E-poetry

I'm just using a screen instead of an easel to do what we've been doing for hundreds of years. Ever finger-paint? If that's the Mac metaphor then the PC version is like painting with chopsticks—and someone else got all the prawns!
— Loss Pequeño Glazier, *Leaving*

Such a system will represent at last the true structure of information (rather than Procrustean mappings of it), with all its intrinsic complexity and controversy, and provide a universal archival standard worthy of our heritage of freedom and pluralism.
— Theodor Holm Nelson, *Literary Machines*

November always seemed to be the Norway of the year.
— Emily Dickinson, *Letters*

Future Tenses

Poetry is a field of writing/programming whose alliance to digital practice seems to be generally unacknowledged. For one not to see the connection between poetic practice and new technology seems to undervalue a literary genre that has seen its innovative practice consistently at the forefront of artistic investigations of the twentieth century. These investigations have included Futurism (social space of mechanization), Oulipo (procedure), the work of Jackson Mac Low and John Cage (determinate generation of texts), and other paradigm-shifting investigations. This is not to assert any direct influence between investigations but to view them in contributing contexts. As to the present, there is no doubt that poetry *has* entered the digital age—programming has notably been used to produce printed texts by Cage, Mac Low, and Charles O. Hartman—but poetry's entrance into the field has been tentative and its presence has not been widely accepted. By contrast, if we look at two other genres, hypertext fiction and scholarly electronic hypertext, we see a presence that is more strongly agreed upon.

Indeed, hypertext fiction and scholarly electronic hypertext both seem clearly self-assured about their relation to digital media. For example, hypertext fiction has a long presence at Brown University and an active marketing and promotion advocate, Eastgate Systems. Eastgate also provides a commercial software package, StorySpace, to further its vision, insisting that it embodies a new paradigm for writing. Scholarly electronic hypertext is supported by a number of academic projects, such as Jerome McGann's Rossetti Archive and Matthew Kirschenbaum's William Blake Archive (both at the University of Virginia).[1] Such practice also has well-organized sponsorship by organizations including the Text Encoding Initiative and the Center for Electronic Texts in the Humanities.

There is no equivalent infrastructure for poetry. True, the Electronic Poetry Center at SUNY Buffalo seeks to provide a similar service for digital poetry, but the absence of professional organizations, the lack of inclusion in literary scholarly conferences, and the sparsity of discipline-specific conferences are notable. A great hindrance is the nonexistence of any commercial or commonly accepted tool for the creation of digital poetry. Part of this could, of course, be attributed to the inattention given poetry in general. But for e-poetry, this deficiency seems to go even further; for e-poetry is neither accepted by other non-poetry digital practitioners nor generally by print poets.

The field of electronic poetry practice is, of course, well established and broadly defined. The possibilities for digital poetry extend from the work of Mac Low and Hartman, whose work at this writing, though making substantial contributions, curiously seems to find its culmination in print. It includes the works of numerous hypertext poetry practitioners, whose language sometimes is nostalgic, appearing to insist on a modernist or other outmoded aesthetic. (Such works sometimes seem ignorant of the investigations of the materiality of language that have characterized late-twentieth-century poetry, instead regressing at times to earlier uses of language, such as the symbolic, the representational, or even the allegorical.) It includes the dynamic and alternative forms of hypertext, news of which seems incredibly absent from the literature. In includes a substantial number and range of visual and kinetic texts. Within the field, additionally, are the presently limited number of programmed poetries that are only very recently becoming available. Clearly, e-poetries have broken important ground, exhibiting significant and multiple potentials. But one wonders if e-poetry's basic sub-fields of practice—hypertext, visual/kinetic text, and works for networked and programmable media—would be commonly recognized, even by innovative poets themselves.

Poetry's Digital Presence

Poetry's entrance into digital culture has been in fits and starts, at times stunted, ironically, by technology itself. Curiously, one of the ways that poetry texts showed themselves en masse on the digital horizon was the self-publication frenzy that occurred when the World Wide Web first became popular. Contrary to heralding any advance into a digital poetics, computer technology was used to "Xerox" thousands of home pages of often sentimental, personalized, and formally conservative poetry. (Unlike the Mimeo ["mi MEE Oh"] Revolution, where a sense of group consciousness was engendered in the 1960s, this 1990s movement might better be called the "me-oh-me" Revolution.) On the other hand, proponents of cybercultural studies envision a mode of literature with a strong emphasis on science fiction (involving little poetry) that employs the tools of new technology to investigate (with a range of visual effects) the important social relations of computer technology. Despite the crucial importance of such investigations, the focus of this study has been innovative poetries: work that explores the material possibilities of writing/programming in a given medium, that is, the electronic one.

What signs are there that the innovative poetries have not developed a clear sense of place in digital textual production? There is the dearth of any mention of digital poetries in most teaching anthologies. Even the two-volume *Poems for the Millennium*, an anthology edited by Jerome Rothenberg and Pierre Joris that focuses on innovative poetries of this century, devotes very little space to e-poetries. Its section "Towards a Cyberpoetics: The Poem in the Machine" devotes 13 out of 1,682 pages (less than 1 percent of its attention) to e-poetry. The fact that such a section even exists is an important acknowledgment of the relevance of e-poetries to the practice of innovative poetries. Nevertheless, considering the significance of computer technology to writing/programming as we proceed into the next millennium, it is striking that this century's most salient advance in writing technology is given such scant attention. Moreover, the selections are cursory, containing two collages of quotations and mostly excerpts of works from sound poets and "cyberpoets" in the same section. The compilers of this volume are accomplished and highly regarded anthologists, and one cannot fault them because their mission in this anthology is more broadly defined.[2] One can, however, claim that this paucity of coverage is a reflection of a general lack of recognition of the many ground-breaking accomplishments of e-poetries.

A distrust of the validity of digital practice is also reflected in the lingering lack of stature accorded electronic publication, particularly in academic circles. This distrust extends to every form of practice, poetry, fiction, and to scholarly work across all disciplines. This resistance to electronic publication clearly presents challenges for the medium, as Vincent Kiernan explains: "No one knows for sure why some electronic journals are having a rough time getting papers and subscriptions from scholars, but several theories are being bandied about by editors, publishers, librarians, and scholars. Scholars are worried, according to the speculation, that electronic publication will not carry much credit toward tenure, or that the electronic journals might fail, carrying prized papers with them into oblivion. Many electronic-only journals publish papers individually, as they are accepted, rather than on a regular schedule" (Kiernan A25). Such a lack of accreditation may also

have spilled over to pollute e-poetry's own sense of validity. Poets them-
selves often regard a poem published in a paper publication as more
substantial than one that is on the Net. As I so often hear: "Go ahead and
put it on the Web; it has already been published." The irony of this state-
ment lies in the fact that the "public" *is on the Net*, not (unfortunately)
clamoring in small press bookstores. Innovative electronic projects rarely
receive the attention one might expect. What's worse, those that are recog-
nized—in what seems an atmosphere of digital Victorianism—are stiflingly
conservative. The truly visionary projects, such as Philippe Bootz's *Alire*,
the works of Jean-Pierre Balpe, Philippe Castellin's *DOC(K)S*—works that
provide an essential vision of the horizon of digital literature—are well known
in the francophone world and in Europe but are rarely mentioned in the
United States. Such works as Balpe's "Une littérature inadmissible" ("An
Inadmissable Literature," *DOC(K)S Alire* 3, 13–16 [1997]) offer a prescient
and inspired view of the future. Yet due to any number of factors, including
a lack of translations, works like these have not yet received the credit they
deserve.

Another barrier to a coalescing of e-poetry's identity has been its audi-
ence. If print-based innovative poetry—or for that matter even conservative
academic poetry—are said to receive scant attention, the audience for e-
poetry is concomitantly minuscule (or, "pequeño" as my relatives would say).
Even worse, this audience is divided, its fragmentation having been exacer-
bated by the incompatibility of computer operating systems. The most
notable controversy here is the PC versus Mac conflict. The Mac presently
controls only a small percentage of the computing market, a fact that I think
has largely limited the audience for such poets as John Cayley, who created
a critical body of Mac-based work. Some of his early works for HyperCard
are seminal works for e-poetry and are barely accessible for the majority of
readers, a significant limitation indeed. Even academically mainstream texts,
such as *Uncle Buddy's Phantom Fun House* and Michael Joyce's *Twilight, A
Symphony*, cannot at this writing be run on Windows.

Text generation programs evidence the same climate of disarray. This is
evident considering that, presently, a single multi-platform program for the
computer generation of poetry does not exist. Indeed, if one were asked to
name *one* such text generation program, most people could not do so. This
might resonate with the way that only a few years ago, only specialists per-
formed word processing; now it is common for most people to do their own
word processing. There may very well be an equal momentum toward end
user production of digital literary texts. Considering this, it is especially
striking to note the present lack of programming/e-poetry generation tools.
Compared to the advances of spreadsheet, animation, and image editing
programs for their disciplines, one must ask where is the literature proces-
sor? Where is the integrated tool to make concordances, word plays,
morphemic substitutions, operations by grammatical structure, word origin
analysis, and other language-based permutations?

Sidebar: Tin Man Weeps Straw Break

The emergence of an identity for e-poetics is further complicated by confusions about the interrelationship between fields of practice. Though I will not address all categories of digital practice in depth, it seems appropriate to devote space to considering the degree to which some of these areas are contested. In this regard, I am thinking of an exchange in December 1997 between John Cayley and Michael Joyce on the ht-lit discussion list (ht_lit@consecol.org). Cayley posted first on the subject of "poesie[sous rature] & informatique" (15 Dec. 1997), offering an enthusiastic announcement of the combined publication of *(soft) DOC(K)S[sous rature]* Series 3 nos. 13/14/15/16 (Fall 1997) and *aLire* 10, "Poesie & Informatique," detailing both print and CD-ROM contents of the issue. In his exuberance, Cayley recommends the publication as: "[A] substantial (quadruple issue) assemblage (mixed bag) of material relating to what I prefer to call 'Poetics in Programmable Media.' The perspectives and engagements of the French/European/non-anglophone/international practitioners is a necessary corrective to the current domination of USA-Net-centric 'classic hypertext' in this emergent field of Writing, so this collection is well worth exploring" ("poesie[sous rature]"). Within hours, Joyce fires back under the subject "back broke camel straw man" (15 Dec. 1997). For Joyce, as the subject of his message suggests, Cayley's comment was the proverbial straw that broke the camel's (clichéd) back. Joyce's stridency is based on Cayley's reference to "domination," and he launches an extended rebuttal:

> Domination indeed?!? who is dominating whom, where, and to what purpose? To speak of any kind of electronic writing as if it were a hegemonic (and imperial, viz. "USA-Net-centric 'classic hypertext'") scheme not only is . . . absurd on the face of it (net rhetoric to the contrary—and in comparison to the literary scene in Paris, London and New York in early 20th C—we are all of us relegated to our small and separate corners in a big room where soidisant "new media" conglomopolies have set up their large screen web teevees and super amplified boom-market boxes) but also, quite frankly, needlessly divisive especially to the extent that it attributes an intention to so dominate. ("Back")

It is true that no intention to dominate is implied. (Though the intention to dominate was not one of Cayley's charges.) Further, Joyce goes on to argue that the literary hypertext community has always been characterized by generosity. He accuses Cayley of falling into the "classic knock" (which could either be "the usual knock" or "knocking someone by calling them 'classic'") by faulting Eastgate for "its ground-breaking work." As a kind of proof of his own generosity, he cites that he has written favorably about "the kinetic poets." A couple of days later, Cayley responds under the subject "tin man weeps straw break" (19 Dec. 1997),[3] acknowledging a less than judicious choice of words in the offending paragraph but elaborating extensively on some of the points Joyce raised. Joyce does not address the topic again.

It should be noted that the spirit of cooperation for which Joyce argues is indeed a desirable one; he is certainly to be commended for stressing its need. (It should be noted that Joyce has, in his professional career, been warmly supportive of numerous literary endeavors. The point of this sidebar is to read closely the tenor and themes of this exchange to reach a clearer understanding of the specific issues that arise here.) Joyce's call for cooperation, however, seems compromised by the stridency with which he responds. His objection to being called "dominant" and his aversion to the idea of "classic" hypertext seem out of proportion to Cayley's indiscretion in word choice. The sound chastisement Joyce delivers demonstrates a certain exercise of authority: this tone is important.

Indeed, if one were to measure authority, and define the term "classic" as practice recognized by the mainstream media, Eastgate would not mind that moniker. (Ironically, Eastgate Systems, in January 2000, ran a "Great Deal" advertisement on its home page that read: "Great savings on the classic hypertext of Michael Joyce,"[4] a fact that suggests even Joyce's publisher does not hesitate to use the term "classic.") Having been lauded for its efforts by Robert Coover in the *New York Times* and having been given substantial attention by the academy, Eastgate enjoys a name recognition far superior to its peers; there is little doubt that "classic" practice is on a much larger scale than *Alire* or the works of Cayley, Kac, or Rosenberg. (Though Joyce feels diminished by "soidisant 'new media' conglomopolies . . . [with] their large screen web teevees and super amplified boom-market boxes" (Joyce, "Back") the evidence is that classic hypertext, in relation to other e-poetic practices, does *not* exist on a diminished scale.) As to Joyce's use of authority, it makes the reprimand he delivers less than collegial because he *is* in a position of power and should be conscious of that fact.

If one were to measure the "authority" of a poet, how would that be done? Is it by presence in anthologies? Of the e-writers discussed here, Joyce is the only one in the *Norton Anthology of Poetry*. Is it through academic appointments? Joyce has an academic position; neither Cayley nor Rosenberg has one. Citations? Recent searches of Expanded Academic Index ASAP gave Joyce more citations than Cayley, Rosenberg, and Kac combined. If we extended these associations and called Joyce-Landow-Bolter the three traditionalists or pedagogists or formalists and referred to Cayley-Rosenberg-Kac as the three action text workers, the former camp receives five times the number of citations as the latter in 1998 and four times the number in 2000.[5] (One may note that the first trio is composed mostly of theorists, and the second group is composed of theorist-practitioners, so the results might be skewed toward theorists. Nevertheless, these results still give us an indication of levels of attention to these different types of practice.

Issues of authority aside, one is led by this exchange to wonder about Joyce's position on emergent media generally. What is the present? What would be its future? In "Forms of the Future," an article referred to in the Cayley-Joyce exchange, Joyce actually offers a highly pessimistic state-of-the-art analysis: "Nor is it likely that a haphazardly swirling chaff of Java tools and plug-ins will suddenly reach a point of spontaneous combustion and bring forth a new light. The current state of multimedia does not repeat the case of the motor-car where widespread parallel technological developments led to a sufficient shift in sensibilities to make the mass distributed assembly line seem a techno-logical event threshold. The form of multimedia itself has no obvious audi-ence, nor any obvious longing which it seeks to fulfill" ("Forms"). These harsh-sounding words emerge from a complex conjunction of reasons. For one thing, Joyce is reacting to a culture in which "we live in an anticipatory state of constant nextness" because "for most technologists the measure of the future is a soundbite, an animated gif, or a mouse click" ("Forms"). He is frustrated with the commercial media; he longs for a revival of high litera-ture. He yearns to have something good come out of technology but sees no indication of an "electronic form yet to emerge."

Yet Joyce's position is highly conflicted, even confusing. On multimedia, he is extremely negative, having declared it to be without audience or direction in the above passage. Then he qualifies this somewhat later to say that he uses "multimedia" for "electronic television and [the] electronic marketplace" in contradistinction to "hypermedia." Yet later he describes Mark Amerika's *Gammatron* as being weighed down by "the already discussed impossibility of multimedia," a work that is neither electronic television nor commerce. A similar confusion emerges about his view of the image. On the one hand he expresses an extraordinary vehemence for the image: "Total belief in the un-mediated image is the behavior of cults. The Heavens' Gate cult knew what it saw beyond Hale Bop. Total belief in the unmediated image is denial of the mortality of the body" ("Forms"). Again, these are very strong words, not just descrying the image but placing it in the category of irrational cult worship and, in the case of Heaven's Gate, mass suicide. This is a strong, almost ex-treme position indeed, his vilification of the image even raising moral or reli-gious implications. Yet, elsewhere in the paper, Joyce discusses his then work-in-progress as being "about the relationships between word and image and the slippages as each lapse into each other." In the context of this article, it is confusing to have it both ways, image first being horrific but then later, curiously interesting. These two tones just do not match. Additionally, by mis-using "multimedia" (which does not, by common usage, mean electronic tele-vision or commercial electronic media), he casts a negative light on multimedia.

Such confusion becomes even more problematic when considered in light of his disagreement with Cayley above. Keep in mind that Joyce cites himself as generous because, in "Forms of the Future," he alluded to Cayley and oth-ers in his quick mention of a magazine. The special issue of the magazine Joyce is citing is *Visible Language,* one indication that the matter of image is not a small one. Further, the new media poets associated with the magazine are known for visual approaches to language. Though he does briefly praise the *Visible Language* special issue, he spends a disproportionately large amount of time detailing the more conservative or centrist fiction writers who are his main concern. The praise he cites himself as having given the *Visible Language* poets barely amounts to a nod in comparison.

It is absolutely central to consider here that the main divide in current debates over digital practice hinge on this matter of the image. One side argues that text must dominate and the other side argues that image will define multimedia (or hypermedia, in Joyce's terminology). Thus I think that the exchange with Cayley and the article discussed here supply crucial perspectives to this debate.

What are Joyce's "forms of future"? In general he is somewhat vague and somewhat utopian about projecting what might constitute such forms. Moreover, a description of his "electronic literature" is not exactly clear. In his article, he likens it to Berlin, the city where he first gave the paper in question, "a Berlin in which the cranes crosshatch a sky whose color, rather than being William Gibson's color of television, is not yet known, a sky whose expanse promises a new clarity." He explains: "The new electronic literature will seem old, as old as any human story, in its newness as old as birth" and also that, "The new electronic literature will restore the circle as it always was and, paradoxically, as it never was before" ("Forms"). It is clear that Joyce's vision is a benign one, that he yearns for a kind of golden age of electronic literature, and he does this earnestly. But inasmuch as he *is* able to describe electronic literature, he seems to see it as a literature of language and not of image. "I am however saying that language—with its intrinsically multiple forms, with its age-old engagement of eye and ear and mind, with its ancient summoning of gesture, movement, rhythm and repetition, with the consolation and refreshment it offers memory—offers us the clearest instance and the most obvious form for what will emerge as a truly electronic narrative art form" ("Forms").

One might note Joyce's suggestion that e-literature will be prose. As to electronic technology itself, one cannot help but wonder if Joyce is not giving careful enough consideration to technologies now being actively explored. As with his metaphor of Berlin, a city of possibilities not of the present, maybe he is overlooking e-literature's present possibilities. For example, as to where his electronic literature of the future will occur, Joyce makes it clear that it will not take place on the Web: "The Web is a pretty difficult space in which to create an expressive surface for text. It seems to me that the Web is all edges and without much depth and for a writer that is trouble. You want to induce depth, to have the surface give way to reverie and a sense of a shared shaping of the experience of reading and writing. Instead everything turns to branches" ("Forms"). But despite these objections, he explains that he did, nonetheless prepare a text, "Twelve Blue," for the Web. He describes it as follows: "With this fiction I decided to stop whining and learn to love the Web as best I could, to honor what it gives us at present and to try to make art within the restrictions of the medium" ("Forms"). Again, there is a conflict here between theory and practice, a conflict that Joyce good-naturedly tries to navigate. But one might point out that the Web is not just an inconvenient interface, but the largest-scale shared art space ever seen. It also offers numerous engaging programming opportunities. As such, it is not merely an inconvenient medium in which to work, but a location with much exciting potential.

Crucial to our considerations here is the relation of the medium to art-making. What Joyce does with the Web, to make the best of it, it seems to me, is what any artist does: engage the medium. In that sense, his yearning for the digital city on the horizon, like his longing for an idealized Berlin of the future, misses the central issue. He notes: "As with Berlin what matters most is not what life goes on beneath but what life emerges and in what light we come to see each other in the act of passing by." I would insist that the life that goes on below is crucial and that scaffolding rising in the sky is what informs digital practice: it is the HTML, it is the structure, it is the *process,* in both a contemporary and Olsonian sense, that gives digital practice its engagement. Like Mexico City's Museo del Universitario del Chopo, a building enshrouded in scaffolding as a permanent architectural feature, contemporary practice recognizes such process as part of, if not central to the act of making. The point here is not to single out Joyce for analysis—his acceptance of diverse practice has been generous and his own prose has explored multiple stylistic possibilities. Indeed, during responses made at the June 2001 Guggenheim "The Brave New Word" program, Joyce reflected on the "timidity" he perceives in present digital media works. He equally includes himself in such a reflection, firmly believing there should be greater risk-taking by those who are defining this art. Combining this comment with Joyce's nearly concurrent announcement that he will cease to work in electronic arts for the present, one sees the degree to which Joyce is committed to his vision. Nonetheless, I do feel it is important to *read* what is said in these exchanges. In the above case I feel that the disagreement with Cayley is more complex than it seems and also indicative of larger issues facing digital media.

Present Tensions

It has been suggested that merely presenting poetries in electronic form does not constitute "electronic" poetries. Eduardo Kac, for example, has written that the Electronic Poetry Center "is not primarily committed to electronic poetry proper, but to the use of the Web to discuss poetics and to publish essays on the topic" ("Selected" 234). This statement elicits a number of possible comments, including considerations about which strategies are best, institutionally and in terms of long-term collection building, for the development of a digital literary center. One might also comment about timing, specifically: When is the right time to create a resource such as the EPC's "E-poetries" library,[6] which was developed some time after the inception of the EPC? That is, does one start early and be over-inclusive, or does one wait when a critical mass might help better delineate a burgeoning field? How does one demonstrate the continuity of the innovative arts from the print through the programmed? Then there is the issue of how you evaluate writing in networked and programmable media, because online texts may not employ elaborate features of electronic media but still manifest certain basic qualities of the electronic text including malleability, transmissibility, and reproducibility. Thus, the definition of what constitutes an electronic text is open to some interpretation.

The point Kac raises highlights the fact that we are faced with not only a lack of a uniform practice in electronic poetry but also an inadequate vocabulary for discussing e-poetries. If one were to extend Kac's line of inquiry further, the question of how specifically to classify an electronic poetry arises. Kac's "Webliography" divides the field into four categories: "Poetry Resources," "Hypertext Resources," "Poets' Sites," and "History of New Media Poetry."[7] None of these include "electronic poetry." Neither is there any hint in his document about where one might locate an "electronic poetry proper."

Useful resources do exist, of course. "TextWorx Toolshed" is an excellent site listing software for the computer generation of text.[8] Macromedia's Flash program has also emerged as a tool that is becoming accepted by e-poets. Of interest also are text analysis sites, sites that provide various text manipulation programs, which can be useful for computer generation of text. Beyond these, searches on the Web for "computer generated writing" yield little of relevance. Programs that are retrieved, ironically, are predominantly Mac-oriented, making such programs minorities (the Mac) within a minority world (poetry). To extend this disparity, poetry is not only a minority activity in the literary world, but even hypertext poetry (of which Eastgate is the most prominent publisher) is a minority citizen of the StorySpace vision of hypertext, one which, if only based on the number of works it has published, seems predominantly prose dominated.

If we wished to locate e-poetry, what terms are at our disposal? There are several terms that might include e-poetry. The "Web," "hypertext," and the "Internet" are terms that identify methods of linking and delivering texts. David Jay Bolter introduces the idea of a "writing space," a differently oriented spatial location for electronic writing (one within an artificially restricted realm for the text). Kac, in "New Media Poetry," labels the body of poetic works in electronic media "new media poetry," emphasizing the hybrid genres present in such works. Espen Aarseth uses the term "cybertext" to embody a range of discourses emanating from the electronic environment, including forms consciously as well as indirectly "written" (such as video game dialogs or transcripts of moo sessions). It is clear that poetry and poetics texts of primary interest in this medium are not merely indirectly written texts but works consciously constructed as "written" or electronically "produced" works of "writing." ("Writing" is used here in a larger sense than its usual sense of typographic characters arranged as transparent carriers of meaning and can involve images, applets, characters that cannot be displayed, scripts, commented text, and other features.) We call such works "electronic poetry" or "e-poetry." "E-poetry" includes poetries with a number of specific qualities. These include the following:

- Works that cannot be adequately delivered via traditional paper publishing or cannot be displayed on paper. This would include innovative works circulated in electronic form.
- Texts with certain structural/operative forms not reproducible in paper or in any other non-digital medium. These include works employing hyperlinks, kinetic elements, multi-layered features, programmable elements and events.
- Digital media works that have some relation to twentieth-century innovative practices.

E-poetry engages economic, ideological, and social factors. It consists of *innovative* poetic practices in various digital media, that is, writing/programming that engages the procedures of poetry to investigate the materiality of language. If we consider these factors, then we begin to approach a working definition. This definition would benefit, at a later date, from a rigorous inventory of the various practices that presently constitute e-poetry. For the purposes of our discussion here, let us make some general observations about the future of e-poetry.

A Prospectus for E-poetry

On the technical level, one must accept that a definitive common ground will never be agreed upon. Further, divergent proprietary programs will repeatedly plague access to various e-poetries. Nonetheless, one can look to the existing shared turf, the Web, and begin to develop an action plan that can be effected in that common space. For one thing, practices that have existed in separate fields may now begin to watershed within the open architecture of the Web, avoiding the platform fracture that has exacerbated existing divisions in poetry.

Though the Web can be characterized as predominantly commercial, it is also a place where Web poetries can begin to incorporate multiple practices into a more generally accessible on-screen performance, extending the reach and impact of those practices. What has yet to be realized is a thorough re-invention of the possibilities of the Web *as medium*.

1. For link-based hypertext, one can begin to think of a future beyond the dull, passive link that would combine radically different uses of the link, unpredictability, self-constitution, single-use, and creation-on-the-fly, with alternatives in visual presentation, including hidden, context-sensitive, and mouseover actions.

2. Metabrowser technologies such as frames, spawned windows, client pull, and other techniques can be used to destabilize the notion of a total or complete reading and add polysemy to on-screen textuality.

3. Programming has produced numerous static, "fait accompli" texts; these can be incorporated into the corpora of poetry on the Web. Programming developments, however, also point to the possibilities of greater interactivity and to performance of real-time reader-unique readings made available to an audience greatly larger than before. (Programmed texts contrast sharply with "interactive fiction" because, rather than providing a set of static choices, texts are literally created as they are read.)

4. Finally, the status of code as writing offers an intriguing area for investigation; experiments in pushing and pulling the code horizon constitute fruitful fields of action.

The prospectus presented in this chapter calls for a collecting of writing/programming practices in a shared terrain where diverse performances may be witnessed. The word's circulation and ability to be viewed regardless of platform, corporate interest, or national boundary is of primary importance. (Packaging of discrete works may still occur in this model.) Though the Web will not necessarily be a permanent medium, it is, like the book, a temporarily stable delivery medium for writing/programming—and use of a shared space is called for. The Web and the writing/programming presently on it barely begin to explore the multi-faceted possibilities of its materiality; this locus for e-poetry is rich with the potentials of a practice that is multiple.

Certainly, the code-reader relation is a fundamental locus for investigating the potentials of e-poetry writing. It is important not to overlook the materiality of the electronic space in the attempt to see who can race to the ends of the Web the fastest. This prospectus does not intend to merely offer an encomium to the Web but to urge an investigation of the possibilities of using it as a bearer of multiple practices and diverse cultural engagements. It is also a call to investigate the materiality of this pliant reading surface; let us begin to fathom the code belying delicious spasms of surface tension. Such an identity, along with voices that are multiple, will mark these emergent poetic forms as constituting the critical mass of work necessary to define a post-millennial poetry that increasingly expands its possibilities.

2001: An E-text Odyssey

To attempt to define what is happening in the digital poetries, it is important to allow alternative conceptions to that of the codex. Though we are typing on keyboards, our fingers are yet, from the point of understanding multiple textualities, stained with print. Such changes have always occurred gradually. We know that early incunabula were exact reproductions of manuscripts, for "the first printers, far from being innovators, took extreme care to produce exact imitations" (Febvre and Martin 77). During the long transition from book rolls to codex, the roll and codex existed side by side for 400 years. (Interestingly, during that time pagan works were usually written on scrolls while Christian works were written on codices, suggesting that writing's interface has ideological implications!) It should not be a surprise that the transition to digital technology will similarly start with imitation and subsequently be slow, involving minute adjustments over great time periods. Further, it can be predicted that during the lifetimes of people born in the twentieth century, poetry will continue to be a hybrid activity, with groundbreaking works appearing in print, in digital media, and in combinations as yet unimagined.

The emergence of a well-rounded vision of the digital text brings to mind some of the issues that were raised at the Digital Arts & Culture 99 Conference that took place in Atlanta in October 1999. It must be stated that this conference, in general, was a tremendous success, one that came from the conference's openness to new forms of digital expression. From the opening reading by John Cayley and me, a certain tone was set. Or I would say, a breadth of expression was allowed. The conference was open to exploring the multiple possibilities for how media works can be envisioned. This was reinforced by the keynote performances at the conference, the fact that the digital salon allowed so many people to show their work, and by the variety of performances at the closing reception (including multimedia, live action, theatre-moo, performance art, cyberpolitical theatre, and more). Most important, these divergent conceptions of digital art were treated with respect and intelligent consideration, something for which the organizers deserve substantial praise. Acknowledging the openness that typified the conference, nonetheless I think it is crucial to also note a certain tension present at the conference about what I would call authority. (I am calling this an authority issue since the persons who argued most strongly for these positions were either conference keynotes and/or are people who occupy positions of academic or literary prominence.) This manifested itself in two main pulls or focuses of attention.

One of these pulls was toward narrative as an implicit concern of digital media. If one is to approach digital media with this bias toward narrative, one is trying to write to a tainted hard drive, since most contemporary conceptions of narrative are very much tied to the Western linear and print imagination. For example, in her electronic textuality tutorial "Electronic Textuality: What Is It?" N. Katherine Hayles describes the reader's role in constructing the text through the functions of "controlling pathways, assembling narrative, and deciding order," a role that strongly reinforces narrative. This focus on narrative as the basis for textuality is not only prose-rooted but denies the possibilities of the kinetic, the programmed, the aleatory, and the deterministic. Indeed, it represents the digital text as somehow knowable (or at least chartable); thus denying the rich possibilities offered by practices that allow the multiple, the ambiguous, and the uncontrollable to create alternative textualities (also explored through ongoing practices in innovative print poetry). The conference's most distinguished panel was the plenary round-table discussion on "The Future(s) of Narrative." In sharp contrast, no panel on the future of non-narrative received equal prominence. (Smaller, session panels on non-narrative did occur, including a Moo panel chaired by Espen Aarseth and a materiality/programming panel chaired by Terry Harpold; these were not, however, given plenary status.)

The second pull was toward text as definitive in literary studies. In this vein, works discussed (masterworks by implication) were consistently skewed to the text-based. Thus Hayles referenced Stuart Moulthrop's "Garden of Forking Paths" in her address, an early text-intensive project (no longer available) that, maybe of all early hypertexts, most closely lies on the line between print and hypertext.[9] Though it must be emphasized that Hayles has been one of the first literary scholars to admit the importance of the image to the work of digital art, the text-biased orientation of some of the examples she chose are open to question.[10] These works often rely on a reductive concept of the digital where images are used as a component in static renderings of narrative. For example, in her tutorial "Electronic Textuality: What Is It?" she lists, under the heading "New Literary Forms" an early hypertext work called "Buddy's Funhouse." The opening screen to this work consists of an image of an older, wood house with labels on entrances and windows such as "Art Gallery," "Oracle," "Hyper Earth," and "Source Code." Though I admire the attempt to bring digital works into academic discussion, if these are works that contribute to an understanding of, in the words of the tutorial's subtitle, "theoretical implications for questions essential to literary studies," then it seems to me crucial to represent visual and dynamic exemplars of digital literature in order to express the diversity of the medium.

As to the definition of electronic textuality, Hayles argues for "a network, not a linear sequence." Such a shift does not call into play the multiple possibilities for the digital medium because a network is simply a collection of multiple linear sequences; it also still predominantly relies on a metaphor of text as meaning. The lack of open-endedness in such a conception also collapses the possibilities for such a network. (A network that is limitlessly open-ended, by contrast, is a much different "text" than a closed network.) This second pull of the conference was truly brought to the front by Robert Coover's keynote address to the conference, "Literary Hypertext: The Passing of the Golden Age."[11] In the words of William Marsh, this address was an "anachronistic call for a 'return to the written word'" (Webartery), and it clearly valorized text hypertexts as somehow representing the zenith in accomplishment for digital technology. Hand in hand with such a claim was, again, a valorization of Michael Joyce's *Afternoon* as a "master text." (It was pointed out at the conference that the German press has referred to Joyce as the "Homer of hypertext"; I would not be surprised if even Joyce himself might agree that such a moniker is not without hyperbole.) Such a valorization, I would argue, is more of a reaction to narrative's expanded power in the medium and less an evaluation on this work as an exploration of the potentials of the digital medium. Indeed, Coover's statements seem to be rushing us into a declaration of the supremacy of a given period rather than allowing the field to fully develop before making such a call. This is supported by Coover's reference to Latin literature in the title of his address, an invocation of the Golden Age of Latin literature (70 BC to AD 18), during which the Latin language was brought "to perfection as a literary medium and many Latin classical masterpieces were composed" ("Golden"). Though it is laudable to honor important works of the past, one might say that the keynote might be implying that such a perfection or high point occurred for hypertext during the time of early hypertext. This is a strong statement for the supremacy of text hypertext. Further, declaring the masterworks of an age at such an early stage can distract one from the possibilities of works taking place in the present.[12]

More important, however, is the fact that such clinging to narrative and the textual taints our ability to perceive the field in front of us. As Aarseth has noted, "The ideological forces surrounding new technology produce a rhetoric of novelty, differentiation, and freedom that works to obscure the more profound structural kinships between superficially heterogeneous media" (14). I would like to use Aarseth's comment to point out that the real affinities of the text hypertexts valorized above, through the rhetoric of novelty, have been obscured. Their affinities are to print, and therefore they may not so much be harbingers of new digital media as last-stage manifestations of works with a sole allegiance to print.

The fields of visual, kinetic, new media, and works for programmable media, now in their infancy, are the biggest news as the dark night of the second millennium pales to the lengthening dawn of the third. What do we find in the twenty-first century? Is Hal speaking in iambic pentameter or in more abstract L=A=N=G=U=A=G=E? The Web continues to bring to light poetry for the screen predicated upon the use of increasingly faster connections. This means that sound, kinetic, and video works will become increasingly abundant. Readers interested in viewing such works may wish to consult the "E-poetry" and "Sound" pages at the Electronic Poetry Center, as well as the Cyber Poetry Gallery and Machine Made of Words,[13] for works that show the way in these emerging idioms.

What examples of such future forms presently exist? Projects such as FIDGET are instructive.[14] The Java applet program by Clem Paulson, based on a text by Kenneth Goldsmith, takes the text and structures it into "a dynamic mapping system that is organized visually and spatially instead of grammatically. In addition, the Java applet invokes duration and presence" (Goldsmith, "FIDGET Online"). This is a project that engages a vision of the future of electronic poetry.

Such a vision can also be seen in the numerous works for computer ex-ecution by Anglo-Canadian poet, John Cayley. Issued under the rubric of his "Indra's Net" series, Cayley coins the neologism "hologography" to clas-sify certain of these highly innovative works, which incorporate a number of visionary electronically modulated literary practices. "Oisleánd" (Indra's Net IX), for example, explores how one written language may be transliterated into another. A HyperCard stack and graphics files are accessed by the soft-ware Cayley has written to use "mesostic techniques to sow the text of either original or translation within the spelt words of the parallel text in its corre-sponding language" ("Procatalogue"). Clearly, Cayley's algorithmically based works makes him one of the premier practitioners of innovative e-poetries.

Finally, the procedural enters computing right from its operating system in my use of UNIX-based grep procedures to generate texts. In this case, it seemed to me that because UNIX was the operating system underlying many Web files, it made sense to build a procedure out of a standard UNIX com-mand. Some of these grep works (described in the earlier, "Grep, A Grammar," in this volume) are available on my author home page at the EPC.[15]

Will Web sites continue to explode in numbers and persist in single ego-orientation? Given increasing Web congestion and the seeming impermanence of many sites on the Web, it might be wise for attention to be given to "libraries" or collections of work that stand a better chance of serving as repositories for poetry in an electronic age. Indeed, these may become key to the survival of electronically delivered poetries. In terms of the integrity of Web-based libraries, it is hoped that as works on the Web continue to proliferate, attention will be given to the maintenance of accu-rate and well-edited collections of files. In this regard, we are the keepers of our own libraries and initiatives are best directed by groups of poets dedi-cated to these ends. Finally, poetry based on or incorporating programming, Java, CGI, or other languages may offer some of the most interesting possi-bilities for the future of electronic poetry. Be sure to watch for articles and sites geared to these burgeoning areas of investigation as poetry moves from the stasis of print into the multiple hybrid possibilities of digital media and the indefatigable glee of the algorithm.

It is most important to remember that on the electronic frontier, just as in the realm of the codex, one's attention can never stray far from the rela-tion between practice and ideology. As we move further and further into the new millennium, it will become increasingly important to maintain a focus on meaningful innovation. What do we hope to gain from these new textualities? What terrain do we wish to explore, and what forms of practice do we wish to make possible? There are specific positions crucial to this discussion.

All digital practice is not contained within the idea of hypertext, and hypertext itself is not limited to multi-pathed fictions or link-node constructions. Neither is innovative literary practice equivalent to the preparation of scholarly electronic editions. Without a doubt, this latter field uses hypertext to consummate effect, but it is a field of its own, one not necessarily related to innovative poetic practice. As Aarseth has noted, "Hypertext is a logical extension—and hardly a revolutionary substitution—of the communication technology that both the Enlightenment and modernist literature is based on" (82). In this regard, I would further like to suggest that simple link-node hypertext may ultimately prove to be the least interesting exemplar of the digital medium. In fact, it is possible that one day it will be looked upon as the last stage of print or linear writing, rather than the first stage of digital or hybrid writing.

Questions about whether the visual is appropriate or lamentable in works of digital media are not primary ones. It may be unproductive, for example, to lionize early hypertext's almost exclusive use of text (such a use of text was in many cases a technological exigency). Text in digital media, inasmuch as it simply sits inertly on the screen, is simply a holdover from print writing and from low threshold technology. One of the most significant strengths of new media writing is to reunite the text with the image, as well as with other media, such as sound and video. The visual has as much to do with new media writing as text did to codex writing. In fact, if we consider the vast role the image has played in writing generally (cave paintings, Chinese writing, Egyptian hieroglyphic writing, Mayan glyphs), the codex era can be considered an aberrant period when text and image were temporarily isolated from one another.

The possibilities for programming stand on the front line of digital media writing. Not only does programming allow for the greatest possibilities for text and image but, when it comes to the position of the writer in relation to the computer, it puts the writer in a key position of agency. As Aarseth notes: "The poetics of computer program writing is constantly evolving, and through paradigms such as object orientation it inspires practical philosophies and provides hermeneutic models for organizing and understanding the world, both directly (through programmed systems) and indirectly (through the worldviews of computer engineers)" (11).

Not only does the activity of programming fall clearly under the aegis of poeisis, but it is a natural undertaking for writing, an understanding that offers plural textual possibilities. It extends the most interesting aspects of codex writing into a field that is dynamic, expressive, and complex, transforming static text into intelligent action. An increase in experimental possibilities is never guaranteed by the turn around any corner; it many cases, the dawn of a new era is simply used to reinscribe old ideologies, the same set of plot progressions, and the same relentless expression of the mediocre, solipsistic "I." It is crucial for poets working in electronic media to recognize the value of new media work that pulls away from the quagmire of already-explored concerns and pushes the experimental forward into increasingly more interesting material spaces and hybrid practices.

Indeed, *Digital Poetics* itself is a book that reaches *from* hypertext *through* visual/kinetic text and *to* writing in programmable media. This book is intended as a journey that starts with the presentation and development of the possibilities of hypertext. Its complication and crisis is located in a consideration of the depletion of the link. It is hoped that the resolution here lies in the ascension of a new horizon, one that might give us a clear indication of what might arise from the materiality of the digital medium. Such a horizon, it might be argued, would be one inhabited by the active or "intelligent" text—text that not only writes and reads but, being software itself, can do a little soft-shoe on the side.

Is this a declaration that hypertext is dead? No, there will certainly be appropriate uses for the mechanisms of hypertext for scholarly electronic editions and a multitude of other document types, especially those that extend the print paradigm. Also, the urge to make conventional narratives into "serious" arrangements through linking will always be a temptation to many. Indeed, this activity, like new formalist poetry and quest adventure games, certainly has a complex and intriguing aesthetic that opens up some narrative possibilities through technology,[16] including non-fixed reading paths. Nevertheless, if we want to look at how technology and art converge to provide our culture with multiple alternative paradigms in writing, link-node hypertext is simply inadequate to bear the whole load. I hope this book not only will have charted the field of digital poetics but also will have served to mark a passage through different levels of understanding—from the discovery of hypertext to the manifold possibilities on the true digital horizon, possibilities that will admit other forms of textual practice alongside the codex in the coming years. Such possibilities provide an enrichment of textual practice, presenting writing that is creolized, writing based on innovative practice, and writing that increasingly engages programmable media.

Epilogue
Between the Academy and a Hard Drive
An E-cology of Innovative Practice

Crisis?   there is no crisis
but tick of the pen
of teeth ticking
the shelled busses
lilies in parentheses, cupped hand of a lens

tiles ticking past
where we, real, wobble
      —Elizabeth Willis, *The Human Abstract*

Hypertext could be commonplace before the century is out.
      —*The Economist* (London), 23 Aug. 1986

I am / an architecture of sounds / instantaneous / on /
a space that disintegrates itself.
      —Octavio Paz, *Selected Poems*

Innovative print poetries have been defined in numerous instances in terms of their investigation of varying forms of textual materiality. Indeed, one way to differentiate an innovative writing from one that is confessional, conservative, or that has not gotten beyond the tropes of modernism, is to look at how meaning functions in the work. Does the poem (or the prose) treat language as a transparent bearer of meaning? By contrast, an innovative work can be said to treat the making of meaning as problematic. Further, this criterion of meaning as problematic cannot be fulfilled by simply inserting vagueness into the text's narrative or by merely serializing elements; it is realized through an investigation of the material elements of writing in the given medium. In other words, from the viewpoint of innovative practice, "literature" is not a heavenly liquid drunk from a clear crystal goblet. It is the struggle with the goblet that presents the problem—its smoothness, its temperature, the way the concept of the liquid is changed by being in the goblet. It is the social group with which the goblet is associated, the dysraphism present at the meniscus, the tension of the curve at the point the liquid makes contact with the surface of the glass. (For example, how different is ginger ale when drinking from a crystal flute compared to a styrofoam cup.) These and other similar dynamics inform innovative practice.

If this struggle between transparency and materiality is at issue in print poetry, then it is of even greater importance in electronic literature. This is especially true where the code/interface relation is concerned, effectively constituting three theaters in which the struggle with transparency can occur: code, interface, and text. How does one investigate these three scenes of activity? How does one describe their dynamics? How does one learn the contours of the digital text, its quirks, its interweaving of strands of code and surface language, the conditions in which it exists? How does one educate about temporality, discontinuity, error messages, material that is there one minute and is not the next, the "not found"? Is it time to enroll in Digital Poetry 404? Can the e-text indeed even be said to be material? Clearly, the argument here is that it *is* material. To substantiate this assertion, a consideration of the criteria for such a materiality will be considered in this epilogue, as will traps in misreading the innovative in digital media.

Such a focus on the materials of digital literature seems particularly germane with the recent establishment of the Electronic Literature Organization (ELO) in October 1999. This is an organization that seeks to "highlight the creative efforts of authors who are producing new forms of literary content based in electronic media," in the words of the flyer announcing the founding of the organization. This is an important goal and such an organization could be a valuable agency in the growth of this literature, a literature, it might be noted, that is not as much "new" as present and active. We look forward to the possibility that this organization will accomplish the goals it has set before itself. More works will, of course, be forthcoming. As we look toward orchestrating the electric light that comprises this medium, it is crucial is to focus on what constitutes electronic literature. That is, work that simply reinscribes literary practice bound with the shackles of modernism and other pre-digital textual modes may offer less than the full potential of the digital medium. Works that engage the technical possibilities of the medium and advance the plural practice that the medium makes possible may offer interesting possibilities. Such works are creating new paradigms for poetic practice based on the textuality of the electronic medium. To explain this, we can consider textuality to be like a precolonial America. Rather than leveling the landscape and pretending it is merely an inert surface upon which to found an empire, let us plant our works within the context of what the medium brings to the scene of art-making, its materiality.

In reference to the investigation I propose, one that seeks an affirmation of the *facts* of the material struggle, I am reminded of the Mexican exclamation, "¡Orale!" "¡Orale!" which means, "Speak it!" or "Indeed!"—but with emphasis to the point of, "Tell it like it is!" The essence of the expression is in orating, or giving a concordant oral message (that's the "oral" in "orale"). "¡Orale!" speaks to the engagement with the real of the activity or fact that is being asserted. It is essential at this point in the development of electronic literature to focus our attention on works that engage the "real" of the activity, continuing innovative practice in poetry and fiction. It is important to engage in practice that has provided a critique of the cultural status quo and of our ways of reading as an apparatus of that status quo. Innovative practice has pioneered not only new media but also new ways of perceiving through a given medium, a practice that has localized art not as a way of *representing* but as a way of *making*. As William Carlos Williams writes: "When a [poet] . . . makes a poem, makes it, mind you, he takes words as he finds them interrelated about him and composes them—without distortion which would mar their exact significances—into an intense expression of his perceptions and ardors that they may constitute a revelation in the speech that he uses. It isn't what he *says* that counts as a work of art, it's what he makes. . . . What does it matter what the line 'says'?" (*Collected* 54). Such a sense of making is what makes *writing* tick. ¡Orale!

What Makes It Innovative?

First, we must acknowledge the extraordinarily innovative work of codex writers Jorge Luis Borges, Julio Cortazar, James Joyce, Gertrude Stein, William Carlos Williams, and Louis Zukofsky, who created hypertexts that pre-date the microchip.[1] More recently, it is appropriate to recognize the artists of "first wave hypertext" (print) and "second wave hypertext" (graphical), periods described by N. Katherine Hayles.[2] These waves do, indeed, break into enticing surf. However, though valuable ground has been covered, I am not sure we have yet framed literary digital practice in a way that would allow us to see the paperless forest for the digital trees. Have any works in recent decades surpassed the codex precursors mentioned above? Or are our reading habits causing us to look at texts that are less than revolutionary? When it comes to locating the great literary works of the digital age, it may well prove that in the present era, the academic lens is focussed too narrowly to pinpoint the forest in front of us.

The problem with the question, "Where can we find hypertexts that will define the digital medium," lies within the question itself. The same confusion exists in the fact that many faculty members consider me "the hypertext guy," despite the fact that I have given talks on "New Media Poetries" and my book is called *Digital Poetics*. In other words, one cannot associate innovative digital practice solely with hypertext. Link-node hypertext only constitutes a small part of the range of possibilities before us and may be a specific ideology within *print* technology, as Aarseth has commented, rather than an actual digital technology.[3] In this sense, link-node hypertext may only remediate print in the electronic medium and does not, by this fact alone, engage the new technology. One cannot assume that if a work is in hypertext, it is by definition, digitally innovative; such an assumption would be like concluding that if I stood before you dressed in a pilot's suit, I would be a pilot and not a poet, a fact that would have horrifying potential if I happened to be in the cockpit on your next flight.

What Criteria Do We Use?

How then do we begin to construct a frame that would define innovative practice in digital literature? Let me suggest the following criteria, not as a definitive list but as a first draft of a list-in-progress.

1. *The position of the "I."* Innovative work avoids the personalized, ego-centered position of the romantic, realist, or modernist "I." Such a sentimentalized "I," often concerned with its own mortality, can be considered as having passed away. Innovative practice is practice that often overcomes the "I" to explore material dimensions of the text. This is, as Robin Blaser has written:

> that matter of language caught
> in the fact so that we
> meet in paradise in such
> times, the I consumes itself
> *(Holy* 61)

Indeed, the "I" does exist in digital literature—but not as an omniscient narrator, raconteur, or master of things to unfold. Rather, it is an initiator of a process that, once begun, "takes over" the way a process executes (thereby consuming the "I") or is an agent that exists in a problemmatized or multiple relation to the text.

2. *The material.* Text grows from code, draws from the drama of code, is rooted in the material of C, or HTML, or Java. Of greatest interest are the convergences and irritations that occur on the boundaries of code and text: it is not interactive fiction but interactive friction that warms the text. To make the work directly related to its semantic-material context is a smart way to work. Smart, the way the URL or Atlanta's subway system, Marta, www.itsmarta.com, can be read both as "www it is Marta dot com" but equally, given an Atlanta pronunciation, "www it's smartah (smarter) dot com." Or, in a more general sense, using landscape architecture as a metaphor, the previous poetic approach was to raze everything that existed at the building site and start with blank ground. The structure is built, then trees are later planted (where others were torn out) to give some natural look to the lot. In this approach there is little consideration given the contours of the land, its ecology, its material, or to what spaces are being covered and uncovered, as Peter Bishop has pointed out in *The Greening of Psychology* (Dallas: Spring Publications, 1991). (If we only consider the undersides of bridges, we will discover the most desolate landscapes in the modern world.) An approach that embodies the innovative is to understand the world that is there and to integrate a building into the natural contours and features of a landscape. This is not merely a logical way to proceed but one that is eco-logical, in the best sense of both words. As John Cage noted in "Aspects of a New Consciousness," art is about becoming open to our environment.[4] Accordingly, the innovative digital literary text employs an architecture that places tex-

tual structures within the contours and values unique to its medium, a practice of textual e-cology.

3. *Enabling of new tools of intelligence.* This quality suggests avoiding the reinscription of authority, totalizing positions, and commodifying of the artistic work. It suggests that writing can be seen, not as an individual personalized achievement, but as a series of strands in a larger social-spatial textual fabric (the network). It points to a sometimes jazz-like cacophony that sets the stage for the outburst of material properties to illuminate the site of the text. The honks, the squawks, the squeals that let you know the jazz instrument is brass, or wood, or reed. Further, new ways and tools to work in the medium, be they morphing programs or animation formats or algorithmic patterns, are not merely methods to realize a personal project. Rather, they are completely different tools in the artist's repertoire, and they expand the metaphoric and creative scope of the human imagination. For a modest example, the "alt" tag to the image of innovative jazz raised above would read, alt="Ornette Coleman, not Kenny G." As to the importance of programming to new modes of intelligence, it is no coincidence that the first program almost every programming student learns to write is called "hello, world," a program that outputs nothing more than the simple statement on the screen, "Hello, world." This output can be seen to indicate a brand-new contact with the world, as if each time a program is written, a new intelligence is born through the algorithm.

What Are Some Traps?

1. *The narrative.* The problem is not narrative itself but, as has been suggested, the fetishization of narrative, or as Markku Eskelinen has described it, "Pompous attempts to master the text."[5] The narratives that are intentional or manipulative may be less compelling than ones that are random, polysemous, or outside traditional plot structures. The idea of plot can give way to a confluence of possibilities for the word to make meaning. One of these future possibilities, Espen Aarseth has commented, is simulation. Indeed, there are many as yet untouched ways to explore character, identity, and action. As to alternative approaches to the game plan in relation to video games, for example, what about the circulation of "cheat codes"? These are codes that, when put into a football video game can allow your tight end to run 100 miles an hour or make every player in the game able to leap twenty feet high. In this light, I always wonder what the video-game makers would think about one young man I know. When he got a new football video game, he played it incessantly. His interest in the video game culminated with his learning to customize two teams, his and the machine's. He, a young man from Buffalo, then created a super team of Bills and a pathetic team of the Cowboys and now plays Superbowl games where the Bills incredibly win by 350 points. In another game, NBA Live 99, he created a custom character

named Charles Bernstein. Subsequently, he created one called Loss Glazier, just in time for a three-point face off with Bernstein. The results of that match will, for diplomacy's sake, remain undisclosed. I'm not sure that these examples are what the game makers had in mind, but I think they show that alternate paths of narrative do exist.

2. *The link*. The link is not, by nature, innovative. (John Cayley has referred to links as "nilsk," an anagrammic rearrangement that, to me, emphasizes their "null" value.)[6] In this vein, it is worth reiterating that link-node hypertext is not the only form of hypertext; it is simply the most common. And yet, its biggest shortcoming is its closeness to print. As Cayley notes, "A node-link hypertext can become a book and vice versa, but text generators require programmatons" (Programmatology). Programmatons, in Cayley's parlance, are computers. Thus he is insisting that the node-link hypertext and the book can be interchanged but the frontier of the innovative, the non-link digital text, *requires* the medium to support it. This is one way to evaluate the relevance of innovative practice in digital media.

3. *The author versus programmer*. The idea of the author becomes richer when considered in relation to the agency of the programmer. The connotations that "author" brings to the text, power, authority, mastery of the text-producing fields, are often unhelpful for innovative writing. Yet the idea of the programmer, on the other hand, or poet-programmer, might offer a potentially interesting alternative. The concept of a poet-programmer or prose-programmer is of a person who works among the tangles of the vines that yield the work. It is of one who sets up a series of events that culminates in the work as an action or execution of procedures. It includes a concept of intelligence that is more concerned with setting into motion a number of variables than with creating a representation. The concern is, more specifically, with the parameters, character, and nuances of that motion as action. The focus is less on any individual product of that process, though individual products can be valuable as documentation of a given process.

Where Do We Want to Go?

1. *Our conception of the field can be considerably broadened*. Similar to the way that Charles Olson re-mapped the concept of the field regarding the relationship between typographic spacing and the codex page, is the way code, the visual, the transient, and the multiple are important to our concept of the field of the innovative digital work. As N. Katherine Hayles pointed out in "Print Is Flat, Code Is Deep," writing is less than exclusively the projection of ideas from the flat, uniform plane of print. (To such a distinction I would also add the "underworld" of the actual mark-up or programming language itself. There are a plethora of new fields to be furrowed.) The text now revels in radical forms of adjacency—a metonymy that comes from overlaying, collage, juxtaposition of visual elements, and forms of mapping. Such

conjunctions of creolized, diverse, and heterogeneous components are forms that innovative print poetry has investigated extensively and will continue to investigate; indeed innovative e-poetry will continue to exist in relation to innovative print poetry. Digital innovative practice can add to the possibilities of print the concept of programming as writing and the real-time action that programs realize.

2. *The Commune/Web.* To consider where our world stands in relation to a concept of open and shared textuality, we only need to consider a newspaper headline like the following: "Global Competition Fells Japan Tradition" (*USA Today*, 27 Jan. 1999, p. 1). It shows that to "go global" is to take the paradigm of U.S. economic competition and, when the scale changes, simply transfer it to the new locale. What is ignored are the implications of "global." Take for example its ecological implications. It is not necessarily culturally productive to fell things, traditions or forests for profit or other reasons. Or again, an enlightened concept of "global" would include the fact that we collectively share a place, an environment, a network. In textual terms, it means that writing is a whole and that as individuals we are just a part of that whole. How much more interesting the "text" of a literary conference becomes, for example, when we consider the whole conference a text, rather than looking to an individual presentation for that sort of breadth.

3. *The non-semantic, the spatial, the polymedial, and the creolized open new registers in possibility for the text.* It is crucial to recognize that emergent forms of expression may not necessarily be recognizable as variants of previous forms. In addition, in the digital medium, forms that are "live," that execute in the presence of the reader, offer experiences in textuality a world apart from the rigidity of fixed paths through a textual field. Such concepts help locate new media within the innovative tradition.

Conclusion: What Are We *Making* Here?

> text breaks into architecture of page
> floating Figs
> scholar riding in Capital C
> —Joan Retallack, *Afterrimages*

Given such a topology of electronic materiality, we are next obliged to examine existing electronic literature to see where it would fit into such a scheme. Indeed, is all electronic literature innovative? Which electronic works push innovative writing practices and which rely on more modernist or new critical understandings of the "word"? Is materiality the way to make this distinction? What attributes constitute the innovative in an e-poetry, hypertext, or other digital works of art? What valence does the visual bear? How do you classify the role of procedure in relation to a text that is produced?

We have clearly entered a new era; it benefits the literary and cultural scholar to take note of this new landscape. The question is whether we take advantage of this transition to diversify and pluralize the possibilities for literary form. Do we incorporate new modes of expression into our discourse and models, or do we simply reinscribe old values onto new media? Most promising are scenarios in which we wrest ourselves away from our moorings so that we allow our bearings to adjust to the medium at hand; we do not want to echo the genre-lapse of the movie reviewer who describes a film as "a voluptuous page-turner of a movie." We do not want to be distracted by the "image versus text," or other essentially analog debates. It is as if we have been given a huge, brand-new, conceptually revolutionary operating system. The question then becomes, do we simply Laplink our old files to the new machine, or do we use this opportunity to reinvigorate, pluralize, and fortify our intelligence? What places us in that uncomfortable position between the Academy and a hard drive? It is the fact that a difficult leap of perception faces us? Can we defy our habits? Our idea of the digital literary work is confined by literary practice that has become habitual by nature; thus it is hard to see something anew and then part with old habits. The hard choice before us is to identify new forms of literature, expand our habits, and not be restricted to old forms in new clothes.

One example of such "old clothes" is the present social condition of the disposable environment; a condition typified by a troubling lack of focus on the material (the planet, our relations with others, our shared intelligence).[7] Art has historically addressed such issues and continues to do so now. What is culturally necessary is to broaden ways of seeing. Digital technologies give us alternative and multiple ways to expand the way we "make" the world. Engaging the materiality of the digital medium is a way to genuinely engage more diverse possibilities for writing and is the path that must be pursued. As culture progresses through innovation, the innovative in digital literature can diversify and pluralize our relation to the text and to the world.

Literary culture in general is still not far from the computer phobia that existed in the early days of word processing. As digital media scholars, our views about the textualities of digital art must be as open as possible, to pull literary culture along a little more. The digital condition is real and present; it is quite urgent that we address the fact of the vibrant digital literature before us and begin the difficult drive to embrace it. What needs to be done? We need to get under the hood of this silicon horse, roll it through the gates of academia, and (if I might refer to the fact that the first digital culture conference occurred in Norway) pour out with brandished fjords. This field offers many opportunities for literary scholars with an interest in innovative literature. Adequate terms and an appropriate discourse to describe the unfathomed richness of the materials of the digital medium are only now in the making. The interdisciplinary facets of digital work offer rich areas of exploration. The relation between technical and aesthetic aspects of such works is an engaging one. We will be well served by demanding more from our monitors and seeing beyond computerized works that could simply exist on paper, the way Imamu Amiri Baraka saw the limits of the typewriter of his generation:

> A typewriter?—why shd it only make use of the tips of the fingers as contact points of flowing multi directional creativity. If I invented a word placing machine, an "expression-scriber," if you will, then I would have a kind of instrument into which I could step & sit or sprawl or hang & use not only my fingers to make words express feelings but elbows, feet, head, behind, and all the sounds I wanted, screams, grunts, taps, itches, I'd have magnetically recorded, at the same time, & translated into word— or perhaps even the final xpressed thought/feeling wd not be merely word or sheet, but itself, the xpression, three dimensional—able to be touched, or tasted or felt, or entered, or heard or carried like a speaking singing constantly communicating charm. A typewriter is corny!! (*Raise* 156)

The electronic medium is physical; it is material. It is valuable to explore its possibilities through the lens of innovative practice. Echoing the passage above we might say that word-processed poems or non-revelatory link-node exercises would be, by Baraka's terms, also "corny." They do not offer a real engagement with digital practice but, borrowing also from Lawrence Ferlinghetti, a "corny island of the mind." Let us take Baraka's suggestion to heart. Explore the multiple possibilities of *making* in this medium. Emerge from the study with wires tangled in our hair, pixels in our spirit, happy to find that physical interaction with the intangible that makes it *making*.

Notes

Although every attempt has been made to provide up-to-date URLs, some may have changed, and some occasionally get changed without warning to sites that may be objectionable. I have attempted to warn readers when a site has changed as of the time this book went to press; however, please be aware that a site can change at any time.

Introduction

1. In general, the term "poetry" is used in this volume to refer to practices of innovative poetry rather than to what might be called academic, formal, or traditional forms of poetry.

2. There is no agreed-upon term for digital poetry. It will sometimes be referred to in this volume as digital poetry, electronic poetry, e-poetry, computer-poetry, or computer-generated writing. See chapter 8, "Future Tenses," for a more complete discussion of the terms and boundaries of electronic poetics.

3. These efforts included Jackson Mac Low and John Cage's use of computer programs to generate mesostic and diastic readings of texts, the publication of Hugh Kenner and Joseph O'Rourke's Travesty program in 1984, Charles O. Hartman's presentation of the program Diastext to Jackson Mac Low, and the development of StorySpace. See chapter 7, "E-poetries," for more on this topic.

4. http://epc.buffalo.edu, http://www.ubu.com, and http://www.burningpress.org (1 Jan. 2001).

5. See the subsection on HTML in the "Sidebar: On Techne" section later in this introduction.

6. This passage plays on a number of technical terms, a poetic play on the multiple possibilities that almost all words, regardless of their technical nature, present. See this book's glossary for some definitions of the terms used in this book.

7. Netscape is chosen in this example as the only alternative to the rigidity of Microsoft's Internet Explorer. IE has established itself as a corporate standard, a position with inherent ideological ramifications. Both browsers should be considered equally "sloppy" in the degree of control that is available for Web-based documents.

8. http://jefferson.village.virginia.edu (15 Jan. 2000).

9. http://scco1.rutgers.edu/ceth (15 Jan. 2000).

10. http://www.kcl.ac.uk/humanities/cch/bib (15 Jan. 2000).

11. *Postmodern Culture* 7, no. 3 (1997), Stuart Moulthrop, issue ed., http://muse.jhu.edu/journals/pmc/v007 [subscribers only] (6 March 1999).

12. *Electronic Book Review*, http://www.altx.com/ebr (6 March 1999).

13. Ultimately, one could argue that, as time passes, each of the systems compared here become more like each other. NT can be used like UNIX to distribute software, allow multiple users access to specific files, and perform various network functions. NT also allows single-user computing to exist within a network environment, a fact that becomes increasingly apparent with the converging interface designs of Windows Millennium Edition (formerly Windows 98) and Windows 2000 (formerly NT 5.0). Equally, you could point to facets of UNIX, its ability to restrict as well as to allow access, and conclude that it can be used like NT. Obviously, these systems can be configured in many ways to do similar things. In this sidebar I seek to point to larger, conceptual issues that underlie these systems.

14. Programming purists will insist that HTML is not code, a term reserved for the executable instructions that constitute computer programs. This is an accurate point. Nevertheless, there is a broader sense of the term "code" that refers to a text that appears unreadable because it is meant to be interpreted by a machine. In this sense "code" is appropriate for HTML.

15. The boxer Oscar de la Hoya once commented that if you put paint on his feet you would see a stunning painting on the ring after he was done with the fight. It is this innate dynamic sense of writing as an underpinning for action that HTML makes manifest. Indeed, this is one of the aspects of writing that has been changed irreversibly by digital writing.

16. See chapter 2, "Our Words," in this volume for more on the rapid pace of development of the Internet.

17. "I thought of throwing it in the fire, but I feared that the combustion of an infinite book would be equally infinite and would engulf the planet in smoke" (trans. Glazier).

18. It is also telling that the narrator trades his own Bible for the new book and that the phrase, "the Book of Sand," in Borges's text is neither italicized nor put in quotation marks, i.e., it is treated like the title of a religious book. (Typically, titles of books, such as *Digital Poetics*, are italicized.) This same convention is followed in the Spanish edition of this book, *El Libro de Arena* (Barcelona: Plaza & Janes, 1991).

19. The term "conventional hypertext" is used here to refer to link-node hypertexts that present readers with a series of choices constructed around a narrative flow. It is not meant to refer to all forms of hypertext. Other forms of hypertext do present more interesting possibilities for the medium, the concept of the link as an occlusion, detailed in this volume, and Jim Rosenberg's investigations of multiple texts occupying a single location, among them.

20. For example, the link can be seen as a king of metaphoric connection, stylistic choices in motifs used for a Web page could be called a conceit (a mixture of text and image as a logically complicated image), and measure and meter are quite tangible as frames/second in a kinetic poem. Both concrete poetry and abstract poetry have direct relevance to types of poetry that

are being investigated in the digital environment.

21. Not all mimeo era productions employed mimeography. Instead, as I noted in my book *Small Press: An Annotated Guide*, "the appeal of the term [Mimeo Revolution] is the idea of self-sufficiency in producing literary texts; this idea fueled the movement and provided a model for decades to come" (3). Certainly, this spirit continues in some of the more innovative digital sites.

22. One must note that the idea of the digital text contrasts sharply with conventional conceptions of the term "hypertext." A hypertext *can* be conditional but only inasmuch as there is variability to the sequence of link choices made by the user. A conventional conception of hypertext presents a much narrower sense of the conditional, and a much smaller range of possibilities, than what is considered here for the digital text.

23. Some of the works discussed here were accessed at UbuWeb, http://www.ubu.com (18 Dec. 1999).

24. In the words of the online ASCII Art FAQ, "ASCII artwork denotes artwork that is created without using graphics at all. Its palette is limited to the symbols that you have available to you on your computer keyboard" (Veland). This, it seems, would also qualify as concrete poetry, with images formed from keyboard (or typeset) characters. Such artwork also characterizes a historical period in the development of the Web, as in the gopher era and the days of VT100 text-only computer terminals (which cannot display images), it was not uncommon for graphics to be formed from typographic characters. In gopher, banners and other textual features were always composed with typographic characters. For example:

```
H   H    I  I  I
H H H       I
H   H    I  I  I
```

might represent a greeting of "Hi" on the top of a gopher page or mainframe computer printout. Currently, emoticons (:>) are probably the most recognizable form of ASCII art, though one limited in scope. For more elaborate ASCII artwork, the reader is referred to The Great ASCII Art Library, http://www.geocities.com/SouthBeach/Marina/4942/ascii.htm (22 Feb. 2000).

25. http://www.vispo.com/animisms/SeattleDrift.html (18 Dec. 1999).

26. http://epc.buffalo.edu/authors/wershler-henry/grain.html, http://wings.buffalo.edu/epc/authors/glazier/viz/fish/fish.html, http://net22.com/qazingulaza/joglars/afteremmett/bonvoyage.html (all accessed 18 Dec. 1999).

27. This is a term I would use for the numerous home computer book publishing efforts that multiplied when home book production software became affordable in the 1980s.

28. The "Beyond Art" conference, for example, explored the following questions: "Are the arts being threatened or inspired by the use of computers? How has the popularization and pervasive nature of digital technology

changed the creative process of the artist, the actor, the filmmaker, the architect, and the writer? What has been the effect of technology on the viewer, the reader, or the critic? And what of those who seek to fund and preserve our cultural heritage?" ("Beyond"). "In the Event of the Text" is an excellent title for a conference, because the title itself signals a fundamental shift from text as a fixed and rigid concept to something that is fluid, active, and spatially located.

29. The relation between interface and ideology is a close one. For one example, consider early books, many of which were Bibles, which had to be read in a standing position. The interface of such quarto and octavo volumes, which implied a certain ponderousness to the word and positioned the reader as a kind of supplicant to the text, contrast sharply with the interface of the dime novel, a book that is meant to be consumed and discarded. Of course, the sizes of the books mentioned above might more properly be called formats, but format and interface present similar dynamics. The arrangement and mechanisms of computer interfaces have a similar range of implications.

Chapter 1. Jumping to Occlusions

1. For example, people see a book and think of "a book" or "the knowledge object" and not "a message fixed into a linear progression of paper pages."

2. Greps are discussed at various points in this book. For the purposes of this volume, a grep is a writing generated by using UNIX's standard grep program to parse a file based on given input characters. The output of this operation is an "interpreted" or "alter" version of the text of a source file, that is, a machine-modulated literary text. For more on this topic, see the section "Grep: A Grammar" in chapter 6.

3. Alberto Moreiras's "Can we define a task of thinking that would refuse to believe in itself above and beyond technique?" (194). Donna Haraway's "A cyborg world might be about lived social and bodily realities in which people are not afraid of their joint kinship with animals and machines, not afraid of permanently partial identities and contradictory standpoints" (196).

4. See chapter 3, "Home, Haunt, Page," in this volume for more on this topic.

5. In this context, it might irk some of the more conservative fine printers to consider mimeo, the flagship of early small press, sensuous. Yet when one considers the weight, feel, appearance—even fragrance—of *C* magazine, *Adventures in Poetry*, or many of the works published by d.a. levy, the tactile experience of mimeo is undeniable.

6. See "A How to Read" in this volume for more on digital materiality.

7. This concept was made famous in Charles Olson's well-known "Projective Verse" essay (in his *Selected Writings*).

8. Note that though link-node hypertext is addressed here, it is only *one form* of hypertext. See also chapter 5 in this volume for more on hypertext.

9. The important hypertext author and critic, Jim Rosenberg, has objected strongly to this view of hypertext as rupture. He comments, "I see hypertext not as about rupture from the linear, but as a *connectivity technology* . . . My vision of hypertext is very intense connectivity, taken down all the way into the fine structure of language, inside the sentence. The question that has motivated me for a very long time is what does it mean to build a poetry where you start with this connectivity and build with it *entirely*" ("Re: Update"). That is, Rosenberg sees hypertext as a tool of manifold connecting possibilities. He notes, "Hypertext gives us new ways to build word objects. It's not about breaking apart the linear, it's about building things." (See Rosenberg's concept of the "episode" in his "Structure of Hypertext Activity" paper, http://www.cs.unc.edu/~barman/HT96/P17/SHA_out.html.) His conception provides an informative alternative to the model expressed here. The difference in conceptualizations really lies in the type of hypertext being discussed. This chapter is concerned with challenging link-node hypertext, particularly as found on the Web. Rosenberg's view of hypertext is concentrated on the potentials of diverse experimental hypertext models. Readers are encouraged to read Rosenberg's essay and his own works of poetry, works that realize the possibility for multiple writings to occupy the same position. His method brings depth and connectivity to hypertext in extraordinary ways.

10. Sigmund Freud, *Introductory Lectures on Psycho-Analysis*, standard ed. (New York: Norton, 1966), 17–98.

11. These are poems that try to thread a path between layers of language, covering two "substructural" languages of the U.S. idiom. First is the discourse of the Net, especially as evidenced by the sensationalism surrounding each release of Windows. The second idiom is Spanish (a language preexisting English in the southwestern U.S. and in much of America), a subterranean presence in our linguistic fabric, a very relevant, if unacknowledged, "mark-up" and linguistic seam for American languages. (One must also consider the seams between American Spanish and the Native American languages, such as Nahuatl, that preceded it and the influences of French in south and northeast North America.)

Chapter 2. Our Words

1. In the words of the *Netscape Handbook*, TCP/IP is "short for Transmission Control Protocol/Internet Protocol, the standard communications protocol required for Internet computers" (http://home.netscape.com/eng/mozilla/1.1/handbook/docs/answers.html#C32 [22 Oct. 1999]).

2. The classic conundrum about the information seeker is this: not only does such a person not have the information they seek—but they do not

even know what they actually want. That is, a person looking for the address of a sporting association might ask for a book on tennis. (What the person actually wants is an encyclopedia of associations.) It is fairly typical for people to be unable to articulate the information source they need. This is further complicated when a person is operating on misperceptions (confusing "etymology" for "entomology," etc.) or errors of fact. When information is sought in person, the first step in satisfying the information-seeker's request is to determine what the person *actually* needs, rather than what the person *thinks* is there. The Web, because it is writing, must negotiate such a situation textually: that is, a screen, if it is to succeed, must, *through its writing*, channel an information seeker's inquiry, provide a path, and textually circumnavigate any common or predictable difficulties for the reader.

3. For example, the works of authors from different countries who worked very closely together would be in different locations on the shelves. Even farther apart in the library would be a novel based on a philosophy and a nonfiction work on that philosophy by the same author.

4. Statistics are based on those reported by Win Treese in *The Internet Index*, available at http://www.openmarket.com/intindex/index.cfm (31 Jan. 2000).

5. Statistic from "Matthew Gray of the Massachusetts Institute of Technology," http://www.mit.edu/people/mkgray/net/printable/internet-growth-summary.html (22 Feb. 1999).

6. http://www.netsizer.com/daily.html (31 Jan. 2000).

7. Three-wheeled cars are much easier to park; they clearly might be superior in some situations.

8. For one example of the relevance of such orders, see Jerome McGann's in-depth exploration of Ezra Pound's "scriptural imagination," how these textual apparatuses function in the first edition of the *Cantos*. McGann suggests that "one of Pound's greatest contributions to poetry lies concealed in his attentiveness to the smallest details of his texts' bibliographical codes" (*Textual* 137). These "codes" are, of course, his texts' "orders"—their references, contexts, and materials.

9. "It is wrong to say: I think. One should say: One thinks (through) me. . . . / I is an other" (trans. Glazier).

10. In this context it is interesting to note that Microsoft's new interface is referred to as Windows ME.

11. The *World Almanac* notes that in 2000, eight hair-thin optical fibers can transmit the equivalent of 90,000 encyclopedia volumes in a second, a somewhat less grand claim but difficult to imagine, nonetheless.

12. "The point is arriving at the unknown through the disordering of all the senses. The sufferings are enormous, but one must be strong, must be born a poet, and I have realized I am a poet" (trans. Glazier).

13. Obviously, such search engines will continue to be developed. Though significant advances can be made in the design of such engines, the assump-

tions of indexing systems must always be questioned.

14. http://epc.buffalo.edu/rift, http://epc.buffalo.edu/ezines/diu, http://epc.buffalo.edu/ezines/passages (all accessed on 22 Oct. 1999).

15. http://www.jacket.zip.com.au/welcome.html, http://www.heelstone.com/meridian, http://www.departments.bucknell.edu/stadler_center/how2, http://epc.buffalo.edu/ezines/deluxe, http://www.jps.net/nada/index.html (all accessed on 3 May 2000).

16. See Bernstein's "Artifice of Absorption, A Poetics," esp. pp. 67–68.

17. 1998 statistic from Win Treese, http://www.openmarket.com/intindex/98-05.htm (21 Feb. 1999).

18. Statistic from Win Treese, http://www.openmarket.com/intindex/93–12.htm (21 Feb. 1999).

19. Another decision about link words involves their appearance. By default, they are a different color than text and an even different color after they have been clicked. Does having them a different color overly foreground their status as link words? Should link words be undifferentiated, i.e., the same color as regular text (invisible)? If they were the same color, would it be apparent enough they should be clicked?

20. Even viewed from Rosenberg's conception of the link as a connective force, the moment of switching from one level to the next can be abrupt and startling.

Chapter 3. Home, Haunt, Page

1. Domain suffixes appear in the address of a home page and, when indicating national origin, give it a sense of location. For example, the URL of the home page of Radio UNAM, the radio station of the National Autonomous University of Mexico, is http://www.unam.mx/radiounam, the "MX" referring, of course, to Mexico. The United States, apparently considered a default location, does not generally employ a country suffix.

2. The word "frame" here is not to be confused with frames as a design option for the Web. It is closest to the term "lexia" or "frame" when used in film studies. "Lexia" is not used because there is no suggestion that a frame is a semantic whole, as J. David Bolter, George Landow, and others have suggested.

3. http://www.soos.com/poetpark (1 Oct. 1995). Please note that this site has now been converted into a gateway for adult sites. How "home" can change. . . .

4. Sites examined include: Prose & Contexts Online, formerly at http://www.interlog.com/~dal (22 Nov. 1997) and now superseded by Bitwalla Design http://www.bitwalla.com (23 Oct. 23 1999); Fingerprinting Inkoperated, http://www.interlog.com/~dal/fi/index.html (22 Nov. 1997); http://www.bitwalla.com/fi/index.html (23 Oct. 1999); Subtext, http://speakeasy.org/subtext (22 Nov. 1997); Grist, http://www.thing.net/~grist (22

Nov. 1997); P-Net, now defunct but formerly at http://www.wimsey.com/
~ksw/pnet/pnet.htm (22 Nov. 1997); and the Electronic Poetry Center, http://
epc.buffalo.edu (22 Nov. 1997).

5. A home page fits many descriptions. This brings us to a popular joke:
Following a burglary, a cultured man is concerned, not so much with the
television, VCR, and stereo he has lost, but with a large painting that was
taken during the crime. He searches the city to find his painting. At last
when he finds it, he discovers that a homeless man (a man without a "page"
of his own?), claiming to have retrieved it from a dumpster, now has it propped
in the alley where he is living. The cultured man demands that he return the
painting. The homeless man puts forth an eloquent argument about the
artistic merit of the painting and its ability to uplift the human spirit. Moved,
the cultured man, in a grand gesture of generosity, allows the other to keep
the painting. After he leaves, the homeless man turns to a friend and com-
ments, "Thank goodness he changed his mind. We almost lost our roof!"
(Interestingly, "hame," in Middle Dutch, is "covering.")

6. Shakespeare, *Romeo & Juliet* III:i, *Scribner's Magazine*, Aug. 1877, and
James Joyce, *Ulysses* (1961), 302, respectively.

Chapter 5. Hypertext/Hyperpoeisis/Hyperpoetics

1. A word needs to be said about approbation. Having an authoritative
agency approve a work reflects the relation between the printed word and
the validating superstructure that mainstream publishing effects. Such an
agency of validation evokes Phyllis Wheatley, the eighteenth-century Ameri-
can slave who was the first published African American. Before her book
could be published Wheatley was summoned to appear before a committee
of eighteen prominent citizens "entrusted with the solemn task of deter-
mining whether or not an African-born slave was capable of writing poetry
in the English language" (Basbanes). The approval of the committee was
certified in an "attestation" provided as a preface to her poetry collection.
Their statement included the following: "We whose Names are under-writ-
ten, do assure the World, that the POEMS specified in the following Page,
were (as we verily believe) written by PHILLIS, a young Negro Girl, who
was but a few Years since, brought an uncultivated Barbarian from Africa.
... She has been examined by some of the best Judges, and is thought qualified
to write them" (Basbanes). Corporate publishing has exercised, it can be
argued, a similar control through the book selection process, the politics of
reviewing, and conglomerates that control circulation and promotion of
books, similarly screening the "uncultivated Barbarians" of unconventional
writing. This resonates with the fact that, after Gutenberg made it possible
for Bibles to be individually owned, schools of religious thought emerged
that would argue for less intervention in the human-deity relation. This
may be seen as a liberation of the word if you are an optimist, a degradation

of the word if you believe more can be less, or a sign of the declining capital value of the written word if you look to an economic model for an explanation. The fact is that it is now possible for anyone to publish just about anything; this inundation characterizes the environment within which Web-based hypertext must function.

2. http://www.csd.uwo.ca/~jamie/hypertext-faq.html (2 Mar. 1999).

3. The Xanadu FAQ describes Xanadu as "An overall paradigm—an ideal and general model for all computer use, based on sideways connections among documents and files. This paradigm is especially concerned with electronic publishing, but it also extends to all forms of storing, presenting and working with information. It is a unifying system of order for all information, non-hierarchical and side-linking, including electronic publishing, personal work, organization of files, corporate work and groupware" ("Xanadu"). John Cayley notes: "I think that actually with the docuverse and his notion of transclusion (the literal, link-evoked *incorporation* of quoted material into any extension to a new part of the docuverse which is in the process of composition), rather than pioneering a first version of the Web, Nelson conceived of a very different form for "the Web" (as if there is only one possible Web) before it existed, one which would have been radically different—not necessarily 'better' but a much stronger challenge to the world of letters than hypertext or the actually-existing Web (which can't even take on copyright it sometimes seems)" ("Chapters").

4. Note that the "Compact for Responsive Electronic Writing," a Web user's/programmer's convention followed by some Web providers, commits itself to the interlinking of documents within the Web in order to foster "new forms of collective intelligence." The guiding statement of the "Compact" is as follows: "Should a fellow user of the World Wide Web request that I include within my own work a link to her or his work, I will make every reasonable effort to accommodate that request."

5. The issue of control is a big one. As a dramatization of how much authorial control is possible in hypertext, my work "That Thing About Client Pull" is subtitled "Hypertext without a Mouse" and uses a Web feature called "client pull" to present a series of hyperlinked screens that move in a timed sequence without any input from the reader. Such control is also the focus of certain software packages that offer visual maps and other aids so that the writer can engineer the possible paths of reading.

6. URLs are as follows: "Hypertext" at The Electronic Labyrinth, http://jefferson.village.virginia.edu/elab/hfl0037.html, 1995 (11 Dec. 2000); Scott Stebelman's "Hypertext and Hypermedia: A Select Bibliography" at The George Washington University, http://www.hfni.gsehd.gwu.edu/gelman/instruct/symposia/biblio96.html, 1997 (11 Dec. 2000); and the "Research & Theory on Hypertext" section of the "Voice of the Shuttle: Technology of Writing Page," http://vos.ucsb.edu/shuttle/techwrit.html#hypertext, 1999 (10 Jan. 1999).

7. The Web page, "Landow's Overview Types" (http://jefferson.village.virginia.edu/elab/hfl0101.html), abstracts material presented in a longer format in Landow's essay "The Rhetoric of Hypermedia" (in Delany and Landow, *Hypermedia and Literary Studies* [Cambridge: MIT UP, 1991,] pp. 81–103). Page numbers on the Web page refer to the book version of this essay.

8. Martin Spinelli, making an observation about David Bolter, writes about a similar lack of engagement with the possibilities of hypertext. Bolter is not using the potentials of hypertext, Spinelli argues, "In fact, the reverse is true, *Ulysses* and *Finnegans Wake* would be flattened out by the type of hypertextual rendering Bolter proposes" (87).

9. See the discussion of the prefix "hyper" on pp. 57–58 in this volume.

10. http://www.heelstone.com/meridian (7 Feb. 2001).

Chapter 6. Coding Writing, Reading Code

1. Grep is a program that enters a file, searches it, and creates a separate entity. Grep gives such an emphasis to process that its default destination (or "standard output") is not even a file, only an impermanent display on the screen.

2. Commands such as grep present interesting alternatives to dominant paradigms for electronic writing, such as those that typify Microsoft products. Indeed, the graphical environment that characterizes most word processing programs is much more imprecise than it would seem. Events such as the sudden unexplainable crashes that have typified Windows result from pile-ups among multitudes of invisible programs, i.e., for reasons the user cannot even see. User vulnerability to unpredictable events increases when the user is restricted from access to source code because it is proprietary. In the UNIX system, by contrast, access to source code is a fundamental tenet of how that computing environment works. Grep also reminds one of the pre-Windows environment of DOS. Like UNIX, the DOS environment included consummately effective flags, undeviating execution of procedure, and starkly literal (and material) textual output.

3. Though short-lived (1850–52), the friendship between Nathaniel Hawthorne and Herman Melville was an intense one. It began with each writer writing about the other's books and ends most markedly with Hawthorne in Melville's books as Vine in *Clarel* and as the subject of "Monody." It was Hawthorne's influence that may have turned *Moby Dick* from a sea adventure into a darker investigation.

4. The full title is "The Fishtail: Arrowhead, or 'The Whale.'" These letters are available at "The Life and Works of Herman Melville," http://www.melville.org/corresp.htm (4 Jan. 2001). Hawthorne's letters to Melville would have also been used but none seem to have survived. (This might be expected because of Hawthorne's lack of interest in Melville during the latter stages of their relationship.)

5. Poetics logs are available at http://listserv.acsu.buffalo.edu/archives/poetics.html (19 Dec. 2000).

6. Though purists will argue that HTML mark-up is not programming, as noted earlier, it is referred to as code here. HTML is often called code, but also note that (1) many of the conventions of programming are relevant to HTML mark-up; (2) with the inclusion of JavaScript in HTML, the line between mark-up and programming becomes even more blurred; and (3) mark-up does involve the writing of instructions for later interpretation and thus might be thought of as an elementary form of programming.

7. See Knuth's, *The Art of Computer Programming* (Reading, MA: Addison-Wesley, 1997–98) for a detailed introduction to writing computer programs.

8. Awareness of the differences between browsers is critical given the intensifying competition between Netscape and Internet Explorer. Many elements are now specific only to one browser or the other, including tags such as background sound, blink, layer, marquee, and multicolumn and some attributes to body, frame, image, and border, among others. It is critical to be aware of these differences since a mis-rendered work of art/literature can display profoundly differently from the artist's conception.

9. It must be emphasized again that there can be immense benefits to writing, or at least reading, unmediated HTML code. For a description of HTML, see the "On HTML" section of the sidebar in the introduction to this volume.

10. Coding errors, such as out-of-place or missing quotation marks, for example, would be obvious.

11. *The Maximus Poems* is a book that, in itself, experiments with such visual dynamics. See esp. pp. 438 and 498–99.

12. The code "&ntilde" is interesting because many people do not even know the name of the "~" character. Hence, when it is used in mark-up, in "Pequeño," for example ("Pequeño"), this somewhat unfamiliar character seems to speak its own name.

13. A playful interpretation of "&amp," for example, reveals a morpheme of the word "ampersand" buried within the concatenation of characters that represents it. This is all the more interesting since we rarely spell "ampersand" or pronounce any part of it; so the "amp" sound is always hidden—except when in code.

14. For example, Luca Cardelli argues that "everything is an Object" and that "everything can be represented in terms of objects." Obviously Cardelli is contrasting objects, here in programming terms, with functions and classes, yet the resonance is striking.

15. Interestingly, Olson's theory of poetry was called "Projective Verse."

16. To reveal the HTML source code in Netscape Communicator 4.51, for example, click on "View" and then "Page Source." A new window will open where the HTML source code will be displayed. Other versions of Netscape and other browsers should offer a similar option.

17. To do this in Netscape Communicator 4.51, for example, click on

"Edit" and then "Preferences." There you will be able to uncheck "Automatically load images." Other versions of Netscape and other browsers should offer a similar option.

18. "Mouseover: Essay in Javascript," *Electronic Book Review* 7, "image+narrative part two" (Summer 1998), http://www.altx.com/ebr/ebr7/ebr7.htm (May 2001).

19. "Mouseover" also contains a significant hypertextual apparatus, not addressed here. For a discussion of this apparatus and for a detailed reading of this work covering issues not undertaken here, please consult Martin Spinelli, "Communication Technology and Literary Community: From Utopia to Paralogy" (Ph.D. diss., State U of New York, 1998), 106-9.

Chapter 7. E-poetries

1. Though American practice continues to be somewhat isolationist, especially in the field of hypertext, the communications breakthrough of the Internet has made interchange with non-U.S. writers more common. A complete look at e-poetries should involve a more sustained look at practitioners working outside the United States, especially John Cayley, Philipe Bootz, Jean Pierre Balpe, writers associated with the French "generator poetry" movement, writers working in Oulipo, and continental Canadian and Australian writers. I attempt to suggest such a breadth of practice in this chapter.

2. The 1960–61 works by Mac Low (poems written by deterministic procedures and indeterminate performance works composed by chance operations or intentionally but realized by guided improvisation) are included in *An Anthology*, edited by La Monte Young (Bronx, NY: Young and Mac Low, 1963; 2nd ed., New York: Heiner Friedrich, 1970). Intentionally composed musical and other performance works by Young and others that are in the book are also indeterminate as to performance, showing that others were then exploring such methods.

3. From 1955 on, Mac Low composed a number of poems and musical works by "translation" procedures whereby notes in musical scores are translated into words, or words are translated into notes. Among these, *Homage to Leona Bleiweiss* is dedicated to the deviser of a *New York Post* word game, whose wordlist solutions are translated into note groups performed improvisationally by instrumentalists.

4. Poems from *Stein* can be accessed from Mac Low's author page at the Electronic Poetry Center, http://epc.buffalo.edu/authors/maclow.

5. It must be noted that the use of a colonial metaphor here could also be considered insensitive to contemporary views on the culture of the Americas.

6. These include Gerrit Krol's *APPI: Automatic Poetry by Pointed Information, Poëzie met een Computer* (1971); Robert Sigmund's *Energy Crisis Poems:*

Poetry by Program (1974); Pedro Barbosa's *A Literatura Cibernética* (1977); Eugen Gomringer's *Kein Fehler im System: Eine Unsystematische Auswahl von Sätzen aus dem Gleichnamigen (Imaginären)* (1978); *The Policeman's Beard Is Half-Constructed: Computer Prose and Poetry* (created in 1984 by Racter, a computer program written by W. Chamberlain and T. Etter); Judith Kerman's *Interactive Poem Demo Animated Picture Poems* (1987); and Fabio Doctorovich's *Bribage Cartooniano* (1994).

7. Charles Bernstein, "Experiments," http://epc.buffalo.edu/authors/bernstein/experiments.html (6 March 1999); "Bernadette Mayer's Writing Experiments," http://www.poetryproject.com/mayer.html (6 March 1999).

8. The Voyager CD-ROM Store is at http://www4.viaweb.com/voyagerco/index.html (6 March 1999); and Eastgate Systems Inc. is at http://www.eastgate.com (6 March 1999). At last visit (26 Dec. 2000), *Poetry in Motion* was not listed in the Voyager catalog.

9. Thomas Swiss has written provocatively about Eastgate's marketing strategies and advertising discourse in relation to its claims to literary innovation. As Swiss sees it, this is a discourse that "positions the company and its authors as both advocates of noise (meant to overthrow the literary mainstream) *and* music (meant to enter the mainstream)" (Swiss). Swiss's argument is informative in the context of Eastgate's position in the hypertext community.

10. http://www.eastgate.com (1 Jan. 2001).

11. Jim Rosenberg has successfully overcome this platform fracture; his work has been available for Windows since 1996. Beginning early in 2000, Rosenberg has also begun to adapt his works for Web-based reading.

12. Kac has noted in his essay "Photonic Webs in Time: The Art of Holography" that the word "hologram" is preferable to the often used "holograph" to describe works in this medium.

13. This figure results from an Alta Vista search for the term "poetry" on 4 June 1999.

14. Grist On-Line Magazine, ed. John Fowler, http://www.thing.net/~grist (6 March 1999).

15. Karl Young, ed., http://www.thing.net/~grist/l&d/lighthom.htm (6 March 1999).

16. Luigi-Bob Drake, ed., http://www.burningpress.org/va/vaintro.html (6 March 1999).

17. Both Karl Young and Luigi-Bob Drake view their sites as forms of extended anthologies.

18. http://www.chbooks.com (6 March 1999).

19. Kenneth Goldsmith, ed., http://www.ubu.com/ (6 March 1999 and 31 Dec. 2000). Unfortunately, due to a serious server crash, Ubuweb lost much valuable data in February 2000, marking a sudden and immense loss of information for the online poetry community. The situation seemed irrevocable and Ubuweb users were in shock at the prospect that so much

excellent material could be instantly lost. Fortunately, recovery efforts succeeded and Ubuweb returned in an expanded version later in 2000. The incident was, however, quite a sobering example of the impermanent nature of the Web environment.

20. Loss Pequeño Glazier, Director, http://epc.buffalo.edu (6 March 1999).

21. LINEbreak is hosted and co-produced by Charles Bernstein and produced and directed by Martin Spinelli.

22. OCLC, an organization that sets library cataloging standards and helps with cooperative efforts by libraries, describes itself as "a nonprofit, membership, library computer service and research organization dedicated to the public purposes of furthering access to the world's information and reducing information costs" (http://www.oclc.org [25 Oct. 1999]).

23. One recent study reported that 88 percent of all Web pages are in English, with 2 percent in French (Dunn C7). Though this statistic seems extreme, it clearly indicates the general tendency for Web pages to be English-oriented.

24. http://huizen.dds.nl/~sdela/wra/IET98 (1 Jan. 2001). See also http://dartington.ac.uk/pw. This latter site features Bergvall's essays.

25. http://www.shadoof.net/in (1 Jan. 2001).

26. http://www2.ec-lille.fr/~book/oulipo (1 Jan. 2001).

27. http://epc.buffalo.edu/orgs/bureau (1 Jan. 2001).

28. http://www.itaucultural.org.br/invencao/invencao.htm (1 Jan. 2001).

29. http://epc.buffalo.edu/authors/menezes/tribute (1 Jan. 2001).

30. http://www.altamiracave.com (1 Jan. 2001).

31. http://www.thing.net/~grist/l&d/biennial/biennial.htm (1 Jan. 2001).

32.   I saw myself when I closed my eyes:
          space, space
          where I am and am not. (trans. Glazier)

33. See "Sidebar: Tin Man Weeps Straw Break" in the next chapter for more on the idea of dominance in this medium.

Chapter 8. Future Tenses / Present Tensions

1. See http://jefferson.village.virginia.edu/public/jjm2f/imagebase.html (Rossetti); and http://jefferson.village.virginia.edu/blake (Blake) (14 Nov. 1999).

2. The influence of the anthologies noted here has been extremely widespread. Particularly in the areas of ethnopoetics, translation, and the literatures of native peoples worldwide, some of these anthologies have made a singular contribution to literature. Rothenberg has edited *Technicians of the Sacred* (New York: Anchor Books, 1969, and Berkeley: U of California P, 1985); *Shaking the Pumpkin, Revolution of the Word* (Garden City, NY: Doubleday, 1972); *Symposium of the Whole* (Berkeley: U of California P, 1983);

The Book, Spiritual Instrument (New York: Granary Books, 1996); and, with Steven Clay, *A Book of the Book* (New York: Granary Books, 2000). Joris has co-edited *Poesie Internationale: Anthologie* (Luxembourg: Guy Binsfeld, 1987), and also, with Rothenberg, *Poems, Performance Pieces, Proses, Plays, Poetics by Kurt Schwitters* (Philadelphia: Temple UP, 1993), sometimes also cited as *pppppp: The Selected Writings of Kurt Schwitters.*

3. John Cayley, regarding the title "Tin Man Weeps Straw Break," wrote that "'Tin man . . .' is just me, a capping subject line to Joyce's original 'back broke camel straw man,' but it is fairly carefully thought out. I was thinking of a cyborg tin man in the Wizard of Oz, how he weeps (discovers 'human' feeling he always had, as representative of programmatonism/AI), over the straw which broke the camel's back and fills the head of the scarecrow, who is a true intellectual, after all" ("Re: Norway").

4. http://www.eastgate.com (16 Jan. 2000).

5. From a universe of 3,322,234 articles in the Expanded Academic Index ASAP database (19 July 1998), the number of citations for each author is as follows: Bolter 16, Landow 19, Joyce 10, Cayley 8, Rosenberg 0, and Kac 1. From a universe of 4,817,001 articles in the same database (repeated on 28 Feb. 2000), the same search resulted in: Bolter 11, Landow 21, Joyce 14, Cayley 9, Rosenberg 0, and Kac 2.

6. http://epc.buffalo.edu/e-poetry.

7. A Web version of Kac's "Webliography" is available at http://mitpress.mit.edu/e-journals/Leonardo/isast/spec.projects/newmediapoetry.html (1 Jan. 2001).

8. http://www.burningpress.org/toolbox (12 Dec. 2000), based on Ficus Strangelensis's site, Computer Generated Writing, http://www.notam.uio.no/~mariusw/c-g.writing (5 May 2000).

9. Moulthrop's "Garden of Forking Paths" hypertext can be considered to occupy the boundary between print and hypertext for a very simple reason. The project takes a print story ("The Garden of Forking Paths" by Jorge Luis Borges) that is a nearly consummate example of how well a hypertext can be presented in print and converts it into an electronic hypertext. Thus a curious inversion occurs because, once the story is adapted to hypertext, it loses the compact and artful density of the original literary work. (Further, part of the hypertextual dynamic of the original can be associated with its linear, print-based presentation.) Indeed, the electronic version is also self-consciously imperfect since its goal was to be an aid to teaching and not a literary work. It is also imperfect since the text was used without permission of the copyright holders. For that reason, it is no longer publicly available. Moulthrop's apologia for the withdrawal of this hypertext is available on the Web (http://raven.ubalt.edu/staff/moulthrop/hypertexts/forkingPaths.html [27 Nov. 1999]).

10. It should be noted that Hayles's later paper, "Coding the Signifier: Rethinking Semiosis in Digital Media" (presented at the Modern Language

Association Annual Conference, Washington D.C., 28 Dec. 2000) embraced a wider range and diversity of digital works than the presentation discussed here. Indeed, her later paper does begin to investigate a number of dynamic works, addressing a wider range of digital media projects.

11. See http://www.feedmag.com/document/do291_master.html (1 Jan. 2001) for the published version of this address.

12. Coover's incredible support of hypertext must be acknowledged. As Jennfier Ley points out, "Coover . . . supported the hypertext community in its early days, and his critical writing about it in places like the [*New York Times Book Review*] definitely helped legitimize early hypertext. As a novelist and a man much in love with 'words' . . . I think he can be forgiven for a bit of nostalgia. And I think that any sense many had that his Golden Age premise was wrong was a sense that hypertext/media is so very new . . . we hated to see anyone roping it into developmental elements or stating that periods in its development had passed" (Ley). Indeed, the discussion here is not meant to criticize Coover but to place his comments within general trends of the conference.

13. http://epc.buffalo.edu, http://www.experimedia.vic.gov.au/~komninos/cybgal.html, http://www.burningpress.org/gallery/gallery.html (all accessed 1 Jan. 2001).

14. Kenneth Goldsmith with Clem Paulsen, http://stadiumweb.com/fidget (1 March 1999).

15. http://epc.buffalo.edu/authors/glazier (1 Jan. 2001).

16. In terms of some of these affinities, note that Stuart Moulthrop's keynote address at the CyberMountain Conference (June 1999) was entitled "Gamely Interstitial: Narrative, Excess, and Artifactual Interstanding." For a copy of the slide show given with this presentation, see http://raven.ubalt.edu/staff/moulthrop/talks/cymount/index.html (26 Nov. 1999), where he examines "the fundamental kinship of any literary project with a feedback loop—hypertext, adventure game, ars combinatoria" (Cybermountain).

Epilogue

1. The Electronic Labyrinth lists the following works as print precursors of non-linear literature: Sterne's *Tristram Shandy*, Robbe-Grillet's *In the Labyrinth*, Nabokov's *Pale Fire*, Cortázar's *Hopscotch*, O'Brien's *At Swim-Two-Birds*, Ballard's *The Atrocity Exhibition*, Calvino's *The Castle of Crossed Destinies*, Pavic's *Dictionary of the Khazars*, and Pavic's *Landscape Painted with Tea* ("The Nonlinear Tradition in Literature," The Electronic Labyrinth, http://web.uvic.ca/~ckeep/hfl0241.html [23 April 2000]).

2. References here are to the paper "Print Is Flat, Code Is Deep: Rethinking Signification in New Media," presented at Digital Arts & Culture 99, Atlanta, 29 Oct. 1999. Robert Coover also addressed first-wave hypertext

in his eulogistic "Literary Hypertext: The Passing of the Golden Age" (http://www.feedmag.com/document/do291.shtml) on that same date. The main difference between these "waves" is that the texts of first wave are almost completely composed of text, whereas those of the second wave are composed of text integrated with substantial amounts of image.

3. Personal conversation with the author, 30 Nov. 1999. Among many reasons, consider that if we define digital literature as literature that cannot be reproduced in print, then link-node hypertext would not be included since elaborate arrangements of cards or charts can be made to represent it. Because of this, its general reliance on static lexia of writing and its inherent bias toward authorial control, it might be more accurately considered the last stage of print technology.

4. "Aspects of a New Consciousness" is an interview with Cage displayed on video as part of the exhibition "The American Century: Art & Culture, 1950–2000," Whitney Museum, New York, 1999.

5. Comments by Eskelinen and Aarseth were made during the roundtable discussion on "The Future(s) of Narrative," at the Digital Arts & Culture 99 Conference, Atlanta, 30 Oct. 1999.

6. Here, I am employing this term for a specific purpose. For general usage, Cayley is more optimistic about this concept, considering "nilsk" as "links" turned inside out, i.e., a conception that allows more multiple possibilities.

7. What I am calling "the disposable condition" includes the climate of competition, growth economics (rather than sustainable economics), and the common practice of people on the "fictions of value" in, for example, the stock market, real estate, and so forth.

Glossary

Acrostic. Poem created by trans-linear alignment of predetermined initial or terminal characters.

Archie. An early Internet-search program.

ASCII. A type of code almost universally readable by different computer systems. ASCII text is basic, unembellished text without control or special characters.

Bot. A robot or small program that, running in the background behind user tasks, often performs mundane tasks, such as indexing.

C. Widely used and robust programming language.

Cello. Early Internet browser predating Netscape and Internet Explorer.

Chmod. "Change mode" or alter access parameters to files in the UNIX system.

Client pull. HTML-invoked feature that causes one page to automatically go to a different page.

Code. Term used for programs, i.e., written instructions to the computer. Used by extension for HTML.

Collocation. The juxtaposition of different data elements through a procedure.

Command line. The line on the screen where commands are entered.

C-shell. A specific UNIX operating system environment.

Diastext. Program by Charles Hartman for creating diastics.

Diastic. Poem created by trans-linear alignment of predetermined characters, variable in position.

DHTML. Dynamic HTML; a convention that adds dynamic capabilities to HTML.

Director. A program for creating interactive computer "movies," often used for CD-ROM production.

DOS. Basic PC operating system.

Dynamic fonts. Convention that allows Web-producers to determine displayed fonts with precision.

Emacs. An idiosyncratic but precise tool often used to edit ASCII text on the UNIX system.

E-poetry. Poetry that engages the electronic medium.

E-writing. Writing that engages the electronic medium.

Flash. A program for creating interactive computer "movies," often used for Web-based display.

Frames. Display convention that divides the Web browser into two or more independent windows.

FTP. File Transfer Protocol; protocol for transferring files between computers.

Gopher. Text-based interface for delivering information through the Internet before the invention of the World Wide Web.

Grep. A procedure, formal method, or program that filters text according to given patterns; it processes input text and produces output, according to user-specified modifiers. To grep ("global/regular expression/print") a given target, is to search across files for instances of a string of characters. (See chapter 6 for a more detailed explanation.)

HTML. Hypertext Mark-up Language; convention for preparing documents for display on the Web.

Hypertext. One of many possible systems for interlinked text. The most basic of these systems is link-node hypertext.

Hypertext fiction. Works employing link-node conventions that allow readers to choose different paths through a narrative.

Impulse chance. Compositional system that allows for spontaneous improvisation based on immediate environmental stimuli.

Java. Robust programming language used with the Web.

JavaScript. Somewhat limited programming language used with the Web.

Kernels. UNIX operating system environment.

Kinetic text. Computer texts that include motion.

Laplink. Program for connecting computers via an external capable for the transfer of data.

Lexia. A unit of reading; often refers to a screen-based unit of information linked by hypertext.

Listserv. Automated list that sends copies of individual messages to numerous e-mail accounts.

Mark-up. The insertion of codes that formats text for Web viewing.

Mesostic. Poem created by trans-linear alignment of predetermined medial characters.

Mimeo Revolution. An era when small literary magazines with often avantgarde literary content were produced through mimeography, chiefly in the 1960s.

Mosaic. Early Internet browser predating Netscape and Internet Explorer.

Networked and programmable media. Web-based and program-based media.

NT. Windows system for linked computers in a local network.

Perl. Programming language often used in conjunction with servers and the Web environment.

Permissions. The UNIX system of permissions provides different levels of access to varying categories of users.

Robot. See Bot.

Server. A server is a computer that supplies information to the Web.

Shell. UNIX operating system environment.

Source code. The computer code or mark-up fundamental to the operation of a program or the display of a page.

Speaking clock. A specific early programmed poem by John Cayley.

Spider. A robot or small program that, running in the background behind user tasks, often performs tasks such as indexing across multiple systems.

Style sheets. System for formatting Web documents.

Symbolic link. In the UNIX environment, a method for displaying a directory or file in a location other than where it actually exists.

TCP/IP. Protocol that makes possible the exchange of Internet data.

Telnet. Protocol for communication with a remote computer.

Thread. A common theme among multiple listserv or message board postings.

Travesty. Early program for generation of poetry texts.

UNIX. An operating system used by many universities and computer scientists, with the C-shell a common UNIX configuration.

URL. Uniform Resource Locator; a Web "address."

Veronica. An early Internet-search program.

Virtual reality. Three-dimensional simulation of a "real" space.

Visual text. Text that uses letters for visual effect by arranging letters in graphical patterns.

VRML. Virtual reality modeling language; language for the creation of 3-D environments on the Web.

VT100. Text-only convention for the communication between computers.

WAIS. An early Internet-indexing program.

Worms. A robot or small program that, running in the background behind user tasks, often performs tasks such as indexing across multiple systems.

WYSIWYG. Graphical user interface, i.e., "what you see is what you get."

XHTML. HTML that allows the use of XML.

XML. Extensible Mark-up Language; a system that allows flexible mark-up coding for Web documents.

Zines. Small literary magazines with defiant themes produced through xerography, chiefly in the 1970s and 1980s.

Works Cited

Aarseth, Espen J. *Cybertext: Perspectives on Ergodic Literature*. Baltimore: Johns Hopkins UP, 1997.

Allsopp, Ric, and Scott de Lahunta. "*Performance Research* On Line: New Media Work for CD-ROM (A Performance Research Supplement)." 4.2 (1999).

"alt.hypertext." http://www.csd.uwo.ca/~jamie/hypertext-faq.html (2 March 1999).

Antin, David. *Selected Poems, 1963–1973*. Los Angeles: Sun & Moon, 1991.

Apollinaire, Guillaume. *Calligrammes: Poems of Peace and War, 1913–1916*. Berkeley: U of California P, 1980.

Aristotle. *On Poetry and Style*. Trans. and with an introduction by G. M. A. Grube. New York: Liberal Arts, 1958.

Aspects of a New Consciousness, Dialogue III. Jack Kroll interview of John Cage. New York: Electronic Art Intermix, 1969. Videocassette.

Baraka, Imamu Amiri. *Raise, Race, Rays, Raze: Essays Since 1965*. New York: Random House, 1971.

Barthes, Roland. *S/Z*. New York: Hill and Wang, 1974.

Basbanes, Nicholas. "The Canon: In Print Before, Again, for All Time." http://www.georgejr.com/may97/gates.html (5 Jan. 2001).

Basinski, Michael. "The Parts." *Basinski: A Zine of the Arts* 1.1 (1998): n.p.

Baudelaire, Charles. *Oeuvres Complètes*. Vol. 1. Paris: Gallimard, 1975.

Baudrillard, Jean. *Simulacra and Simulation*. Ann Arbor: U of Michigan P, 1994.

Beckett, Samuel. *Stories & Texts for Nothing*. New York: Grove, 1967.

Bennett, James Richard. "Style." *The New Princeton Encyclopedia of Poetry and Poetics*. Eds. Alex Preminger and T. V. F. Brogan. Princeton, NJ: Princeton UP, 1993. 1225–27.

Bergvall, Caroline. "Fourth Tableau." *Out of Everywhere: Linguistically Innovative Poetry by Women in North America and the UK*. Ed. Maggie O'Sullivan. London: Reality Street, 1996. 207–9.

—. "Writing Out of Space: The Performance of Writing as Sited Practice." Paper presented at Assembling Alternatives, U of New Hampshire, Durham, 29 Aug.–2 Sept., 1996.

Bernstein, Charles. "Alphabeta." http://www.ubu.com/contemp/bernstein/alphabeta.html. 1997 (1 March 1999).

—. *Content's Dream: Essays 1975–1984*. Los Angeles: Sun & Moon, 1986.

—. *Dysraphism*. Los Angeles: Sun & Moon, 1987.

—. "An Mosaic for Convergence." *Electronic Book Review* 6.1 (1997): http://www.altx.com/ebr/ebr6/ebr6.htm (1 March 1999).

—. "Making Words Visible." *The L=A=N=G=U=A=G=E Book*. Ed. Bruce Andrews and Charles Bernstein. Carbondale, IL: Southern Illinois UP,

1984. 284–86.

—. *My Way: Speeches and Poems.* Chicago: U of Chicago P, 1999.

—. *A Poetics.* Cambridge: Harvard UP, 1992.

—. "Politics." http://www.ubu.com/contemp/bernstein/politics2.html. 1997 (1 March 1999).

—. "The Response As Such: Words in Visibility." *MEANING* 9 (1991): 3–8.

—. *The Sophist.* Los Angeles: Sun & Moon, 1987.

Berrigan, Ted. *The Sonnets.* New York: United Artists Books, 1982.

Bey, Hakim. *The Temporary Autonomous Zone, Ontological Anarchy, Poetic Terrorism.* Wiretap Electronic Text Archive Ed.: gopher:// wiretap.spies.com:70/00/Library/Document/taz.txt. 1991 (27 Nov. 1999).

"Beyond Art." http://info.ox.ac.uk/ctitext/beyond/index.html (9 Sept. 1999).

"Biblia pauperum." http://www.lang.uiuc.edu/LLL/etexts/bp-lat.html (28 Feb. 1998). Now defunct.

Blaser, Robin. *The Holy Forest.* Toronto: Coach House, 1993.

Bök, Christian. *Crystallography: Book I of Information Theory.* Toronto: Coach House, 1994.

Bolter, J. David. *Writing Space: The Computer, Hypertext, and the History of Writing.* Hillsdale, NJ: L. Erlbaum Associates, 1991.

Bonington, Paul. "Publishers Note: The Fourth Media." *Internet World* 6.4 (1995): 6.

Borges, Jorge Luis. *Collected Fictions.* New York: Viking, 1998.

—. *El Libro de Arena.* Barcelona: Plaza & Janes Editores, 1975.

—. *Ficciones.* New York: Grove, 1962.

Brontë, Emily. *Wuthering Heights.* Wiretap Electronic Text Archive Ed.: gopher://wiretap.spies.com:70/00/Library/Classic/wuther.txt (27 Nov. 1999).

Bush, Vannevar. "As We May Think." *From Memex to Hypertext: Vannevar Bush and the Mind's Machine.* Eds. James M. Nyce and Paul Kahn. Boston: Academic, 1991. 85–110.

Cano, Linda. "Place Names." 5 Aug. 1997. Online posting. Nahuat-l Discussion List (5 Aug. 1997). Available e-mail: nahuat-l@server.umt.edu.

Cardelli, Luca. "Everything Is an Object." n.d. http://ftp.digital.com/pub/ DEC/SRC/publications/luca/talk/EverythingIsAnObject-abs.html (8 Nov. 1999).

"Catalog." *Multimedia Encyclopedia on CD-ROM, Version 5.1.* Novato, CA: Software Toolworks, 1992.

Cayley, John. "Beyond Codexspace: Potentialities of Literary Cybertext." *Visible Language: The New Media Poetry* 30.2 (1996): 164–83.

—. "From NYC." E-mail to the author (27 Feb. 2000).

—. "Indra's Net or Hologography." http://www.shadoof.net/in/prog/ progseto.html (28 Feb. 2000).

—. "Of Programmatology." http://www.shadoof.net/in/prog/progseto.html (27 Feb. 2000).

—. "poesie[sous rature] & informatique." 15 Dec. 1997. Online posting. Discussion List (15 Dec. 1997). Available e-mail: ht_lit@consecol.org.

—. "Re: Norway." E-mail to the author (5 Oct 1998).

—. "Re: The Chapters - 1 of 3." E-mail to the author (27 April 2000).

Clark, Tom. *Robert Creeley and the Genius of the American Common Place: Together with the Poet's Own Autobiography*. New York: New Directions, 1993.

Clay, Steven, and Rodney Phillips. *A Secret Location on the Lower East Side: Adventures in Writing, 1960–1980*. New York: New York Public Library and Granary Books, 1998.

Consenstein, Peter. "Memory and Oulipian Constraints." *Postmodern Culture* 6.1 (1995): http://muse.jhu.edu/journals/postmodern_culture/voo6/6.1consenstein.html [subscribers only] (13 March 2000). For nonsubscribers see http://jefferson.village.virginia.edu/pmc/text-only/issue.995/consen.995.

Coover, Robert. "Hyperfiction: Novels for Computer." *New York Times Book Review* 29 Aug. 1993: 1.

Creeley, Robert. *Charles Olson & Robert Creeley: The Complete Correspondence*. Ed. George F. Butterick. Vol. 1. Santa Barbara: Black Sparrow, 1980.

—. *The Collected Essays of Robert Creeley*. Berkeley: U of California P, 1989.

—. *The Collected Poems of Robert Creeley*. Berkeley: U of California P, 1982.

Crystal, David. *The Cambridge Encyclopedia of Language*. Cambridge: Cambridge UP, 1987.

"Cybermountain Moo Session." 2 June 1999 (transcript). http://cmc.uib.no:8000/899 (26 Nov. 1999).

"DAC 98: Digital Arts & Culture 98." http://cmc.uib.no/dac (21 Feb. 1999).

Davie, Donald. *Ezra Pound*. Chicago: U of Chicago P, 1975.

Davies, Kevin. "Thunk." *Open Letter* 10.1 (1998): 71–76.

Delany, Paul, and George P. Landow. *Hypermedia and Literary Studies*. Cambridge: MIT UP, 1991.

Denver, John. "Take Me Home, Country Roads." *Alfred's Basic Adult All-Time Favorites, Level 1*. Ed. Taffy Nivert Words and Music by Bill Danoff, and John Denver. Van Nuys, CA: Alfred Publishing Co., Inc., 1988. 43–45.

Dickinson, Emily. *The Complete Poems of Emily Dickinson*. Boston: Little, Brown, 1960.

—. *The Letters of Emily Dickinson*. Ed. Thomas H. Johnson. Vol. 2. Cambridge: Belknap Press of Harvard UP, 1986.

Disch, Thomas M. "Hartman/Muse." http://www.dartmouth.edu/acad-inst/upne/f9622a.html (18 Oct. 1998).

Dragomoshchenko, Arkadii. *Xenia*. Los Angeles: Sun & Moon, 1994.

Drake, Luigi Bob. "Burning Press Home Page." http://www.burningpress.org (15 Oct. 1998).

—. "CybpherAnthology Proposal Home Page." http://www.burningpress.org/va/vaintro.html (15 Oct. 1998).

Drucker, Johanna. *Figuring the Word*. New York: Granary Books, 1998.

—. "Process Note: Marshall Reese, Writing." *The L=A=N=G=U=A=G=E Book*. Ed. Bruce Andrews and Charles Bernstein. Carbondale, IL: Southern Illinois UP, 1984. 263–66.

Duncan, Robert. "As an Introduction." *Sulfur* 35 (1994): 80–86.

—. *Ground Work: Before the War*. New York: New Directions, 1984.

—. "The H.D. Book, Part II, Chapters 5, 7, 8." *Credences* 1.2 (1975): 50–94.

—. *The Opening of the Field*. New York: New Directions, 1960.

—. "A Preface." *Maps* 6 (1974): 1–16.

Dunn, Ashley. "It's a Very Wide Web: 1 Billion Pages' Worth." *Los Angeles Times* 20 Jan. 2000: C7.

Dupriez, Bernard. *A Dictionary of Literary Devices, Gradus, A–Z*. Toronto: U of Toronto P, 1991.

Eigner, Larry. *Selected Poems*. Berkeley: Oyez, 1972.

"E-Poetry 2001." http://epc.buffalo.edu/e-poetry/2001 (2 Jan. 2001).

Febvre, Lucien, and Henri-Jean Martin. *The Coming of the Book: The Impact of Printing, 1450–1800*. London: Verso, 1984.

Galarneau, Andrew. "Boot Up a Book." *Buffalo News* 19 Sept. 1999: E1–2.

García Lorca, Federico. *In Search of Duende*. New York: New Directions, 1998.

Gelernter, David. *The Aesthetics of Computing*. London: Orion, 1998.

Glazier, Loss Pequeño. "(Go) Fish." http://epc.buffalo.edu/authors/glazier/viz/fish. 1999 (17 Feb. 2000).

—. *Leaving Loss Glazier*. Buffalo: Paisan, 1997.

—. "An Online Defense." http://epc.buffalo.edu/authors/glazier/defense.html (17 Jan. 2000).

—. *The Parts*. Buffalo: Meow Press, 1995.

—. *Small Press: An Annotated Guide*. Westport, CT: Greenwood, 1992.

—. *Tango*. Unpublished MS, 2000.

—. *Uniform*. Unpublished MS, 2000.

"Golden Age." *Encyclopædia Britannica Online*. http://www.eb.com:180/bol/topic?eu=37970&sctn=1 (14 Nov. 1999).

Goldsmith, Kenneth. "FIDGET Online." 5 July 1998. Online posting. UB Poetics Discussion Group (23 Oct. 1998). Available e-mail: poetics@listserv.acsu.buffalo.edu.

Hagen, Steve. *Buddhism Plain and Simple*. New York: Broadway Books, 1999.

Haraway, Donna. "A Manifesto for Cyborgs: Science, Technology, and Socialist Feminism in the 1980s." *Feminism/Postmodernism*. Ed. Linda J. Nicholson. New York: Routledge, 1990. 190–233.

Hartman, Charles O. *Virtual Muse: Experiments in Computer Poetry*. Hanover, NH: UP of New England, 1996.

Hartman, Charles O., and Hugh Kenner. *Sentences*. Los Angeles: Sun & Moon, 1995.

Hawthorne, Nathaniel. *Passages from the French and Italian Note-Books*. Vol.

1. Boston: J. R. Osgood, 1872.

Hayles, N. Katherine. "Electronic Textuality: What Is It?" http:// englishwww.humnet.ucla.edu/individuals/hayles/lectures/electext.htm (14 Nov. 1999).

H.D. *Kora and Ka*. New York: New Directions, 1996.

Heath, Steve. *Newnes UNIX Pocket Book*. Second ed. Oxford: Newnes, 1994.

Hillis, W. Daniel. *The Pattern on the Stone: The Simple Ideas That Make Computers Work*. New York: Basic Books, 1998.

Hocquard, Emmanuel. *Theory of Tables*. Trans. Michael Palmer. Providence, RI: Oblek Editions, 1994.

Howe, Susan. *The Nonconformist's Memorial*. New York: New Directions, 1993.

"Hyperbook." The Electronic Labyrinth. http:// jefferson.village.virginia.edu/elab/hfl0038.html (10 Dec. 2000).

"Hypertext." The Electronic Labyrinth. http://jefferson.village.virginia.edu/ elab/hfl0037.html (10 Dec. 2000).

"Hypertext Now." Eastgate Web Site. http://www.eastgate.com/ HypertextNow (23 Feb. 1998).

"Hypertext Resources on the Web." Eastgate Web Site. http:// www.eastgate.com/hypertext/WebHypertext.html (14 Feb. 1998).

"In the Event of Text: Ephemeralities of Writing." http://www.hku.nl/events/ iet. See also http://huizen.dds.nl/~sdela/wra/IET98. 1999 (1 Jan. 2001).

Joyce, James. *Ulysses*. Paris: Shakespeare, 1922.

Joyce, Michael. "Back Broke Camel Straw Man." 15 Dec. 1997. Online posting. HT_LIT Discussion List (15 Dec. 1997). Available e-mail: ht_lit@consecol.org.

—. "Forms of Future." http://media-in-transition.mit.edu/articles/ index_joyce.html. 1997 (29 Feb. 2000).

—. "Nonce upon Some Times: Rereading Hypertext Fiction." *Modern Fiction Studies* 43.3 (1997): 579–97.

—. *Of Two Minds: Hypertext, Pedagogy, and Poetics*. Ann Arbor: U of Michigan P, 1995.

Kac, Eduardo. "Holopoetry." *Visible Language: The New Media Poetry* 30.2 (1996): 184–212.

—. "Holopoetry: Complete List of Holopoems." http://www.ekac.org/ allholopoems.html (20 Oct. 1998).

—. "Introduction." *Visible Language: The New Media Poetry* 30.2 (1996): 98–101.

—. "Invenção—Announcement." 10 Nov. 1998. Online posting. HT_LIT Discussion List (1 March 1999). Available e-mail: ht_lit@consecol.org.

—. "Photonic Webs in Time: The Art of Holography." http://www.ekac.org/ Photonic.Webs.ISEA_95.html (20 Oct. 1998).

—. "Re: Back Broke Camel Straw Man." 20 Dec. 1997. Online posting. HT_LIT Discussion List (1 March 1999). Available e-mail:

ht_lit@consecol.org.

—. "Recent Experiments in Holopoetry and Computer Holopoetry." http://www.ekac.org/recent.experiments.html (20 Oct. 1998).

—. "Selected Webliography." *Visible Language: The New Media Poetry* 30.2 (1996): 234–37.

Kendall, Robert. "Writing for the New Millennium: The Birth of Electronic Literature." *Poets & Writers Magazine* (Nov./Dec. 1995). Formerly reprinted at http://www.wenet.net/~rkendall/pw1.htm (17 Oct. 1998). Now at http://wordcircuits.com/kendall/essays/pw1.htm.

Kiernan, Vincent. "Why Do Some Electronic-Only Journals Struggle, While Others Flourish?" *Chronicle of Higher Education* (1999): A25. http://chronicle.com/free/99/05/99051701t.htm (8 Nov. 1999).

Kinsella, John. *The Undertow: New and Selected Poems.* Todmorden, UK: Arc Publications, 1996.

Koskimaa, Raine. "From Afternoon till Twilight." *Electronic Book Review* 7 (1998). http://www.altx.com/ebr/reviews/rev7/r7kos.htm.

Kuszai, Joel. *Report on Community.* Buffalo: Meow, 1996.

Landow, George P. "Landow's Overview Types." http://jefferson.village.virginia.edu/elab/hfl0101.html (23 April 2000).

—, ed. *Hypertext: The Convergence of Contemporary Critical Theory and Technology.* Baltimore: Johns Hopkins UP, 1992.

"Landow's Overview Types." http://web.uvic.ca/~ckeep/hfl0101.html (2 March 1999).

Lazer, Hank. *3 of 10.* Tucson: Chax, 1996.

Leggott, Michele. *Reading Zukofsky's "80 Flowers."* Baltimore: Johns Hopkins UP, 1989.

Ley, Jennifer. "Re: [webartery] DAC, media boys & girls, *time*." 11 Nov. 1999. Online posting. Discussion List (15 Nov. 1999). Available e-mail: webartery@onelist.com.

Mac Low, Jackson. *42 Merzgedichte in Memoriam Kurt Schwitters.* Barrytown, NY: Station Hill, 1994.

—. *Barnesbook.* Los Angeles: Sun & Moon, 1996.

—. *Bloomsday.* Barrytown, NY: Station Hill, 1984.

—. "Re: A Footnote." 1999. E-mail to the author (7 March 1999).

—. "Re: 'Aleatoric' ['-ory']." 1998. E-mail to the author (31 Oct. 1998).

—. "Re: My Article." 1998. E-mail to the author (25 Oct. 1998).

—. "Re: Revised." 1999. E-mail to the author (16 Feb. 1999).

—. *Representative Works: 1938–1985.* New York: Roof Books, 1986.

—. "See Them Together (Stein 59)." *http://epc.buffalo.edu/authors/maclow.* 1999 (2 March 1999).

—. *The Virginia Woolf Poems.* Providence, RI: Burning Deck, 1985.

—. *Words nd Ends from Ez.* Bolinas, CA: Avenue B, 1989.

Marchand, Jim. "10.0493 (a)esthetics of programming." 4 Dec. 1996. Online posting. Humanist Discussion Group (14 Jan. 1999). Available e-mail:

[Unknown]. Vol. 10.493.

Marinetti, F. T. *Selected Writings.* Trans. R. W. Flint and Arthur A. Coppotell. Ed. R. W. Flint. New York: Farrar, Straus and Giroux, 1972.

Marsh, William. "Paragram as Is Hypertext." *Witz* 5.1 (1997): 8–13.

—. "[webartery] DAC, media boys & girls, *time*." 9 Nov 1999. Online posting. Discussion List (15 Nov. 1999). Available e-mail: webartery@onelist.com.

Maso, Carole. "Twilight, A Symphony." http://www.eastgate.com/catalog/Twilight.html: 18 Oct. 1998.

McCartney, Scott. *ENIAC: The Triumphs and Tragedies of the World's First Computer.* New York: Walker & Company, 1999.

McGann, Jerome. *Black Riders: The Visible Language of Modernism.* Princeton, NJ: Princeton UP, 1993.

—. "Radiant Textuality." http://jefferson.village.virginia.edu/public/jjm2f/radiant.html (Rev. 10 Feb. 1996) (1996): 4 Jan. 2000.

—. "The Rationale of HyperText." http://jefferson.village.virginia.edu/public/jjm2f/rationale.html (Rev. 6 May 1995) (1995): 4 Jan. 2000.

—. *The Textual Condition.* Princeton, NJ: Princeton UP, 1991.

McLuhan, Marshall. *Understanding Media.* Cambridge: MIT P, 1994.

Melnick, David. *PCOET.* San Francisco: G. A. W. K., 1975.

Melville, Herman. *Moby Dick.* Wiretap Electronic Text Archive Ed.: gopher://wiretap.spies.com:70/00/Library/Classic/mobydick.txt (27 Nov. 1999).

Mirapaul, Matthew. "An Approach to Poetry That Rhymes with HTML." *New York Times* 3 April 1997. Reprinted at http://www.nytimes.com/library/cyber/mirapaul/040397mirapaul.html [subscribers only] (17 Oct. 1998).

Moreiras, Alberto. "Hacking a Private Site in Cyberspace." *Rethinking Technologies.* Ed. Verena Andermatt Conley. Minneapolis: U of Minnesota P, 1993. 191–204.

Morison, Stanley, and Holbrook Jackson. *A Brief Survey of Printing History and Practice.* New York: Borzoi, 1923.

Motte, Warren, ed. *Oulipo: A Primer of Potential Literature.* Normal, IL: Dalkey Archive, 1986.

Nelson, Theodor Holm. *Literary Machines 93.1.* Sausalito, CA: Mindful, 1992.

Nielsen, Jakob. *Hypertext and Hypermedia.* New York: Academic, 1990.

—. "Nielsen's Definition." The Electronic Labyrinth. http://jefferson.village.virginia.edu/elab/hfl0038.html (12 Dec. 2000).

Odier, Daniel. *The Job: Interviews with William Burroughs.* New York: Penguin, 1989.

Olson, Charles. *The Maximus Poems.* Berkeley: U of California P, 1983.

—. *Muthologos: The Collected Lectures & Interviews.* Ed. George F. Butterick. Vol. 2. Bolinas, CA: Four Seasons Foundation, 1979.

—. *Selected Writings of Charles Olson*. New York: New Directions, 1966.

O'Sullivan, Maggie. "Narcotic Properties." *Out of Everywhere: Linguistically Innovative Poetry by Women in North America and the UK*. Ed. Maggie O'Sullivan. London: Reality Street, 1996.

Pastior, Oskar. "Poempoems." *The Printed Head* 1.5 (1990): 1–37.

Paz, Octavio. *Selected Poems*. New York: New Directions, 1984.

Pecor, Amanda. "Cinderella at Dusk, Before the Promenade." *American Poetry Review* 28.5 (Sept./Oct. 1999) (1999): 13.

Perloff, Marjorie. *The Dance of the Intellect: Studies in the Poetry of the Pound Tradition*. Cambridge: Cambridge UP, 1985.

—. *Radical Artifice: Writing Poetry in the Age of Media*. Chicago: U of Chicago P, 1991.

Pinsky, Robert. "The Muse in the Machine: Or, the Poetics of Zork." *New York Times*, 19 March 1995. http://www.nytimes.com/ [subscribers only] (26 Oct. 1998).

—. *The Sounds of Poetry: A Brief Guide*. New York: Farrar, Straus and Giroux, 1998.

Powell, Thomas. *HTML: The Complete Reference, Second Edition*. Berkeley: Osborne/McGraw-Hill, 1999.

Preminger, Alex, and T.V.F. Brogan, eds. *The New Princeton Encyclopedia of Poetry and Poetics*. Princeton: Princeton UP, 1993.

"Procatalogue." Formerly at http://www.demon.co.uk/eastfield/in/incat.html#OISLEAND. Now at http://www.shadoff.net/in/incat.html (7 March 1999).

"Prose and Contexts Desktop Publishing and Web Design." http://www.interlog.com/~dal (6 March 1999).

Quasha, George. "Reference." *Io* 41.Being = Space X Action (1988): 231.

Queneau, Raymond, et al. *Oulipo Laboratory: Texts from the* Bibliothque Oulipienne. London: Atlas, 1995.

Reid, Calvin. "Poetry and the World Wide Web: 'A Vast Literary Space.'" *Publishers Weekly* 243.13 (1996): 16.

Retallack, Joan. *Afterrimages*. Hanover, NH: Wesleyan UP, 1995.

—, ed. *Musicage: Cage Muses on Words, Art, Music*. Hanover, NH: Wesleyan UP, 1996.

"Riding the Meridian—Lit [art] ure." http://www.heelstone.com/meridian/writing4.html. 2000 (11 Dec. 2000).

Rimbaud, Arthur. *Collected Poems*. Baltimore: Penguin, 1969.

Rosenberg, Jim. "Re: Update." E-mail to the author (2 Oct. 1999).

Rothenberg, Jerome, and Pierre Joris, eds. *Poems for the Millennium: The University of California Book of Modern & Postmodern Poetry*. Vol. 2, From Postwar to Millennium. 2 vols. Berkeley: U of California P, 1998.

Ryan, Marie-Laure, ed. *Cyberspace Textuality: Computer Technology and Literary Theory*. Bloomington: Indiana UP, 1999.

Siegel, David. "Foreword." *Designing with JavaScript: Creating Dynamic Web*

Pages. Nick Heinle. Sebastopol, CA: Songline Studios, Inc., 1997.

Silliman, Ron. "For L=A=N=G=U=A=G=E." *The L=A=N=G=U=A=G=E Book*. Eds. Bruce Andrews and Charles Bernstein. Carbondale: Southern Illinois UP, 1984. 16.

—. "Interview." *The Difficulties* 2.2 (1985): 34–46.

—. "Language, Realism, Poetry." *In the American Tree*. Orono: National Poetry Foundation, 1986. xv–xxiii.

—. *The New Sentence*. New York: Roof Books, 1989.

Spinelli, Martin. "Communication Technology and Literary Community: From Utopia to Paralogy." Ph.D. diss., State U of New York, 1998.

Stein, Gertrude. *How to Write*. New York: Dover, 1975.

—. *Stanzas in Meditation*. Los Angeles: Sun & Moon, 1994.

—. *Tender Buttons: Objects, Food, Rooms*. Los Angeles: Sun & Moon, 1990.

Swiss, Thomas. "Music and Noise: Marketing Hypertexts." *Postmodern Culture* 7.1 (1996): http://muse.jhu.edu/journals/postmodern_culture/v007/7.1r_swiss.html [subscribers only] (16 Nov. 1999). A text-only version is available at http://jefferson.village.virginia.edu/pmc/text-only/issue.996/review-4.996.

Topham, Douglas W. *Portable Unix*. New York: John Wiley & Sons, 1992.

Turkle, Sherry. *Life on the Screen: Identity in the Age of the Internet*. New York: Simon & Schuster, 1995.

Ulmer, Gregory L. "The Miranda Warnings." *Hyper/text/theory*. Ed. George P. Landow. Baltimore: Johns Hopkins UP, 1994. 345–77.

Vaughan, William. *William Blake*. London: Tate Gallery, n.d.

Veland, Erik K. "ASCII Art FAQ." http://wigwam.askoyv.no/Ascii/ASCII_art_FAQ.html: 22 February 2000.

Weinstein, Norman. "Digitized Avant-Garde Writing." *Intelligent Agent* 2.2 (1998): 60–61.

Weintraut, J. Neil. "Introduction." Trans. *Architects of the Web: 1,000 Days That Built the Future of Business*. Ed. Robert H. Reid. New York: John Wiley & Sons, 1997. 370.

"What Is the Internet?" *The World Almanac and Book of Facts 2000* (1999): 623–25. Accessed through OCLC, Accession No: wa00com00050 (4 Jan. 2001).

Whitman, Walt. *Leaves of Grass: The First (1855) Edition*. New York: Penguin Books, 1985.

Wilkins, Don. "10.0441 aesthetics of programming." 18 Nov 1996. Online posting. Humanist Discussion List (18 Nov. 1996). Available e-mail: [Unknown]. Vol. 10.441.

Williams, Emmett, ed. *An Anthology of Concrete Poetry*. New York: Something Else, 1967.

Williams, William Carlos. *The Collected Poems of William Carlos Williams, Volume 2, 1939–1962*. Ed. Christopher J. MacGowan. New York: New Directions, 1988.

—. *Imaginations.* New York: New Directions, 1970.

Willis, Elizabeth. *The Human Abstract.* New York: Penguin, 1995.

"Xanadu FAQ." http://www.xanadu.com.au/xanadu/faq.html (2 March 1999).

Index

About the Author

Loss Pequeño Glazier is Director of the Electronic Poetry Center (EPC), and a poet, professor, and webmaster at the State University of New York at Buffalo. His previous publications include the poetry collections *White-Faced Bromeliads on 20 Hectares (An Iteration)*, *Leaving Loss Glazier*, and *The Parts*, as well as *Small Press: An Annotated Guide*. A selection of his digital works is available at his EPC author page (http://epc.buffalo.edu/authors/glazier).